DEPRESSION
IN CONTEXT

Other books by Neil S. Jacobson:

Integrative Couples Therapy
(with Andrew Christensen)

Acceptance and Change in Couple Therapy:
A Therapist's Guide to Transforming Relationships
(with Andrew Christensen)

A NORTON PROFESSIONAL BOOK

DEPRESSION IN CONTEXT

Strategies for Guided Action

CHRISTOPHER R. MARTELL

MICHAEL E. ADDIS

NEIL S. JACOBSON

W. W. Norton
New York • London

The text of this book is composed in Electra
Composition by Bytheway Publishing Services
Manufacturing by Haddon Craftsmen

Library of Congress Cataloging-in-Publication Data
Martell, Christopher R.
  Depression in context : strategies for guided action / Christopher R. Martell, Michael
E. Addis, Neil S. Jacobson.
    p.   cm.
  Includes bibliographical references and index.
  ISBN 0-393-70350-9
  1. Depression, Mental — Treatment.   I. Addis, Michael E.   II. Jacobson, Neil S.,
1949–1999.   III. Title.

RC537 .M37 2001
616.85'2706 — dc21   2001018040

W. W. Norton & Company, Inc., 500 Fifth Avenue, New York, N.Y. 10110
www.wwnorton.com

W. W. Norton & Company Ltd., 10 Coptic Street, London WC1A 1PU

5   6   7   8   9   0

Contents

List of Illustrations

Acknowledgments and Thoughts on Neil S. Jacobson

THIS BOOK IS ABOUT CONTEXT and an understanding of its development requires a contextual explanation about the authors. I have been privileged, as a psychologist doing primarily clinical work, to become involved in this project. Many years ago I obtained graduate training in a program that was theoretically "broad-based behaviorism," which translates as cognitive and behavioral in some mixed fashion. I received some of my first therapy training by rational emotive therapists; most of my research was conducted with behavior analytic advisors who criticized any writing that was "too cognitive." My theoretical thinking was fragmented, considering functional analyses of behavior when doing research about developmental disorders or neurological impairments, and working cognitively with higher functioning psychotherapy clients. When I read the literature, I loosely translated all models into behavioral theory but still practiced primarily cognitive treatments. For years I maintained separate ideas, fitting them into what I believed were the proper places in my technically eclectic world. Then I met Neil Jacobson.

After having begun work as a research therapist with Robert Kohlenberg and Mavis Tsai, and adding a functional analytic component to cognitive therapy, I began working with Neil and Andy Christensen on their couple therapy project. Neil asked me to work as a cognitive therapist on a depression study he was conducting, and I readily agreed. I was completely absorbed with involvement in psychotherapy outcome research. Shortly after I began the pilot phase of the study, one of the therapists working in the behavioral activation condition of the study dropped out, and Neil asked me to switch treatment conditions. Working with Neil changed my eclectic thinking and allowed me to look back to behavioral roots to explain treatment success. While working on this project, not only did I begin to learn behavioral activation techniques but I also became involved in developing the current theoretical model. Opportunities such as this do not come along that often in the life of the average practitioner psychologist, and I am glad to have been caught up in the enthusiasm surrounding this research.

With our behavioral activation team in place, we set out to expand a treatment condition that was originally about "not doing cognitive therapy." The work was exciting. Neil watched videotapes of the therapists working hard to adhere to behavioral approaches, and he would begin to formulate the approach that would eventually develop as the new version of behavioral activation. Neil, Michael, and I also began to work on this book during that time. This led to many e-mail discussions and early morning phone conversations about theory and technique.

My original ideas about cognitive therapy as the higher functioning alternative and behavioral therapies as the techniques to promote basic change began to merge as I started to think functionally about all human behaviors. This book is the result of many conversations between the three authors, our supervision groups with two other behavioral activation therapists, and the clinical consultants for behavioral activation. Neil's death in 1999 was a terrible loss to his colleagues, family, friends, and to the field of psychology. Prior to his death, however, he had set the course for his work to continue. The research team has continued to conduct excellent work; we await the outcome of the study, and Michael Addis and I have continued to write. Neil had been very excited about getting the word out about behavioral activation to those who wish to conduct research or use the treatment in their clinical work.

There are so many people to thank who have contributed in some way to the development of this book. The excellent team at the University of Washington, Center for Clinical Research, and investigators from other universities in the United States and Canada all provided needed resources and guidance throughout this process. In particular I would like to thank the Principle Investigators on the Depression Study, Keith Dobson, Ph.D., from the University of Calgary who also serves as a consultant for the behavioral activation therapists; Steve Hollon, Ph.D., from Vanderbilt University; David Dunner, M.D.; Karen Schmaling, Ph.D.; and Robert Kohlenberg, Ph.D., from the University of Washington [U.W.]. Their work on the depression study provided the background from which this book has emerged. Sona Dimidjian, who coordinated the Depression Study, has been one of the most outstanding graduate students I have ever met. My fellow behavioral activation research therapists, Ruth Herman-Dunn, Ph.D., who was kind enough to read early drafts of this book, and Thomas Linde, M.S.W., helped to shape the treatment by taking a contextual approach to the treatment of depression. The office staff, including Catherine Holmes, Melissa McElrea, and Elizabeth Schilling, was always helpful in gathering needed journal articles or providing a timely bit of logistical advice. Jackie Gollon and Eric Gortner were instrumental in coordinating the project and monitoring treatment adherence early in the study. I would also like to thank Lisa Roberts for her help early in the study. Merri Lee Jacobs, Ph.D., took time to read the first draft of this book and deserves my warmest appreciation, and David R. White assisted with developing the figures.

At Norton Professional Books, both Susan Munro and Deborah Malmud were gracious and helpful, trusting Neil's judgment in his choice of co-authors. Their belief in this book and in the ideas that were so important to Neil and the rest of us was a great support. Regina Ardini and Christine Habermaas provided excellent copyediting.

Thanks must extend further than just the people who directly contributed through their involvement in the research that initiated this work, or to the book itself. Virginia Rutter has been a dear friend and champion of this book, maintaining the hope that her late husband's work will continue for years to come. I wish to thank two colleagues and friends who provided emotional support from the very beginning of my career. They have been two of the most influential people in my life: Barbara Barry, Ph.D., and the late Mark A. Small, Ph.D., beloved friends.

This book would not have happened without my skillful co-author Michael Addis. Working with him has stimulated my thinking, clarified my writing, and increased my excitement for the science of psychotherapy. I enjoyed the exchange of ideas with Michael throughout this project more than any other aspect of the work. We were able to continue the discussion and writing that had begun in a group of three. Our third author, Neil, is deeply missed. He was a consummate academician, a prolific researcher and author, and a major figure in the field of behavior therapy. He was also open to the knowledge and understanding that could be provided by people who had devoted their careers primarily to the delivery of clinical services. He had little tolerance for pop psychology or seat-of-the-pants clinical lore that had no empirical backing and he liked to be provocative. However, he had respect for talent and intellect, whether used in a research laboratory or a therapy office, regardless of the fame or notoriety of the professional. The time I worked with Neil was far too short, but it was a time that profoundly shaped my professional behavior. Neil was an exemplary scientist-practitioner, a humanist, and an entertaining man. My work and friendship with him profoundly and positively changed my life context.

—Christopher Martell
Seattle, Washington

When I began graduate school in 1988, I was extremely interested in existential and psychodynamic theories of human behavior. My how times have changed! How do you get from Sartre and Freud to Skinner, Ferster, and Jacobson? Perhaps the journey is not as far as it seems. Existentialists, psychodynamic theorists, and behavioral folks all would agree that the claims we come to make about the nature of things evolve in the different contexts we experience over time. In my own case, I have a long history of being surrounded by very thoughtful, generous, and warm colleagues and friends who have helped me to think and talk in ways central to this book. For those in my past and current contexts I am extremely grateful.

Bob Kohlenberg was the first radical behaviorist I ever met. I had read about them in college and had concluded, as I was instructed to, that they were simply wrong. I met Bob during my initial interviews to attend U.W's clinical Ph.D. program. We discussed behavioral interpretations of consciousness, cognition, and the self. Prior to that interview I simply had no idea that behavioral ideas could be so elegant, precise, and widely applied to "higher order" human activities. Bob's courses on behavioral theory and technique were equally stimulating, and I continue to benefit from his friendship and intellectual mentoring to this day.

Shortly after my first meeting with Bob, I was helping to paint our departmental clinic one day when I heard the sound of footsteps and laughter down the hall. I turned to see a friendly face with a big warm smile belonging to a man who bore a strong resemblance to a young Fritz Perls in a T-shirt, shorts, and sandals. This was my first meeting with my future graduate advisor, Neil Jacobson. Neil has been recognized internationally for his contributions to psychotherapy development, research methodology, behavioral philosophy, and community interventions. He was truly a jack of all scholarly trades, in addition to being a wonderful father, partner, colleague and friend to many. However, the greatest tribute I can pay to Neil is not for his more widely known accomplishments, but rather for his ability to nurture the development of those around him. Neil always encouraged me to believe in myself, to follow the paths of things that interested me, to write and to write often, and to share my ideas with others. I think of him often and feel extremely fortunate to collaborate with him on this final project. His loss was a great one to the psychological community, but even more so to those who were fortunate enough to know him personally.

In addition to Neil and Bob, I was surrounded by other students and faculty members who provided a very reinforcing context for discussing research and clinical issues. Marsha Linehan was an exceptional clinical supervisor who taught me a great deal about the humanistic implications of behavioral philosophy and treatment. James Cordova, Amy Wagner, and Jennifer Waltz were wonderful friends and colleagues with whom I shared cups of coffee, office space, and a context of close support for personal and professional development.

I brought much of my history with me when I became an assistant professor at Clark University in 1995. Since then, I have again been fortunate to be in a context of strong intellectual curiosity and scholarly commitment. Clark has a long history in psychology of exploring the major assumptions behind our work. Thus, when Neil, Christopher, and I began to work on this book I had no shortage of colleagues here who were willing and quite able to discuss contextualism, post-modernism, varieties of behavioral approaches, and the nature of truth. I am particularly grateful for the friendship and professional support of Leonard Cirillo, and for the critical thinking of an exceptional group of graduate students: Kelly Carpenter, Mary Davis, Sandi Fulton, Christina Hatgis, Genevieve Iselin, Karen Jacob, Inna Khazan, and Aaron Krasnow.

There are numerous colleagues in the larger academic community who have provided valuable feedback and taken an interest in my career over the last decade. I particularly appreciate the contributions of David Barlow, Gary Cox, Keith Dobson, Steven Hollon, Jim Mahalik, and Jackie Persons. All established scholars in their own right, they have generously taken the time to provide feedback on my own work at critical junctures.

I have thoroughly enjoyed my collaboration with Christopher Martell. It is all too common to hear colleagues lament the lack of true scientist-practitioners in our profession. When they do, I think of Christopher and I'm easily reassured that researchers and clinical practitioners have much to offer each other. Christopher is a top-notch clinician who is able to integrate a great deal of clinical artistry with a hard-nosed respect for science. His clinical and scholarly work is both innovative and well-grounded in basic clinical research. He has been an ideal co-author and I hope this book is the first of many future collaborations.

I recently addressed an incoming freshman class about when learning is or is not reinforcing. I considered my own history in this regard — particularly my early experiences with my family. I remembered my father playing hooky from work (and myself from school!) so that we could tour the used bookstores in southern California. I remembered my mother reading all my papers and providing both encouragement and critical feedback on my writing. I remembered the dinner table discussions about falling trees and forests, psychology, and the nature of people and why we do what we do. There was always reading, and always talking, in my family context and for that I am extremely grateful. Finally, I want to thank my life partner Dina Lees-Addis. Everything shifted for the better the day I met you. You have been a constant source of love and support and have made my life a truly enjoyable context indeed!

— Michael Addis
Worcester, Massachusetts

ACKNOWLEDGMENTS ON BEHALF
OF NEIL S. JACOBSON

When Neil died, his offices at home — he had two of them — were crammed with what seemed like every piece of research on depression and its treatment, and every academic and popular book on the topic that had been published in the past 10 years. He read William Styron and Kaye Redfield Jamison as well as Klein, Beck, and Valenstein. As he began work on *Depression in Context*, our VCR was stacked high with training tapes from the depression study that he watched most mornings starting at around 5 A.M. and then later carefully supervised. Two or three times a week our living room was filled with graduate students, research therapists, and occasionally the other co-investigators on the (current and ongoing) study. His research therapists, including Sandra Coffman, Christopher Martell, Ruth Herman-Dunn, Tom Linde, Steve Sholl, and David Kosins were the "Dream Team." His graduate students, Sona Dimidjian, Eric Gortner, Jackie Gollan, and Lisa Roberts, were "The Big Unit" and were absolutely crucial to the study. His co-investigators, Steve Hollon, Keith Dobson, and Dave Dunner, were his friends. It was hard, and undesirable, to contain Neil's excitement about behavioral activation, and the conversations he had with Christopher and Michael about the treatment described in this book were rich and satisfying for him. He was also working on a book for popular audiences with Judith Woodburn, and conversations with her also fueled his thoughts about the humanity and pragmatism of behavioral activation.

As Christopher and Michael explain in their introduction, the ideas behind behavioral activation were a long time coming and related to Neil's growing and powerful identification with ideas of contextualism — also known, obscurely, as radical behaviorism. He valued deeply his dialogues with Bob Kohlenberg, Steve Hayes, and Bill Follette. Likewise, Neil's work with Andy Christensen on acceptance therapy (also known as "integrative behavioral couple therapy") gave him another domain to apply contextualism. Pieced together, Neil added to and created a world of ideas about human suffering that became more of a universal than something specific to marital distress, or depression, or a host of other problems in living. Neil was first and foremost a scientist, but he was a scientist with a political and social conscience — complete with the requisite history of 1960s and '70s political activism. For Neil, looking at depression and other forms of human suffering in context constituted a pragmatic approach but also a politically meaningful approach.

Neil himself explains the evolution of these ideas in his 2000 article with his dear friend and former graduate student Eric Gortner, "Can depression be de-medicalized in the 21st century: Scientific revolutions, counter-revolutions and the magnetic field of normal science," in *Behavior Research and Therapy*, and in "Behavioral activation: Returning to contextual roots" in *Clinical Psychology: Science and Practice* (2001). For those who are interested in Neil's epistemology and the development of his ideas, I will recommend to you several key (non-empirical) articles that expressed his big picture thinking: "Contextualism is dead: Long live contextualism" in *Family Process* (1994); "The politics of intimacy" in the *Behavior Therapist* (1989); "My perspective on psychotherapy integration: An outsider who is out of it," in the *Journal of Psychotherapy Integration* (1999); and "Studying the effectiveness of psychotherapy: How well do clinical trials do the job," in *American Psychologist* (1997).

I could go on at length about Neil's big picture thinking, but that is not my job here. Instead, as Neil's wife, I'd like to bring to life a little more of the personal story of this work. In 1996, Neil applied for the funds for the behavioral activation study. This followed up his first depression study, the component analysis of cognitive therapy, which indicated that behavioral activation was as good as cognitive therapy. But, for the first time in his life, he was turned down by the NIMH for these funds.

At that point, Neil insisted that his friends and students refer to him as "Deadwood." Seriously. One former student had Neil in her e-mail directory as "Deadwood." The irony of this was delightful: Neil was at the time the most widely cited marital researcher, had been continuously funded by NIMH since graduate school (usually with more than one major grant at a time), and his main component analysis article (with Steve Hollon) on the first depression study was immediately what Neil's friend Don Baucom referred to as a citation classic. He joked about not getting this grant, but at the same time, he was intensely focused on making the depression study a reality. In 1997, he got the grant. On the day Neil called his grant officer to get the "back-channel" word on the funding decision, I carried my cell phone to U.W. where I taught. The phone rang. And much like Dave Neihaus, the Seattle Mariners' baseball announcer, shouting when the home team made it into the playoffs at the last possible moment, Neil cheered into the phone, "Jacobson got the grant! Jacobson got the grant!" And this chant continued for several weeks after that.

You will read about the study in the pages of journals, hear about it at conference presentations, and also read about it in the pages that follow. The work constitutes Neil's greatest contributions, and he was so pleased to be doing it. Neil was lucky enough by the age of 50 to have had colleagues and collaborators that made his working life tremendous fun, and rewarding (if exhausting) for everyone. And while he was a demanding and unconventional leader, he gave back to all those who worked with him in spades. If he were here, he would eloquently champion the contributions of the many others involved in this book and the work on the depression treatment study, but allow me to express thanks in his stead.

Thanks to current and former graduate students who worked with Neil on the current and previous depression studies, including Eric Gortner (completing a J.D. that followed his Ph.D.), Jackie Gollan (post-doc at Massachusetts General), Sona Dimidjian (doctoral candidate at U.W.), Lisa Roberts (doctoral candidate at U.W.), Joseph McGlinchey (doctoral candidate at U.W.), Mandy Steiman (at U.W.), Mark Whisman (now at University of Colorado-Boulder), Alan Fruzzetti (now at University of Nevada-Reno), Stacey Prince (now at the Seattle V.A.), Michael Addis, Paula Truax, Kelly Koerner (a researcher at U.W.), post-docs Kirk Strosahl (now at Group Health of Puget Sound), and Shepard Salusky (private practice in Seattle). Thanks also to Neil's assistant, Catherine Holmes, who managed his increasingly rigorous schedule and the demands of two major clinical trials with gusto and flexibility and who appreciated

Neil's expansive spirit. Before Catherine, Judith Kelson contributed tremendously to improving the computing in Neil's lab, the Center for Clinical Research.

Neil was very thankful to the research therapists on his past and present studies. Joyce Victor and Sandra Coffman were on the first study. Sandra made Neil very happy by continuing from the first onto the second study, as the local head of the cognitive therapy Dream Team. In the current study, Steve Sholl and David Kosins are also valued cognitive therapists on the Dream Team. Ruth Herman-Dunn, Tom Linde, and Christopher Martell make up the behavioral activation team. Neil valued the contributions and give-and-take with these therapists who helped to hone his own thinking and keep the treatments strong and authentic.

Neil's original collaboration with Keith Dobson made this work possible. Keith was always an honorable collaborator who shared Neil's readiness to let the data speak, come what may. And Neil's correspondence and, finally, on the present study, collaboration with Steve Hollon kept Neil smarter, more excited about doing the research, and more precise about the questions and answers he sought regarding cognitive therapy and its components. The collaboration with David Dunner, too, enhanced the work, and enhanced Neil's thinking about paradigms of depression treatment as well as paradigms of research.

The appreciation that I express above takes us to the time that Neil died. I must say, however, something about the work that people have done since Neil has died. Karen Schmaling, a professor of psychiatry at U.W. and a former student of Neil's, has been a loyal, spirited, and invaluable leader in the depression study. Her contributions to the study demonstrate that she was trained very well — but also that she is a dedicated and talented scientist and mentor. Likewise, Bob Kohlenberg has honored Neil and their friendship with his dedication to this enormous study as well as with the extent to which I know that he misses Neil. Bob, who is director of the clinical program in the U.W. Department of Psychology, has given generously to this study through his leadership and through his ability to maintain and carry on Neil's legacy as a contextualist and as a rabbinic scientist. Steve Hollon and Keith Dobson have been loyal and generous to the study by giving their special attention from a long distance to assure the strength and continuity of this study, and they have shown enormous compassion to the folks here in Seattle since Neil's death. And David Dunner, who is now principal investigator in Neil's stead, has been an honorable and caring helmsman. This is all great for the research. But to me, I know how moving this would be to Neil, and so I am grateful.

Likewise, Sona Dimidjian, who, as Neil's graduate student, had become his right hand, has given her loyalty and brains to the depression study, as she has been the coordinator of the study. What Neil admired about Sona was her understanding of the principals of research; her understanding of the theoretical, practical, and political ideas that flow together in behavioral activation; and her recognition of the power of the ideas in the larger, more universal sense. These talents have meant that she has given much more to the study than one could imagine that a young graduate student (or anyone) could do. Neil was delighted to work with Sona; he would be so delighted at what she continues to do and be in the lab; and he would be eager to follow the evolution of her own powerful ideas, as well.

Michael Addis, a former student of Neil's, has given much intellectual integrity and spirit to the depression study. His work on this book — like all of his work — has been penetrating and original. And it has also been very generous.

In Neil's last 18 months, Christopher Martell had become one of Neil's most regular interlocutors, in part because Christopher was involved with both the couple therapy study and the depression study. It was a felicitous relationship for Neil and for Christopher, and Christopher has done an incredible job on this book. I know that Neil looked forward to continuing work with him and had deep respect for his clinical work and thinking. Christopher's efforts in advancing and disseminating behavioral activation are the most generous things he could do for Neil and so I am very grateful.

There are several editorial thank yous as well: Thanks to Susan Munro of Norton for her loyalty to this book, and for her many, many years of constructive collaboration with Neil on various book projects. I would like to thank David Barlow for his consideration of Neil's final journal manuscript, with Sona Dimidjian and Christopher Martell, on behavioral activation, which he completed five days before he died, and which you can see in 2001 in the journal *Clinical Psychology: Science and Practice.*

As busy as Neil was, he always had lots of time for his children, Emily and Jesse Jacobson, and Matthew Hempleman. And I believe that they helped him to stay optimistic about all his endeavors. Shortly before Neil died, his conversations with his daughter Emily about depression and behavioral activation assured that the kids, too, have a taste for the great ideas you'll read about in these pages.

So, in short, I think I know how thankful Neil was to the folks who influenced him — his colleagues, friends, and students, and especially Christopher Martell and Michael Addis in completing this wise and useful book. He was thankful because the work gave him pleasure and the ideas provided optimism for himself and for those who paid attention to the ideas. His gratitude to his collaborators and students has been earned by the work in these pages, and the work and friendship of all the folks working on the behavioral activation study and papers. I, like Neil, believe deeply in the ideas and ideals underlying behavioral activation. Since I'm not a psychologist involved in the research, I await the wider dissemination of behavioral activation, because I would like to find, for myself and for many of the sad or depressed folks I know, knowledgeable and compassionate behavioral activators.

—Virginia Rutter
Seattle, Washington

Introduction

ONE OF THE THEMES THAT RUNS throughout this book is the idea that things make more sense when we view them in context. Our activation approach to treating depression did not arise spontaneously. It evolved out of a research context, a philosophical context, and a broader intellectual context shared by many creative and insightful clinical researchers and practitioners. In the remainder of this chapter we describe the evolutionary context of behavioral activation.

THE RESEARCH BACKGROUND

In 1989 Neil Jacobson and his colleagues at the Center for Clinical Research at the University of Washington began a study to determine the mechanisms responsible for change in cognitive therapy (CT) for depression (Beck, Rush, Shaw, & Emery, 1979). Cognitive therapy had a strong track record of research supporting its efficacy in treating unipolar depression (Dobson, 1989). However, the treatment is multifaceted and includes a range of interventions aimed at changing clients' thinking and behavior. Just because a treatment has been demonstrated to work doesn't mean it works for the reasons assumed to be responsible for its effects. In other words, treatment efficacy says little directly about change mechanisms.

Neil, along with Keith Dobson and a highly committed group of graduate students and research therapists, set out to conduct a component analysis of Beck and colleagues' (1979) treatment. David Coppell, Stephen Sholl, Susan Snyder, and Joyce Victor served as research therapists and did an exceptional job learning and implementing the different treatment protocols. Michael Addis, Jackie Gollan, Eric Gortner, Kelly Koerner, Stacey Prince, and Paula Truax were at various times responsible for patient recruitment, diagnostic interviewing, grant coordination, data analysis, and assessing therapist adherence to the treatment protocols. In terms of research design, CT was broken down into three separate treatments. The first was a pure behavioral activation approach that focused on increasing pleasant events and clients' mastery experiences while decreasing unpleasant and punishing experiences. There were no cognitive interventions at all in this treatment. The second treatment added self-statement modification to the behavioral interventions. In addition to increasing pleasant events, clients were taught how to respond to negative thoughts. The final treatment was the complete cognitive therapy package described by Beck and colleagues, which involved behavioral interventions, self-statement modification, and the challenging of core beliefs or depressive underlying assumptions about the self, the world, and the future.

One hundred-fifty clients with moderate to severe major depression were randomly assigned to 20 sessions of one of the treatments. We took several steps to carefully control the study. First, most of us at the Center for Clinical Research shared a behavioral orientation. This made it possible that the behavioral approach would appear more effective simply because of the researchers' enthusiasm for the treatment. To guard against this possibility, Keith Dobson, an internationally recognized expert in cognitive therapy, joined the research team to supervise the cognitive therapists and balance the possible allegiance in favor of the behavioral condition. As it turned out, if the deck was stacked at all, it was stacked against the behavioral treatment. The research therapists all had been previously trained in cognitive therapy and believed strongly that clients must change their thinking to affect their moods. So strong were the therapists' beliefs that they often expressed considerable frustration when they were assigned a client in the behavioral condition (Jacobson & Gortner, 2000).

All of the sessions were audiotaped and closely monitored for therapist adherence to the three treatments. Reliable ratings made by coders blind to the client's treatment condition indicated that the therapists adhered to the treatments and did not use proscribed interventions (e.g., therapists did not use cognitive interventions in the behavioral condition). Our own ratings also suggested that therapists were performing the treatments skillfully as indicated by scores on a commonly used measure of therapist competence in cognitive therapy (Jacobson et al., 1996). We also sent the tapes to experts in cognitive therapy who were unaffiliated with the study. Their ratings also suggested that the therapists were competent. Finally, the study had the usual characteristics of a well-controlled clinical trial, including standardized outcome measures, evaluators blind to client's treatment condition, and long-term client follow-up.

The results were as clear as they were surprising. After 20 sessions we found no differences between the three treatment conditions on any outcome measure (Jacobson, Dobson, et al., 1996). Nor did we find any differences between the treatments one or two years after treatment (Gortner, Gollan, Dobson, & Jacobson, 1998). Moreover, the rates of recovery, improvement, and relapse were very similar to other controlled research trials of cognitive therapy for depression. The take-home message seemed fairly clear: Treating depression by helping to activate people is just as effective as helping them to change their thinking. Perhaps, on average, cognitive interventions are unnecessary.

ORIGINS OF ACTIVATION

The idea that depression could be effectively treated with relatively "simple" behavioral techniques was neither new nor without controversy. Behaviorally oriented psychologists had been writing about theories of depression and developing treatments for several decades (e.g., Ferster, 1973; Lewinsohn, 1974). The early behavioral approaches conceptualized depression as a set of responses to decreased rates of positive reinforcement and increased avoidance behaviors in a person's repertoire. In support of this approach, several studies during the 1970s (e.g., Lewinsohn, Biglan, & Zeiss, 1976; Lewinsohn & Graf, 1973; Lewinsohn & Libet, 1972) found that increasing pleasant events could be an effective treatment for depression. At the same time, the "cognitive revolution" was busy declaring behaviorism untenable. It had become increasingly obvious to researchers and clinicians that people's thoughts have an impact on their mood and behavior above and beyond particular environmental events. Behaviorists in the Skinnerian tradition had never really denied the importance of private events such as thinking and feeling. They simply thought of thinking and feeling as more behavior to be explained, not as nonphysical entities in the mind capable of causing depressive behavior independent of an environmental context. If a person thought, "I am worthless" and subsequently felt depressed, it was granted that such thinking might make depressive behavior more likely, but why did the thinking occur? (Hayes & Brownstein, 1986; Skinner, 1974). Ultimately, causes were reserved for events that can be directly manipulated, such as those found in the environment.

Thus, behavioral and functional analytic approaches continued to develop and were being creatively applied to problems such as depression and anxiety. However, during the early 1980s cognitive therapy was clearly the most popular and well-supported psychosocial treatment for major depression. In their original treatment manual, Beck and his colleagues (1979) devoted an entire chapter to behavioral activation interventions. But the authors were quite clear that behavioral interventions were assumed to be effective because they changed clients' cognitions. If a client had difficulty getting out of bed in the morning, scheduling pleasant morning activities helped to combat the belief, "I am incapable of doing anything enjoyable." Thus, cognitive therapy theorists and researchers always assumed that cognitive change was the final mediating process in treating depression. We were not surprised then when the results of the component analysis caused a stir in the cognitive therapy community (Jacobson & Gortner, 2000), particularly the suggestion that cognitive change may not be necessary to treat depression and that a behavior activation approach might be more parsimonious (Jacobson et al., 1996).

ACTIVATION STANDS ALONE

The results of the component analysis were as encouraging as they were unexpected and controversial. The idea of developing behavioral activation as a standalone treatment (rather than as a component of cognitive therapy) appealed to us for a number of reasons. First, behavioral activation appeared to be a relatively straightforward treatment approach. Cognitive therapy, on the other hand, appeared to require relatively intensive amounts of training and supervision to reach competent levels of therapeutic skill. The parsimony of the treatment made it seem possible that an activation approach could be relatively easy to disseminate to clinical practice. Neil had always been a strong believer in the need for clinical practice to be guided by research findings. He also had a track record of developing and disseminating empirically supported treatments for marital distress (Jacobson & Christensen, 1996; Jacobson & Margolin, 1979) and demystifying myths about the necessary ingredients for effective psychotherapy (Christensen & Jacobson, 1994).

The second reason that behavioral activation was an attractive approach is that it fit well with our interest in contemporary contextual and functional analytic approaches to treating adult outpatient problems. The common philosophical and theoretical viewpoint shared by many at the

Center for Clinical Research might be called contextualism (Hayes, Hayes, Reese, & Sarbin, 1993; Pepper, 1942), contemporary radical behaviorism (Chiesa, 1994), or molar functional analysis (Baum, 1994; Rachlin, 1991). Regardless of the name we give it, this way of thinking and talking has been so influential in developing our activation approach that it's worth delving into a bit here, if only to provide a preview of what's to come.

A DIFFERENT SORT OF BEHAVIORISM: CONTEXT IS EVERYTHING

Many people have what we would call an avoidant response to the word "behaviorism." It tends to call up associations with rats, mazes, M&Ms, and an obsession with predicting and controlling people's actions. Even those who don't think of behaviorism as antihumanistic often are convinced that behavioral approaches are overly simplistic and cannot deal meaningfully with complex problems such as depression, anxiety, fear of intimacy, low self-esteem, and so on. Indeed, as we asked above, how could one take seriously a theory that denies the existence of thoughts and feelings?

When we present our approach to students, colleagues, and practitioners we often find ourselves quickly saying, "This is a different sort of behavioral approach; it's not what you think." We explain how the model is quite empathic in its view of the human condition, able to deal with complex problems, and concerned with how clients feel and think. So what are the assumptions of this approach? In short, our approach is based on (a) avoiding defect models of depression, (b) viewing depression as a set of actions in context rather than a biological or psychological entity inside a person, (c) viewing depression as understandable and predictable given a person's life history and current context, (d) helping people make targeted changes that result in new behavior-context transactions, and (e) viewing the therapist as an expert coach, consultant, and personal trainer. Each of these is explored in detail in the body of the book, but we sketch them out briefly below.

Avoiding Defect Models of Depression

Most theories tend to explicitly or implicitly conceptualize depression as some sort of internal defect. The problem may be a neurotransmitter imbalance, cognitive distortions, an unconscious conflict, or simply low self-esteem. All of these explanations locate depression somewhere inside the person. It may be hard to think of alternatives — after all, isn't depression some sort of illness, and where do illnesses reside if not inside individual people? There are numerous scientific and philosophical problems with conceptualizing depression as an internal defect (e.g., Valenstein, 1998). Here our concern with defect models is not so much with their scientific status (e.g., are they ultimately true?), but rather with some of the potential consequences of thinking and talking about depression in this way. One consequence is that such characterizations tend to draw our attention away from the contexts of people's lives. We become so preoccupied with internal biological or psychological "things" that we miss the flow of transactions between people and the worlds in which they live.

Another consequence is that defect models tend to pathologize problems in living. On the one hand, the idea that depression is some sort of physical disease is an attractive one; our culture severely stigmatizes problems in living and constructs depressed behavior as a physical disease, which tends to reduce criticism and blame. At the same time, this model again constructs depression as some sort of object inside a person (e.g., Sheila *has* major depression) rather than a set of understandable responses to particular life contexts.

Depression as Shifting Contexts: *Verbs are Better than Nouns*

One of the fundamental assumptions we make is that people's experiences are a function of their history and current context. In fact, actions are so dependent on the contexts in which they occur that they simply make no sense without viewing them in context. We may be told, for example, that Lisa is "sad and lonely." But we really won't know what this means in the context of Lisa's life until we know something about Lisa's history, her current environment, and the sorts of transactions between her actions and their consequences. What sorts of responses to lonely contexts has Lisa learned over the course of her life? Does she sit and think about how lonely she is? Does she become extremely active, filling her day with busy activities to avoid feeling lonely? Or does she take steps toward becoming less lonely? What happens in Lisa's environment when she feels lonely? Does she feel lonely all day long every day, or does the context of loneliness shift from day to day, week to week, or hour to hour?

These sorts of questions lead us to conceptualize depression as a change in context rather than a thing inside of a person. Depression is not some sort of entity located in a person, in his or her behavior, or in the environment. Rather, depression is a context characterized by certain sorts of behavior-context transactions. Generally, we assume that depression occurs when people's actions are less likely to be met with positive reinforcement and more likely to be met with punishment, but this is rather simple and does not always hold true. Much of this book is about exploring variations in the context of depression.

Depressed Behavior Makes Sense

Two things happen when we take depression out of a person and put it in context. The first is that our attention shifts to things we can directly influence and thereby help people make contextual shifts. Jacobson and Gortner (2000) describe it this way:

> The behavior analytic framework emphasizes functional analyses of the environmental events that have impinged on individual clients to generate the depression, and formulates cases in a way that looks outside rather than inside the person for targeting change. That is, instead of emphasizing faulty thinking, our revisionist BA treatment conceptualizes depression in terms of environmental events that created contextual shifts, which in turn have denied the client access to those reinforcers which normally functioned as anti-depressants. (p. 112)

It is easy to see that this approach shares much with traditional behavior therapies, most notably the focus on directly changeable behavior-context relations rather than hypothetical internal entities (e.g., low self-esteem, poor self-image). Because it is difficult to directly change feelings and thoughts, we teach clients to make changes in what they are doing and to observe the relationships between different actions and their consequences.

Another consequence of putting depression in context is that depressed behavior begins to make sense on a continuum with nondepressed behavior. For example, both nondepressed and depressed activities often serve avoidance functions. We go to the doctor to avoid getting ill, sleep to avoid feeling tired, review notes before a presentation to avoid being unprepared, and so on. When people are experiencing depression they often engage in behavior that successfully avoids short-term pain (e.g., not calling a friend on the phone because of the risk of rejection), but leads to long-term negative consequences (e.g., remaining lonely). One of the fundamental laws of behavior is that actions that are followed by avoidance or escape from something aversive become more likely. Thus, we're not surprised when we see clients stuck in avoidance contexts; it makes perfect sense to us!

Targeted Activation: Taking a Strategically Functional Approach

Behavioral approaches are sometimes characterized as superficial, overly simple, or focused on symptoms rather than causes. Reading just this far, one might conclude that we simply tell clients to act less depressed. In fact, we sometimes do just this, but only for very specific reasons with particular clients. In general, our approach is to gather focused data on the relationships between activity, context, and mood. We want to know what people are doing in their lives, what the short- and long-term consequences are, and what effect each has on a client's mood. This is where our approach diverges considerably from approaches based on simply increasing pleasant events (e.g., Lewinsohn & Graf, 1973; Lewinsohn & Libet, 1972). We assume that what needs activating varies from person to person and may vary within a person depending on different contexts. Some clients need to increase pleasant events. Others need to become more assertive in some contexts and less so in others. Other clients need to spend less time ruminating, while still others need to spend more time thinking about their experiences. What matters is what works, and what works is defined by the relationship between different activities and their consequences in different contexts.

Thus, our approach to activation tends to be very targeted and based on a functional analysis of the contexts of people's lives. We encourage clients to make specific changes and observe the consequences. In this way, the approach is similar to the collaborative empiricism described by Beck and his colleagues (1979). Our approach to a client's thinking, however, is quite different. Whereas cognitive therapists tend to be concerned with the content of a person's thinking, we are concerned with the function or consequences. A cognitive therapist might attempt to help a person change the thought "My life is a complete failure" by showing how it is based on dubious evidence, selective attention, and a negative self-schema. Our approach is simply to ask clients to observe the consequences of engaging in such thinking: Does it help you to sit and think this way? What are the consequences, and what are the alternatives?

The Therapist as Coach, Consultant, and Personal Trainer

Those who have spent a good deal of time doing psychotherapy, and those who have spent a good deal of time studying it, tend to agree that the therapeutic relationship is a critical ingredient of the change process (Horvath & Greenberg, 1994; Safran & Segal, 1991). This is certainly true in BA. It is impossible to help people change ingrained patterns of behavior without creating a collaborative and supportive working relationship. However, we do not view the therapeutic relationship de facto as *the* context in which change occurs. Instead, we assume that change occurs when shifting contexts support new repertoires of nondepressive behavior.

Sometimes these new behaviors occur in the context of the therapeutic relationship (Kohlenberg & Tsai, 1991) and sometimes they don't. For example, if a client who has difficulty asking for what he or she wants tries out a new behavior with a therapist (asking for an extra session one week), the therapist would be wise to reinforce the more adaptive behavior (e.g., granting the session or expressing pleasure that the client is asking for what he or she wants). Other times a client may make contextual shifts outside of the therapy session and the role of the therapist is to coach, consult, and train the client as change occurs.

A coach is someone who helps another person learn and implement a set of skills that are likely to be effective. A consultant is someone who observes, analyzes, and makes recommendations about working with particular problems or situations. A trainer's role is similar to that of a coach, but a trainer selects very specific skills to work on and helps a person develop a systematic plan for change. These are the sorts of interpersonal contexts or relationships that seem to work best in BA. The therapy is directive, though the direction is jointly chosen by the therapist and the client. There are core sets of skills to be learned but their particular form varies from client to client. Thus, a good therapist is flexible, skillful, and able to work effectively as a coach, consultant, and trainer with a range of clients.

FINAL POINTS AND STRUCTURE
OF THE BOOK

Much like people's lives, BA is an evolving context. Each client with whom we work, and each case we discuss, provides us with new and challenging ways to think and talk about the diversity of experiences called depression. We are also involved in a large clinical trial aimed at replicating the initial positive findings by comparing BA to cognitive therapy, a selective serotonin reuptake inhibitor medication (SSRI), and a pill placebo. This study is in process and we look forward to the results. In the meantime, this book is the first formal step toward disseminating our ideas to a larger clinical audience. No doubt the treatment will grow with those who use it. Although the word "manual" may run counter to traditional ways of thinking about psychotherapy (Addis, 1997), this book might be thought of as a flexible treatment manual. Our hope is that it will help you adhere to the fundamentals of BA as you work with people to shift the contexts of their lives.

The book is arranged in three parts. Part I looks at theories of depression and treatment for depression, particularly pharmacological treatments, cognitive therapy, and behavior therapies. This part also reviews behavioral terms and ideas and gives a full explanation of our use of the term "contextual." Part II describes the specific behavioral activation treatment approach and provides ample case transcript material. Finally, part III looks at problems that can arise in the therapy and at future opportunities for the use of behavioral activation. Readers who wish to focus mainly on clinical techniques may read part II of the book first without spending a great deal of time on the theory portion in part I. However, there is a warning. A major part of this therapy is to help clients to view their lives from a contextual point of view and in order for a therapist to do so, he or she must become facile with the language of contextualism as it is presented here. Therefore, it is recommended that readers fully understand the concepts in part I prior to applying the techniques presented in part II.

DEPRESSION
IN CONTEXT

PART I
Behavioral Activation: Something Old, Something New

CHAPTER 1

The Search for Internal Causes

M AJOR DEPRESSIVE DISORDER (MDD; American Psychiatric Association, 1994) is a problem familiar to all mental health professionals. Most have treated numerous clients suffering from depression, and odds are that many professionals have experienced it themselves. Since World War II the incidence of people diagnosed with major depressive disorder has doubled. In the United States alone, depression affects 18 million people (Schrof & Schultz, 1999). It is estimated that between 3 and 20 percent of the adult population have met criteria for MDD at some point in their lives, with 20–50 percent experiencing more than one episode of depression. Rates among women are about twice as high as men (Antonuccio, Danton, DeNelsky, Greenberg, & Gordon, 1999). Other correlated demographics besides gender are race and having been divorced or separated (Horwath et al., 1992). The prevalence of depression in adolescence is roughly 28 percent (Lewinsohn & Clarke, 1999). Although depression is not directly indicated, suicide attempts are made by as many as 20–35 percent of gay youth (Gibson, 1994), compared to suicide accounting for approximately 14 percent of overall teenage deaths in the U.S. (Remafedi, 1994). In short, not only is depression a ubiquitous clinical phenomenon, but groups of individuals who have histories of oppression or nonacceptance by society are more likely to receive the diagnosis.

Given the pervasiveness of major depression it is somewhat comforting to know that so much research and clinical expertise has been devoted to trying to understand and treat the problem. We now have effective psychosocial and pharmacological treatments and new biological and psychological theories are developed all the time. With few exceptions the majority of these treatments are about trying to change things "inside" a person. Our approach to treating depression is based on a not-so-obvious theory of human behavior; it is about helping people activate themselves to shift the contexts of their lives. Techniques for activating depressed people have been around for several decades, as has the general idea that activity can be an effective way to combat depression. What the field has missed, and what we hope to provide, is a comprehensive way of engaging clients in changing their own behavior and depressive life situations. The approach is grounded in a very different way of viewing human activity. In short, the focus is on the context of people's lives rather than their thoughts, neurotransmitters, beliefs, or the psychological conflicts thought to be inside them. In this chapter we consider the most common psychological and biological approaches to depression. We then contrast them with our approach to behavioral activation (BA). By first considering common assumptions in two current popular approaches to depression, it will become clear what BA shares with these approaches and where it departs.

THE ZEITGEIST OF
INTERNAL CAUSATION

Theories of internal causation have dominated our understanding of depression for quite some time. By internal causation we mean that the determinants of depressive behavior and feelings are inside an individual. Many have postulated that these internal determinants are biological (e.g., low levels of certain neurotransmitters) and, indeed, this is the predominant rationale for drug treatments for depression. Others have postulated that certain psychological variables inside a person (e.g., depressive thoughts, beliefs, and conflicts, or chronic low self-esteem) cause depression. These approaches did not come out of the blue; considerable bodies of research finding correlation between internal states and observable behavior support both approaches. Both approaches also make sense intuitively. The biological approach is modeled after our understanding of physical diseases where the cause is something inside the individual. Cognitive and psychodynamic approaches are consistent with, and in fact have shaped, lay psychology so much so that it is hard for us to imagine a cause of behavior that is not internal to a person.

When we speak of internal causation we are talking about the idea that there is an underlying mechanism, structure, or process at work that effects the publicly observable behavior of a person. If we ask why Jane is crying (behavior), we are likely to hear explanations such as: because she is sad, because she's thinking about the death of a loved one, because she has an illness called depression, and so on. Some accounts might appeal to Jane's experience, for example, She's crying because she just saw a sad movie, but these are typically considered incomplete until a hypothetical internal mechanism is provided: The movie made her cry because it *triggered memories* of painful life experiences.

This way of thinking and talking is very common. We say that we eat because we are hungry, we scream because we are angry, and so on. It's the way we talk about behavior, and particularly the behavior accompanying problems such as depression and anxiety. Centuries ago, problems in living were attributed to mystical spirits and hidden ghosts. It was easy for people to believe that someone shouted at the sky because he was possessed by a devil, or that a man could fall in love with a particular woman because she had bewitched him. Attributing behavior to what is going on inside a person is so much a part of our way of explaining problems that we rarely stop to recognize it. But internal causes are assumptions or hypotheses rather than facts. They also have numerous implications for how we go about helping people who are suffering with depression.

WHY ARE INTERNAL CAUSES SO APPEALING?

It is not only because people have attributed their behavior to internal causes for centuries that the current zeitgeist exists. We believe there are several factors that make internal causes appealing.

Research Evidence

There are large bodies of research supporting the role of internal causes in depression. Some studies show differences in biological or psychological markers in depressed and nondepressed people. Others show correlations between internal variables and depressive symptoms or behavior. Moreover, some individuals appear to be more vulnerable to stressful life events than others, and there may be a genetic component to depression (Kendler & Karkowski-Shuman, 1997; Kendler et al., 1995). There is also evidence of dysregulation of neurotransmitter systems related to depression (Siever & Davis, 1985). Although the evidence is less clear, there may be differences in the neurological structures of persons with emotional disorders (Pearlson & Schlaepfer, 1995). Changes in brain structures have been demonstrated to result from life experiences such as exposure to enduring stress. Thus, both biology and life experience are implicated in mood disorders (Free & Oei, 1989).

Antidepressant medications have revolutionized the treatment of depression. Beginning with monoamine oxidase inhibitors (MAOs) and into the present with the development of selective serotonin reuptake inhibitors (SSRIs), antidepressant medications have been demonstrated to have increasingly greater efficacy with fewer side effects. New antidepressant medications are developed routinely. Several medications that were still under investigation only six months ago are now being marketed and tried in clinical settings.

A plethora of research indicates that for many people, antidepressant medications are helpful and, in some cases, essential treatments (e.g., Blacker, 1996; Fein, Paz, Rao, & Lagrassa, 1988; Hirschfeld & Schatzberg, 1994; Schatzberg, 1996). Antidepressant medications produce relatively rapid improvement that is maintained while clients are on the medication, but for severe cases of depression (those very people for whom medications are often seen as the first line of defense) there is a relatively high rate of relapse without long-term treatment (Kupfer & Frank, 1992). For people who do not experience side effects this is not necessarily a problem; they can choose to remain on the medication, although some people don't like to be on medication long-term. For those who do experience side effects, the choice is either to take other medications that mitigate the side effects or to try different antidepressant medications. In the event that an individual does not improve (so-called "treatment resistant" depression), different classes of antidepressants are sometimes tried in combination and have been shown to improve efficacy (e.g. Perez, Gilaberte, Faries, Alvarez, & Artigas, 1997; Thase & Rush, 1995).

Neurotransmitters such as serotonin, dopamine, and norepinephrine play some role in either the vulnerability to or maintenance of emotional disorders (Maes & Meltzer, 1995; Schatzberg & Schildkraut, 1995). Yet despite much correlational evidence, there are no studies that show that biochemical abnormalities cause depression. Nonetheless, our culture is increasingly oriented toward biological explanations for problems in living. Thus, evidence of associations between biological variables and behavior is typically interpreted as demonstrating that the biological variable causes the behavioral one. Although the scientific community does its best to maintain a critical stance toward such evidence (e.g., Valenstein, 1998), the popular media typically present such findings as evidence that emotional disorders are de facto caused by biological processes.

The major psychological theories of depression have also produced evidence supporting internal causes. Cognitive theories of depression suggest that people who are depressed possess a negative bias about themselves and the world (Beck, 1976). Some individuals are believed to be more susceptible to depression as a result of activation of a schema or organizing structure in response to negative life events (Beck, 1983). Negative "automatic thoughts" are associated with negative mood states (Beck, 1976). For example, a person who has the thought "I am not going to impress anyone at this party" will feel sad or anxious about attending the party. The person may also behave in a way that undermines social success at the party, and the cognitive theorist would see the behavior as resulting from the negative automatic thought. In other words, the internal thought would be seen as the primary cause of the mood, though not all cognitive theorists insist that there is always a direct causal primacy (Clark, Beck, & Alford, 1999).

In practice, most cognitive therapists focus on negative thinking as the target for clinical intervention in cases of depression. The approach makes good sense and is based on a body of research showing correlation between naturally occurring or experimentally induced negative thinking and negative mood, or depression. For example, people who are depressed selectively attend to unpleasant events (cf. Beck, 1976; Fuchs & Rehm, 1977) and depressive episodes are exacerbated and prolonged by ruminations on negative symptoms and events (Nolen-Hoeksema, Morrow, & Fredrickson, 1993).

There is also a strong body of research demonstrating links between interpersonal processes and depression (Joiner & Coyne, 1999; Nolen-Hoeksema, 2000). For example, people who are depressed tend to elicit negative reactions from others (e.g., Hokanson, Rubert, Welker, Hollander, & Hedeen, 1989). Brown and Moran (1994) showed that the duration of episodes of depression is predicted by interpersonal problems. Although these studies do not strictly refer to internal causes of depression, many interpersonal approaches focus on individual interpersonal deficits such as lack of social skill and excessive reassurance seeking (see Joiner, 2000; Klerman, Weissman, Rounsaville, & Chevron, 1984).

Scientific Limitations of Research
on Internal Causes

The types of studies described above show that when people are depressed they may demonstrate changes in biochemical processes, stereotyped negative thinking patterns, and interpersonal difficulties. However, these studies do not indicate unequivocally that such hypothesized mechanisms actually cause depressed behavior. Although a thorough critique of biological, cognitive, and other internal psychological theories is beyond the scope of this book, here we briefly summarize some major concerns. First, evidence of treatment effectiveness does not speak to the etiology of a problem. Just because medications help in alleviating depressive symptoms for a percentage of people, it does not necessarily follow that the cause of the depression is biochemical. Likewise, if changing negative thinking patterns is helpful, a direct causal link cannot be made between negative thinking and depression. Rest, relaxation, and chicken soup may help reduce the symptoms of a cold, but it does not follow that colds are caused by lack of sleep, tension, and too little chicken soup in the diet.

A second problem with the research on internal causes has to do with methodological limitations. In a thorough review and critique of drug treatments for mental illness, Valenstein (1998) suggests several problems with biological theories. First, several studies have demonstrated that marked reductions of norepinephrine, serotonin, or dopamine does not produce depression in humans. Second, the major biological theories have difficulty explaining why some drugs alleviate depression when they have little or no effect on norepinephrine or serotonin. Third, antidepressant drugs take a relatively long time before they produce an elevation in mood despite the fact that they produce maximum elevations of serotonin and norepinephrine activity in one or two days. Although it is argued that this phenomenon occurs due to a "down regulating" of serotonin receptors, it is also possible that the success of SSRIs are due to a more complicated process than is explained simply by neurotransmitter levels. After reviewing the evidence, Valenstein concludes that, "Contrary to what is often claimed, no biochemical, anatomical, or functional signs have been found that reliably distinguish the brains of mental clients" (p. 125).

Many of the same limitations of research on biological causes apply to theories of internal psychological causes. For example, studies finding correlation between certain types of beliefs or thinking patterns and mood do not demonstrate that the former cause the latter. Experimental manipulations of attributions or other thought processes may lead to depressed mood in some individuals, but there is an obvious gap between such analogue research and major depression as it occurs in real life contexts. Even if we could demonstrate that manipulating cognitive processes in real life led to an increased likelihood of major depression, we would still wonder what caused the change in cognitive processes.

Nonscientific Reasons for the Appeal of Internal Causes

The zeitgeist of internal causation is not only a development of science. There are several nonscientific, and perhaps less honorable, reasons for the current focus on internal causation and for the "medicalization" of emotional difficulties, particularly depression (Jacobson & Gortner, 2000).

THE CULTURE OF BLAME

Regardless of what causes are postulated, depression is increasingly depicted as an illness. The negative stereotypes faced by sufferers of emotional problems provide strong motivation to find explanations that function to reduce blame and increase empathy. There is more money available from social services, eligibility for disability benefits, insurance benefits, and compassion for people considered to be suffering from a legitimate disease or illness. In contrast, when we assume that people rather than illnesses are the cause of their problems, we are more likely as a culture to respond with blame. Note, for example, the troubling notion that there are "innocent victims" of the AIDS epidemic (e.g., infants) and those who "get what they deserve" (i.e., sexually active gay men and intravenous drug users).

Medical illnesses are treated as negative life events that happen only to people, and for which they deserve empathy and concern. Such illnesses are understood to be caused by the body (or an infectious agent to the body) and are therefore not the fault of the person suffering the illness. Problems not caused by the body but by the mind, personality, or behavior of an individual are, on the other hand, more likely to be considered the fault of the person suffering. Thus, the science of internal biological causes converges with the pragmatic social advantages of constructing depression as an illness. Both support the zeitgeist of internal causation. In this context, it is not hard to understand why people whose behavior does not meet an accepted social standard would appeal to a genetic or physiological theory to explain problems in living. Our point is not that people who suffer from depression and anxiety aren't suffering; the pain and suffering are quite real. What we're suggesting is that when you live in a culture highly critical of deviant behavior, and a culture that offers "biological absolution" for such behavior, it is quite adaptive to support illness-oriented theories of emotional disorders.

MENTAL HEALTH ADVOCACY

Mental health advocacy groups often emphasize the medical aspects of depression and the efficacy of medications, while underrepresenting the evidence that short-term psychotherapies are as effective, or perhaps more effective, than medication (Valenstein, 1998). Given the culture of blame described above, this strategy makes sense. Politicians are not easily convinced of the need to provide funding for services for emotional and behavioral problems. In order to gain services for behavioral problems at parity with those provided for physical illnesses, advocates argue that money needs to be available for the biochemical treatments of mental illness. There seems to be an implicit assumption that problems with a biological basis are real, serious, and deserving of financial resources, whereas those without a biological basis are not as pressing, more attributable to lifestyle issues, personal choice, and so on. Once again, the cultural context supports the primacy of biologically oriented theories of internal causation.

PRESSURE FOR FAST CURES

These are the days of fast foods, fast communication over the Internet, and fast cures for human problems. Current guidelines for primary care providers (PCPs) recommend psychotherapy only after failure on two antidepressant medications (Agency for Health Care Policy and Research, 1993). This represents a rather narrow view of the data supporting medication as a first-line treatment (Persons, Thase, & Crits-Cristoph, 1996). Many studies have demonstrated that psychotherapy is equally effective in treating major depression (Persons et al., 1996), although the results may not be as rapid. Nonetheless, despite little evidence (Antonuccio, Thomas, & Danton, 1997), many insurance companies consider medications a more cost-effective alternative, and it has become common practice for some preferred provider organizations to approve continued psychotherapy sessions for clients only after they receive a medication evaluation by a medical specialist. Frequently this requirement is made regardless of the client's desire to consider medication as an option.

CONVENTIONS AND LIMITATIONS OF EVERYDAY LANGUAGE

It is remarkably common in everyday language to attribute our actions to internal causes. We say we cry because we are sad, eat because we are hungry, shout because we are angry, and vote for certain laws because we believe in social justice. In our day-to-day discourse with others, these attributions have some useful functions. For example, telling a friend that we are crying because we are sad is a very good shorthand way to summarize a wealth of recent and past history. Telling people that we believe in social justice allows them to predict all sorts of behaviors we are likely to engage in the future (e.g., voting democratically, contributing to charities, and so on). At other times, attributing our behavior to internal causes can deter others from encouraging us to change (Addis & Jacobson, 1996). If I say, "I'm leaving this meeting because I'm disgusted with what's going on," no one can dispute that I am disgusted; it is understood by all as something private that is causing my behavior. People may take issue with my behavior, but they are unlikely to dispute its cause — if they do, they likely do so for their own pragmatic reasons. Attributing my behavior to lack of sleep, for example, could function to criticize me, absolve themselves of blame, and warn me that future similar behavior will not be tolerated.

It is clear that in the pragmatics of everyday discourse, attributing behavior to internal causes can have some pretty useful consequences. Unfortunately, there is a slippery slope from using internal attributions casually to treating them as if they are "things" that actually govern behavior. In other words, our convenient linguistic strategies get reified into objects; in effect, we come to believe what we say and our verbal community continues to reinforce talk about internal causes of behavior (Baum, 1994; Hayes & Hayes, 1989). Of course, people often make use of external causal attributions as well. Citing situational causes of behavior can absolve someone of blame if the event was negative and make someone appear modest if the event was positive. Our general point is that the distinction between internal and external causes of behavior is so common in everyday language that it is usually taken for granted. Even though the majority of our actions are likely to be multiply determined by our histories, current environments, current biological processes, and current thinking, our language gives us virtually no way to summarize economically these complex transactions. Thus, we fall back on a pragmatic heuristic; we separate the world of behavior into internal and external causes.

The Alternative: Assets of a Contextual Approach

There is nothing inherently wrong with the search for internal causes. In fact, an enormous body of research and many helpful treatments have

developed from the basic assumption that there is something dysfunctional inside people suffering from depression. Our goal in the remainder
of this book is not to disprove or dispute the idea of internal causation,
but to explore an alternative way of thinking about and treating depression. Oftentimes, alternative ways of looking at problems can open up
creative and effective ways to promote change.

Our guiding assumption is that depression can be usefully conceptualized as a process occurring in the context of people's lives; that is, depression can be understood as a series of actions and events rather than some
sort of internal object or mechanism. When we say the *context* of people's
lives we are referring to evolving transactions between people's actions
and the environments in which they occur. Much of this book is about
developing these basic ideas and applying them to the treatment of
depression. For now, the important point is that depression might be
meaningfully approached as relationships between people and their environments, where the relationships themselves are the focus. In other
words, it is precisely at the nexus of human activity and its surroundings
that problems such as depression take form. Such an approach clearly
runs counter to the zeitgeist of internal causation. Why consider it?

Much like internal models, the contextual approach is consistent with
a good deal of empirical research. We have known for some time that
depression is associated with all sorts of stressful life events, as well as
chronic stresses in interpersonal and work domains (Hammen, 1999;
Holahan, Moos, & Bonin, 1999). These events occur as people live their
lives. How someone interprets such experiences is certainly an important
part of the context, but so are the nuanced relationships between his or
her actions and their consequences. It is here that behavioral theories
and interventions can be usefully integrated into a contextual approach.
Behavioral activation provides an alternative to looking inside a person
for change, and asks instead that client and therapist work to make
changes in clients' life contexts more broadly. Sometimes these changes
are about shifting directions (e.g., looking for a new job, getting out of
a painful relationship). Other times they are about changing the way
people respond more generally to stressful life situations; often toward a
more proactive and goal-directed strategy rather than a passive, reactive
one.

The idea that we can help clients become less depressed by helping
them to become more active is not particularly revolutionary. Inactivity
is, in fact, one of the central features of depression. Peter Lewinsohn
(Lewinsohn, 1974; Lewinsohn, Antonuccio, Steinmetz-Breckenridge, &
Teri, 1984; Lewinsohn et al., 1976; Lewinsohn & Graf, 1973; Lewin-

sohn & Libet, 1972; MacPhillamy & Lewinsohn, 1972), Aaron Beck (Beck et al., 1979), and their colleagues have developed effective treatments for major depression that include components designed to increase people's ability to activate themselves. But activating oneself in a context of depression can be extremely difficult. The depressed context supports inactivity, hopelessness, rumination, and withdrawal. If these behaviors are dominant in peoples' lives, how are they to become active? In our view, this is the central dilemma in depression; there is little doubt that strategically activating oneself is effective, but the right strategy can be hard to determine, and even harder to implement. Because a contextual approach focuses precisely on people's day-to-day actions it can illuminate patterns that maintain a sense of being "stuck" and suggest creative pathways to change.

Perhaps the most compelling asset of a contextual viewpoint is that it helps therapists take a different view of clients. Working with people when they are depressed can be extremely challenging. Because other people's pain can be aversive for us, and particularly so when it is unremitting, therapist frustration can lead to subtly blaming and criticizing a depressed client. Yet viewed in context, depressive behavior usually makes sense. Given a particular history and current life context, withdrawal, avoidance, inactivity, and even rumination can be understood as adaptive coping strategies. Needless to say, such a perspective supports a context of empathy rather than blame.

CHAPTER 2

Creating a Coherent Framework for Behavioral Activation

IN THE LAST CHAPTER WE PRESENTED some of the concerns about current approaches to treating depression and the emphasis on internal causation. In this and the following chapter we delve more deeply into the theoretical and conceptual models guiding BA. In developing BA as a standalone treatment there was a goal for it to be a coherent set of interventions. In other words, therapists and clients should be able to know when treatment is about behavioral activation and when it is not. At the same time, we wanted to develop a treatment that could be flexibly tailored to the needs and presenting problems of different clients. One way to work effectively in the tension between adherence to an empirically supported treatment and flexible use of that treatment is to ground oneself clearly in the conceptual and theoretical bases of the treatment. Thus, this chapter is about specifying clearly what it means to think like a behavioral activation therapist.

MECHANISM AND CONTEXTUALISM

Thinking and acting like a BA therapist means thinking and acting contextually and functionally. Viewing people contextually means seeing the person in his or her environment. If we drew a stick figure to represent a person and a circle to represent the environment, cognitive models would look like figure 2.1: There would be an arrow going from the circle to the head of the stick figure, and another arrow from the head back to the circle—but they would be separate. This represents social learning—we learn beliefs and thoughts from the environment and then these beliefs and thoughts shape our perception of the environment.

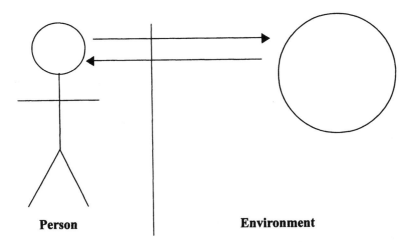

Person   **Environment**

FIGURE 2.1 A *cognitive or social learning model: The environment shapes people's perceptions and beliefs, which in turn shape perceptions of the environment.*

Contextualism would have the figure in the circle and this becomes an inseparable unit of analysis. To represent contextualism in its truest sense our stick figure within the circle would eventually disappear into the circle and the circle into it, forming no artificial boundaries between environment within or without the person (figure 2.2).

When we view things contextually we cannot understand the meaning of something like depression without understanding the context in which it is occurring. In fact, according to contextualism, depression is not a "thing" inside a person, but rather a set of actions or behaviors occurring in a set of depressive contexts. For example, given a long history of not attaining desired goals, and then losing an enjoyable position in a new

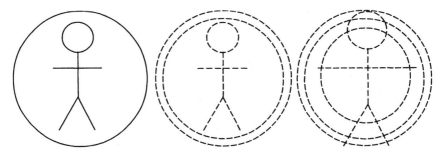

FIGURE 2.2 A *contextual model of the person-environment relationship: Behavior and context are analyzed as one. Dashed lines represent increasing dissolution of arbitrary boundaries.*

company, a person may begin to exhibit some of the symptoms that are recognized as depression. This is a radical idea. The traditional view of depression and other "mental" disorders is that they occur somewhere inside the person, be it inside the neurotransmitter system (as in biological theories) or inside the mind (as in cognitive theories), but both are placed in the brain of the individual person. Treatment then necessarily focuses on changing some particular cause inside the person. Even traditional behavioral views have considered skill deficits inside the person as causal factors for a variety of emotional problems. A contextual view of depression leads us to focus on changing actions and contexts. We're interested in what people are doing when they're depressed, where they're doing it, how they're doing it, and what the consequences are.

Contrasting it with mechanistic thinking highlights the nature of contextual thinking. Both rely on certain root metaphors for describing the world (Hayes, Hayes, & Reese, 1988; Pepper, 1942). A root metaphor is a comprehensive way of representing things in the world. The root metaphor in mechanism is the machine. When we think and talk mechanistically we treat the object of our discourse as if it were a machine. We're interested in how all the different parts fit together. If we want to fix a broken machine, we generate hypotheses about where the dysfunction lies. We assume that if we can locate the broken mechanism in the causal chain then the whole machine will return to proper working order.

It has been suggested that traditional behavioral, cognitive, and biological theories of depression are guided by machine metaphors (Hayes et al., 1988; Jacobson, 1997a). Neither of these theories ignores the environment, but they see the environment as something outside of the person. The environment acts upon the person, and then the person has an impact on the environment. Traditional behavior therapy, though guided by the mechanistic metaphor in theory, may not be so in practice. When biological psychiatry researchers search for the proper regulation of neurotransmitters to explain depression, or search for other neurological correlates, they are trying to find the broken part of the machine and alter it so that it functions properly. Cognitive theory looks for underlying structures that have become dysfunctional and create problems for the person when they are triggered by an environmental event. In BA we speak of triggers, but philosophically we see the environment and the person as one context. As Jacobson (1997b) pointed out, contextualists advocate:

> identifying functional relations; intervening to alter problematic functional relations; shaping desirable behavior by natural contingencies; relying on

natural rather than contrived reinforcers; and avoiding the dualism inherent in the arbitrary definition of behavior as only that which can be observed by others. (p. 631)

In other words, contextual therapists help to change transactions in the environment that will increase the likelihood that natural reinforcers will be available to the client. Cognitive and cognitive-behavior therapists work with clients to change the dysfunctional belief structures; in other words, they have identified the broken piece and attempt to repair it in order to restore the overall machine. They have been highly effective in doing so. Contextualism offers a different approach, one that is only recently beginning to be tested as a philosophy that can guide clinical practice (e.g., Hayes, Strosahl, & Wilson, 1999).

If we think about depression in the way that we just discussed, how do we treat it? Some have taken a behavioral activation approach that is different from ours. Behavioral activation as presented in this book is a new application of the behavioral principles that have been in the literature for decades. Getting depressed clients activated has been an aspect of both cognitive and behavioral treatments. What we are adding is a functional component and have made the treatment more idiographic. By empirically testing such an approach, this updated version of BA allows clinicians to follow several basic principles and work with clients to better understand the function of their behaviors and provide a means for them to begin to make changes in their lives that can alleviate depressive symptoms.

PREVIOUS EXPLORATIONS OF BEHAVIORAL ACTIVATION TREATMENTS FOR DEPRESSION

The two major therapies that have used activation strategies are the behavioral treatment of Peter Lewinsohn and colleagues and the cognitive therapy of Aaron Beck and colleagues. We wish to both acknowledge these pioneers and great thinkers, as well as to demonstrate where our approach to behavioral activation differs from these approaches.

Peter Lewinsohn's Coping with Depression Course

The first attempt to apply behavioral theories such as Ferster's into clinical practice came from the work of Peter Lewinsohn and colleagues (Lewinsohn, Weinstein, & Shaw, 1969). Basing their theory on social learning theory (Bandura, 1969, 1977), Lewinsohn and colleagues (Lewinsohn, Youngren, & Grosscup, 1979) described depression as being associated with a decrease in pleasant events and an increase in unpleasant person-environment interactions. Based on this premise, Lewinsohn's approach to the treatment of depression consisted of developing a measure of pleasant events (MacPhillamy & Lewinsohn, 1982) and working with individuals to use activity scheduling to increase the number of pleasant events and decrease the number of unpleasant events in their lives.

As Lewinsohn's treatment developed it became a broad-spectrum, cognitive-behavioral approach. In the "Coping with Depression Course" (Lewinsohn et al., 1984), the treatment had developed into a comprehensive program to be run in groups. Clients were provided instruction in self-monitoring of activities, particularly of pleasant and negative events. They were also taught relaxation techniques, cognitive restructuring, and social skill techniques. Using lectures, homework, and group activities the treatment was provided by instructors who were presenting a "course." This was an attempt to destigmatize the depressed individuals who participated in the treatment program. Following the recommendations of Zeiss, Lewinsohn, and Muñoz (1979), the authors of the Coping with Depression Course tried to develop a short-term therapy that began with an elaborated rationale, provided training in skills that allowed the participant to feel more effective in managing daily life situations, emphasized the independent use of the skills by the participant outside of therapy, and encouraged the participant's attributions that improvement was caused by her or his own work and not that of the therapist or leader.

Behavioral activation therapy as currently presented differs from this earlier model. First, the approach to BA is an idiographic and functional approach. It is not assumed that there is a broad class of pleasant events that are missing from a client's life. Furthermore, in BA we look at reinforcement as that which increases a behavior and are, therefore, less likely to assume that pleasant events are always positively reinforcing. We try to explore with the client the functions of his or her behaviors and look at the contingencies that may maintain the behaviors. Second, our BA model focuses on activation exclusively, and at the barriers to activation, but we do not include cognitive treatments in the standalone BA approach. We believe that a purely behavioral rationale can account for the changes that we see in client behavior. Finally, we help clients to schedule activities that will help to move them toward some personal goals or block the avoidance patterns that are identified during our functional analysis.

Behavioral Activation in Beck's Cognitive Therapy

Behavioral activation was also utilized by Beck and colleagues (1979) in the treatment manual for cognitive therapy for depression. In cognitive therapy (CT), behavioral activation is used in the early stages of therapy for individuals who are more severely depressed. In some cases, when the client is severely depressed, behavioral activation may be used as the primary strategy more than cognitive interventions. Behavioral activation in cognitive therapy consists first of teaching the client to monitor his or her behavior using an activity schedule. The client is asked either to rate her or his mood during each hour on the activity schedule or to provide an overall rating for the day, or to do both. After several days of monitoring, the therapist and the client evaluate the activity schedule and the therapist helps the client to make conclusions about the relationship between the level of activity and mood.

Once the client has learned to monitor activity, the therapist develops a list of activities with the client that is believed to provide a sense of either mastery or pleasure (or both). The client is instructed to increase the amount of these activities and the therapist works with the client to schedule such activities on the activity chart to increase the likelihood that they will be done. Such activity scheduling and mastery/pleasure ratings are assigned as homework for the client in the early sessions of cognitive therapy. If homework is not completed the therapist helps the client to discover the thoughts that may have interfered with completing the assignment. As the client's mood improves, standard cognitive interventions are implemented and the client is taught to use the Dysfunctional Thoughts Record (Beck et al., 1979) to record automatic thoughts (Beck, 1976) and to find alternative responses to the automatic thoughts.

Behavioral treatments are utilized throughout cognitive therapy. Good cognitive therapists make ample use of behavioral experiments to test clients' assumptions and beliefs. When particular beliefs are identified in a session, the therapist and client work collaboratively to develop experiments to test the belief. This type of collaborative empiricism (Beck et al., 1979) is a hallmark of the cognitive approach to treatment for depression and other emotional disorders. Behavioral experiments allow clients to test the absolute truth of their assumptions. Take an example of a young man who believes that he cannot engage in small talk at social gatherings because he cannot think of anything intelligent to discuss. The therapist may ask questions regarding the client's beliefs about the types of topics others discuss when they make small talk. Once the client has identified several ideas, like a belief that people talk about art, history, technological advancements, etc., the client would then be instructed to test out his assumptions. One way to do this may be to go to a mall or delicatessen and eavesdrop on conversations. The client could carry a notepad and record a list of topics that were overheard. It is likely that the client will hear the sophisticated topics that he fears everyone discusses, but he will also hear chatter about prices of food, misbehaving children, hairstyles, etc. The therapist and the client would then discuss the implications of the discoveries made during the experiment for the client's strongly held belief that he is not smart enough to engage in small talk.

In cognitive therapy, behavioral activation, behavioral experiments, and other predominantly behavioral techniques are used toward the ultimate goal of changing beliefs and assumptions. Consistent with a cognitive theory of emotional disorders, it is change in the thinking that is believed to be a mediator of other behavior that is essential. Lasting change is believed to take place when clients are able to modify core beliefs about themselves and the world that lead them to form erroneous and biased conclusions. The component analysis study (Jacobson et al., 1996) discussed in the first chapter was designed to test the hypothesis that the behavioral components of CT were sufficient in both the treatment of depression and prevention of relapse. Obviously, our approach to BA sees the activation of the client as the sufficient and complete treatment for depression. It is not seen as a means toward an end of changing thoughts or beliefs.

Although BA is used in cognitive therapy, our current treatment of BA differs in that the goal is activating clients, not changing cognitions. We believe that a behavioral formulation is sufficient without proposing underlying structures such as core beliefs or schemas. In the final analysis, if helping a client to change his or her behavior alleviates depression then it is a useful treatment. Given Ferster's (1973) description of depression, there is a strong theoretical rationale for increasing activities that will allow clients to break a passive approach to life and bring them in contact with natural, positive, reinforcement.

When people have experiences that have come to be labeled as depression it is common for them to reduce overall activity. The activity becomes reactive, sleeping at odd times because they feel fatigued, closing the shades because the world appears too hectic, perseverating on negative thoughts because that is what comes to mind. This is the context of depression. In BA, we work with acting and doing. Although we do not propose to fully understand a cause-and-effect relationship, and leave the reinforcement of behaviors up to the natural contingencies that will inevitably maintain them, we try to help the person to increase the opportunity for behaviors to be reinforced positively. In short, cognitive, cognitive-behavioral, psychodynamic, and biological therapists, although coming from very different theoretical orientations, follow the basic philosophy of mechanism and look inside the person for the resolution of conflict and problem behavior. The BA therapist, and other contextualist therapists, look at the entire life of the person, and pay less regard to what is going on "inside of" the person and attempt to encourage individuals to engage or reengage in the events of their lives. We attempt to shift the context from a depressant one to an antidepressant one. Ferster (1973) speaks of environment in the following manner:

> A behavioral analysis requires that we talk about how the environment prompts and otherwise controls a person's activity rather than our accustomed patterns of perceiving the inside and outside world. Nevertheless, the event that influences the person is the same in both the clinical and behavioral descriptions however we may talk about them. The behavioral description is more useful than the mentalistic one because it uses more objective details of how a person comes to act distinctively toward the various features of his inside and outside environment. An objective view of clinical interactions can lead to procedures with a larger rational component. (p. 862)

A SHORT PRIMER OF BEHAVIOR ANALYSIS

Functional behavior analytic theories have made a significant contribution to the development of BA. To think like a BA therapist is to recognize that all behavior is important, that everything has a function, and to attend to the functions of behaviors that clients report that occur outside of sessions as well as to those that occur during the session. The main, overarching premises of behavior analysis (also referred to as radical behaviorism) are contextualism (as we have explained above and will elaborate on in chapter 3), antimentalism, and a focus on the function rather than the form of behavior.

Antimentalism

To the radical behaviorist, it is important that behavior can be observed, and that it is explained parsimoniously. This has often been misinterpreted to mean that behaviorists are only interested in things that can be seen. If this were the case, then behaviorists would have no interest in thinking or emoting, since these processes are difficult to see. This is not the case, however. Radical behaviorists have never had a problem accepting that there are private events that occur and are experienced only by the individual. The behaviorist contention has been that these events are either covert verbal behaviors or verbal behaviors applied to bodily sensations. In essence, what we feel are our bodies. When a life event occurs, such as the death of a loved one, we experience something in our body. We may experience disruption in our gastrointestinal tract, feelings of lightheadedness; we may begin to weep, to feel weak in the knees. Based on our cultural and familial backgrounds, we will have learned to associate certain words such as "grief" and "sadness" to these experiences.

Some of the things that we experience privately (e.g., changes in our bodies) are unconditioned. Our culture and environments condition the words that we use to describe the experiences. In other words, they are learned. The experiences that we call "sadness," "depression," "euphoria," for example, are all learned associations based on our families and cultures. The radical behaviorists denounced the need to reify these associations into things that exist within the "mind." To the behaviorist, one does not "have an emotion" nor does one "have a thought." Instead, these experiences are seen as behaviors and responses to context based on the learning history of the individual. So, one does indeed "emote," usually in response to some current change in the environment, or because of a history of doing so in similar contexts. Likewise, one also "thinks." These activities are regarded as verbs rather than as nouns. The behaviorists simply eschewed talking about these activities as structures because doing so obfuscated the learning process in exploring human behavior. Both thoughts and emotions are seen as dependent variables by behavior analysts in the same way as observable behaviors are seen as dependent variables (Biglan & Hayes, 1996). Since thoughts and emotions cannot be directly manipulated, they cannot be seen as independent variables, which are subject to direct manipulation by the researcher. Only environmental events can be manipulated and the subsequent changes in behavior, thinking, or emotion would be the subject under study, hence the dependent variable. Looking at how thinking and acting interact is to look at a "behavior-behavior" relationship, and therefore one cannot imply that one behavior "causes" another behavior; although one behavior can set up the occasion for another behavior to occur. In other words, the behavior can be a setting variable, also referred to as an establishing operation, or it can serve as a discriminative stimulus (Dougher & Hackbert, 2000). For example, food deprivation establishes food as a salient reinforcer for the individual that is food deprived, that is, it is an establishing operation. This example from a situation familiar to clinicians will clarify. Let's say that Althea has suffered great humiliation at the hands of her peers as an overweight child. She may be particularly sensitive to the criticism of others given her repeated history with other children and the isolation and sadness that accompanied many childhood experiences. Seeing herself in the mirror and hearing words like "fatty" become associated with feeling humiliated and sad. As an adult, regardless of Althea's current weight, if she sees herself in the mirror and says to herself "I'm getting fat," the image and the words associated with the experience of humiliation set up an establishing operation for the reinforcement of dieting behavior. In other words, as she sees the numbers on the scale decreasing she is reinforced for dieting. The numbers on the scale are salient reinforcers given her prior experiences. Hence, her thinking is an establishing operation, there is a behavior-behavior relationship. The act of thinking is related to the act of dieting although it does not cause dieting.

Function Rather than Form

In order to make sense of behavior, the behaviorists look at the function that the behavior serves by observing its outcome. When dealing with complex human behaviors, it is often difficult to truly know the function, but it is important to recognize that the function is important, and that it is, in fact, more important than the form of the behavior. Many behaviors have the same form, but different functions. A man may walk out of his house at 6:00 P.M. carrying a bag of garbage and place it in a metal container. One may say that he is "taking out the garbage," which is the form of the behavior. However, there can be several reasons or functions of the "taking out the garbage" behavior. He could be responding to the odor of the garbage in his kitchen, in which case the behavior functions to remove the aversive stimulus of the odor. He could also be taking out the garbage as a response to a request from his partner, in which case the behavior functions as a consequence (or reinforcer) of the partner's behavior. Another possibility is that he is taking the garbage out to walk away from an argument with his partner. To the radical behaviorist, the function of the behavior is the subject of interest.

Types and Schedules of Reinforcement

Now that we have explained a few of the overarching assumptions of the behaviorist view, we will offer a little more detail about the terminology of behaviorism. For readers who are not trained in behavioral theory or who have not read their learning theory for a number of years we will provide a very brief discussion of schedules of reinforcement in relatively nontechnical terms. First, it may be necessary to clear up the distinction between positive reinforcement, negative reinforcement, and punishment. The concept is very simplistic to the behaviorally trained clinician, but most others confuse the terms. A behavior that is reinforced is always increased; a behavior that is punished is always decreased. When a behavior is followed by a consequence that is pleasurable, rewarding, or otherwise positive, that behavior is said to have been positively reinforced. An example would be seeing a chocolate-covered ice cream cone and taking a bite. If it tastes good to the person she will take another bite, and so on. Having had a history of the good taste of the ice cream, she will likely take a bite when presented with a chocolate-covered ice cream cone in the future. In even simpler terms, "positive" means that something was introduced following a behavior. A behavior that is followed by the removal of a noxious or aversive condition is said to be negatively reinforced. To use a similar example of food, if a young woman has been deprived of food for 24 hours and is offered a piece of bread, the eating of the bread will be followed by a reduction in hunger. She may then seek another piece of bread to further reduce the state of deprivation. We have intentionally used examples of the same behavior, eating, because it is important to recognize that the topography of the behavior is not important when it comes to positive or negative reinforcement. It is the function of the behavior that is important. Simply put, "negative" means that something was taken away.

In the first instance, when a behavior is positively reinforced, the individual engages in the behavior for the positive effect. In the second instance, when a behavior is negatively reinforced, the person engages in the behavior because she experiences the reduction in an aversive condition and has done so in the past. Reinforcement means that behavior increases. So, "negative reinforcement" means that the consequences of the behavior were that something aversive was removed but that the behavior increased in its probability in the future. The important point is that engaging in the behavior is increased due to either the addition of something positive or the removal of something negative.

Punishment decreases behavior. When a behavior is followed by a noxious stimulus, that behavior is said to have been punished. So, if either the young woman eating the ice cream cone because it tasted good, or the second woman eating the bread to reduce hunger, were to be given an electric shock following each bite of food, she would most likely stop the behavior. We would say her behavior had been "positively punished," in other words, something (the electric shock) was added. The same behaviors could be punished negatively by removing something; for example, the women may be required to give up their coat and wallet after either eating the ice cream or bread.

Reinforcement occurs on various schedules (Ferster & Skinner, 1957). Reinforcement on a fixed ratio (FR) schedule occurs after a fixed number of responses on the part of the organism. In other words, a pigeon may receive food pellets after it pecks a key six times. On a FR schedule it will receive the pellets after every six key pecks. Reinforcement on a variable ratio (VR) schedule occurs after a certain number of responses, but the number of the responses are varied. For example, the pigeon may receive the food pellets after it pecks the key six times on the first presentation of the pellets, two times on the second presentation, ten times on the third, five times, six times, two times, and so on. Reinforcement can also occur at intervals of time. By now this should be quite obvious. A fixed interval schedule (FI) occurs when a behavior is reinforced when it occurs after a specified and fixed amount of time. For example, a behavior will be reinforced every five minutes. On a variable interval schedule (VI) the time needed prior to the onset of reinforcement is varied. There are other more complex schedules of reinforcement, consisting of some combination of the above, but such detail is not needed for the present discussion. The point is that reinforcement is not as simple a process as providing a raisin every time a child says a word correctly.

Although the basic concepts of behaviorism are quite simple, they are far reaching in their implications. It really is the parsimony that underlies behavioral activation. In the following section, we will show how early behaviorists used these relatively straightforward concepts to explain complex behaviors, such as depression in context. The concepts, while explaining complex behaviors without relying on ideas that seemed mentalistic or not parsimonious, became quite technical and difficult to understand for many nonbehaviorists.

EARLY BEHAVIOR ANALYTIC FORMULATIONS OF DEPRESSION

Ferster (1981) suggested that when an individual experiences depression characterized by cessation of simple activities that were formerly stable parts of the person's life, such depression may come from a sudden change in the life cycle or an upheaval of the larger social environment.

When an individual functions under a schedule of reinforcement that requires a relatively fixed and large amount of activity for reinforcement to occur, he or she may become depressed. In other words, opportunities for positive reinforcement are limited to the person. According to this view of depression it could be argued that, at least in part, the symptoms experienced by the individual that we refer to as "depression" may serve to signal the individual that he or she needs to make a change in his or her life. In other words, depression is not the result of a "chemical imbalance" in the person, or of "faulty thinking," but rather, it is the response to problems in life.

Radical behavioral theorists have proposed since the 1970s that depression resulted from problems in the individual's interaction with the environment that resulted in the individual not engaging in behaviors that will be positively reinforced and that would allow that individual to exert control over her environment. The antimentalistic language of the radical behavioral theory of depression is both its strength and perhaps the very thing that has placed it in relative obscurity compared to the "sexier" (and more commonsensical) cognitive, interpersonal, or biological theories. While the behavioral view is also rather straightforward, the tendency in the 1950s and 1960s by radical behaviorists to eschew any terminology that could be considered "mentalistic" led to the development of a new language which became useful mostly to other radical behaviorists. It was difficult for meaningful dialogue to occur between the radical behaviorists and other psychological investigators because the radical behaviorists refused to use accepted psychological terms and instead developed a unique language (Staats, 1995).

Ferster's (1981) description of his behavioral theory of depression contains vocabulary that only the most highly specialized behaviorist is likely to understand. When describing depression as a verbal phenomenon, he states:

> The main diagnostic characterization — grief, mourning, self-debasement, and impaired thought — refer to verbal behaviors that are tacts under the discriminative control of private events (Skinner, 1957). A proportion of the total verbal repertoire might consist of complaints, criticism, demands for relief, or assertions of distress, all functionally avoidance and escape behaviors. (p. 185)

This statement is understandable to those trained in radical behaviorism, who understand that a "tact" is a Skinnerian word for a unit of verbal behavior, generally equivalent to a "description." For individuals used to talking in terms referred to as "mentalistic" by radical behaviorists, the language of radical behaviorism is arcane and obscures the theory. Although Ferster described a phenomenon that hundreds of clinicians see in their offices daily, the technical description was difficult to understand. Radical behavioral theory, like psychoanalysis, requires the clinician to develop a specific vocabulary.

It is our contention that the radical behaviorists were correct in their functional analysis of depression. This position accounts for the success of the behavioral approach of Lewinsohn and colleagues (Lewinsohn & Graf, 1973; Lewinsohn & Libet, 1972; Lewinsohn et al., 1969; Youngren & Grosscup, 1979), Rehm (1977), as well as the cognitive approach of Beck and colleagues (1979). Lewinsohn was, in fact, the first clinical researcher to make attempts at applying Ferster's theories to the treatment of depression. Radical behavioral concepts needed to be translated into language that makes sense to those trained in other schools of thought because the ideas hold great validity and promise for the study and treatment of depression and other human problems. Lewinsohn and colleagues (1969) began this endeavor and behavioral activation currently takes Lewinsohn's work further by targeting the avoidance behaviors and other processes suggested by Ferster.

Ferster's Theory of Depression

At this point the reader may ask, "Why go back to earlier behavioral formulations of depression when there has been so much research into cognitive-behavioral and interpersonal approaches?" The answer is simple. There were several important ideas presented by the radical behaviorists that have been lost in the translation. We believe that these ideas present an essential understanding that is important to clinicians as well as to future research on the nature of depression. We will present three main ideas from Ferster's work on which much of BA rests.

RESPONDING TO DEPRIVATION

Ferster (1981) hypothesized that the learning history of people who become depressed may contain many situations wherein behavior is reinforced on a relatively fixed ratio schedule requiring a large amount of activity prior to being reinforced. Also, behaviors that are maintained by negative reinforcement contribute to the development of a passive approach to life. The learning process is inadequate in this situation and the person does not learn that certain behaviors result in positive consequences. For example, if a loving, concerned parent, who interacts with the child frequently, attends to a child, the child will learn that its coos and gurgling result in a positive experience with the parent. The cooing and gurgling will then be positively reinforced, and the child's interactions with the parent will increase. On the other hand, if the child is neglected or attended to inconsistently, it may cry or fidget when it is hungry or need a change, and occasionally the parent will attend to this behavior. The connection is not made, however, between the behavior and its consequence due to the need for a large amount of activity prior to the application of the consequence.

In depression, individuals' levels of deprivation influence the accuracy of their observations about their environment. A person's ability to talk about her life is subject to distortion and incomplete description. This is consistent with the cognitive theory of Beck that there is a negative cognitive bias in depression. It is also explained in behavioral terms by the self-control model (Fuchs & Rehm, 1977; Kanfer, 1971; Rehm, 1977).

Ferster's functional analysis of depression provides a possible explanation for some people's difficulty recognizing the situational antecedents and consequences of their behavior (i.e., self-monitoring) given that learning has taken place in an environment of noncontingent reinforcement and punishment. For example, if a young child has inconsistent parenting and is punished for minor infractions like being several minutes late for a meal in the presence of major successes like having helped clean the kitchen, the child does not have the experience of relating behavior to consequences. If this pattern persists, the growing child will not develop the ability to self-monitor. According to self-control theory, without the process of self-monitoring, it is impossible to evaluate one's own performance or to be able to reinforce oneself. According to Ferster's theory, the child will make responses according to her own deprivation and will not actively respond to the external environment whereby her behavior will be positively reinforced. In extreme cases, the person's behavior will become controlled primarily by negative reinforcement (i.e., the alleviation of the deprivation) and the passive style will continue. Clinicians frequently see behavior that is controlled by negative reinforcement. A client's complaints or withdrawal may function to attain sympathy, for example. However, regardless of whether or not the environment is reinforcing — or the sympathy attained — the client continues to emit the behavior because of a response to deprivation (i.e., the person is, in a sense, sympathy deprived).

NARROWING REPERTOIRES

When an individual learns a passive style of responding, and responses are controlled by the alleviation of deprivation or some other aversive state, that individual does not develop a broad set of behaviors that we would see as adequate for negotiating all of the positives and negatives of life. To speak poetically, the person does not learn how to "live life to its fullest," and mostly reacts to a felt sense of need. This concept is important, because what has usually been regarded by therapists as a skills deficit, that is, something wrong inside of the person (remember the mechanistic/contextualist distinction), is explained in the context of the reinforcement history of the person. In behavioral activation, we try to increase the opportunities for individuals to engage in new behaviors, essentially to expand their repertoires. We do not make the assumption that they lack skill, but rather we assume that, given the context of their lives, they have lacked or lost opportunity.

Ferster (1973) notes that most activities occur for many reasons and are occasioned by multiple sources and that depression may represent weakening of one or more of these sources. The complexity and multiple sources of activities may explain why even physiological processes such as sex and eating are lessened in frequency for people who are depressed. There are also collateral social correlates for these activities and the reduction in these behaviors may lessen the effectiveness of the reinforcers closely connected with the physiological process. A second activity seen in depressed individuals is a high frequency of escape and avoidance from aversive life experiences and a reduced frequency of positively reinforced behavior.

ESCAPE AND AVOIDANCE AS MOTIVATING GOALS IN DEPRESSION

One of Ferster's central ideas that has been underemphasized in the cognitive and behavioral literature on depression is that when people become depressed many of their behaviors come to function as avoidance or escape. Ferster (1973) suggested several characteristics of depression. The depressed person not only engages in certain activities but also demonstrates increased avoidance and escape behaviors. Escaping from an aversive environment (internal or external), or avoiding aversive conditions altogether, becomes the predominant mode of action. Ferster suggests that many of the escape or avoidance behaviors, such as complaining, pacing, and, we would add, ruminating, serve to avoid aversive conditions like silence, inactivity, or activities that produce anxiety for the individual. Depression may occur either because the individual efficiently avoids aversive stimuli and therefore lacks sufficient amounts of positive reinforcement, or because there has been a sudden loss of positive reinforcement, and the individual then begins to engage in escape and avoidance behaviors as a means of alleviating the aversive condition of the sudden loss. Lastly, the depressed individual develops a passive repertoire. In other words, activities that are positively reinforced occur less than those that are reinforced negatively through escape/avoidance. The individual does not develop a repertoire of behaviors that keep him or her actively engaged in problem solving, achieving goals, etc.

It is important for the behavioral activation therapist to be aware of the three ideas proposed by Ferster:

1. Depressed people may respond more to their level of deprivation than to external, environmental contingencies.
2. They develop narrowed repertoires of behaving which makes them more vulnerable to depression.
3. They utilize escape and avoidance behaviors more frequently than nondepressed people do.

These ideas are central to the approach that the behavioral activator takes to each case. Trying to increase activity is a means to increase the repertoire of behaviors that a person engages in, and in order to do this it is important to help the person recognize escape and avoidance so that he or she can begin to approach situations and fully engage. The following clinical example illustrates these theoretical points.*

Clinical Example

Stan sought therapy because he was disturbed by his complete lack of motivation and inability to get out of bed and accomplish the tasks in his life that he believed would improve his situation. He had suffered a recent blow by losing a professional position that had provided structured activity for close to a year. Making preparations and bidding for an important business contract had occupied nearly all of his time during that period. The contract was given to another bidder, however. Now, he was discouraged and had very little to do on a daily basis. The things that he needed to do were unpleasant, including sending letters of gratitude to people who helped him with the bid, and forced him to face the areas of his life where he had not been successful. During the initial interview

---

*Cases presented in this book are partial composites of clients seen in the depression treatment study at the University of Washington, Center for Clinical Research, with identifying information changed. It can be argued that case material is data to be reviewed in actual detail, and in some cases actual conversations between client and therapist will be used to illustrate interventions. However, portions of several cases have been combined in order to protect client confidentiality.

it became obvious to the therapist that Stan's "lack of motivation" was understandable given the fact that the activities he needed to "motivate" himself to do were nearly universally aversive. Stan's current situation is an example of a sudden change in the environment leading to a decrease in activity and a change in reinforcement schedule. However, Stan also had a history that could easily be suspected of leading to the development of a passive style and of behavior maintained by negative reinforcement.

Childhood histories are always difficult to reconstruct. We must rely on clients' recollections, and the details of memory can become obscured by the process of remembering (Loftus, 1980). However, many current behavior patterns make sense in the context of the individual's life, and it is important to try to gain an understanding of what makes sense about the client's current behavior in light of the narrative about historical events. In Stan's case, he described his childhood as being unhappy and inconsistent. His father was a violent man who punished Stan no matter what he did. He recalled being punished for doing poorly in school, but also being punished when he did well because he "did not do well enough." He was never allowed to finish a task because he was told by his father that he should be doing something else and would be punished if he did not "hop to it" at his father's command. Likewise, his mother was very concerned about her own needs and would frequently pit her children against one another to win her approval. It was little wonder that Stan the adult complained of not being able to focus on a task. Stan's interpersonal relationships were either troubled or lacking in intimacy. Relationships with family and lovers were contentious and had even resulted in legal disputes in some cases.

Stan was responding according to his deprivation and had developed a limited repertoire shaped by negative reinforcement and noncontingent punishment. When he felt lonely, he would visit a woman friend, not to develop a relationship, but mostly to end the loneliness. His relationships with people were filled with conflict and involved his attempts to get others to meet his need. He did not appear to have the ability to elicit positive reinforcement from his relationships. Avoidance of aversive situations was Stan's mode of operating. He avoided being taken advantage of by frequenting the courts, he avoided facing his dark and damp house by staying in bed and reading the paper, he avoided having to face his lackluster career by getting distracted from completing his resume, and the list of avoidance maneuvers goes on. Stan provides a good example of how, when an individual has not learned to recognize the antecedents and consequences of his behavior, he responds to his environment by trying to get short-term, immediate relief by avoiding negatives. However, avoiding aversive experiences does not allow one to be reinforced by positive experiences. This avoidance pattern is characteristic of depressed individuals.

Stan's case demonstrates what Ferster (1981) described as a process whereby the individual's overt and covert behaviors become a catalyst for further entrenchment in the pattern and the individual's repertoire becomes narrow. Stan was not able to interact with people in a way that allowed him to experience the positive nature of relationships. He could interact on a casual basis, and had a neighbor with whom he would share stories while they worked in their yards, but the relationship did not go deeper than an occasional "bull session." He could also respond to conflict situations. He was trapped in a cycle of experiencing his own frustrations and needs, responding to others who apparently were thwarting his needs, repeatedly experiencing failure in relationships and vocational choices, and his depression worsened.

At the time he came to therapy Stan was so demoralized that he completely blamed himself for being "unmotivated" and would frequently say "If I could just get myself motivated to do these things I could get beyond this." It was the therapist's job to help Stan see that "motivation" often comes from the outside rather than originating from inside the person, and that his attempts at moving ahead with his life were being punished in the current context. He needed to be taught how to break the avoidance pattern and face the aversive condition of his life, and to act productively in order to contact positive, rewarding aspects of the world. Stan's depression, observed in context, made sense. His world had been shaped by a schedule of reinforcement requiring a large amount of activity prior to receiving a reward, and by a schedule of negative reinforcement — that is, by the alleviation of distress rather than the experience of pleasure. Given this formulation of the problem, it was important that therapy provide Stan with experiences that would allow him to learn the connection between the antecedents and consequences of his behavior. The therapy with Stan was laborious to some degree, and initially looked like it was only minimally successful. However, Stan reported on follow-up that he had returned to a vocational training program and had recognized that he needed to get involved in his life rather than sitting around letting boredom and malaise control his behavior. He felt hopeful about his future.

In this case there are four things operating from a contextual perspective in Stan's depression. First, current contexts carry their controlling properties largely as a function of an individual's history in similar contexts, as evidenced by Stan's repeated conflicts with friends and family that were very much like the same conflicts he experienced as a child. Second, Stan's repertoire of behavior was narrow, as evidenced by his difficulty engaging in activities that brought pleasure or a sense of accomplishment for him. Third, the behaviors he did engage in functioned to avoid or escape his discomfort and/or to get him out of conflict situations. Finally, as Stan began to disengage and remain inactive, others around him responded in a similar fashion, no longer calling or encouraging him. His environment became increasingly punishing.

UNDERSTANDING TERMS: IS PLEASANT AND ENJOYABLE ALWAYS REINFORCING?

The basic approach to BA is straightforward. Individuals who have developed a narrow repertoire of behavior that prevents them from obtaining maximum reinforcement from their environment must be taught to develop a broader and more flexible repertoire. That is, the therapist works as a consultant to the client and helps the client to achieve satisfaction and an increased sense of autonomy and control in his or her world. This is accomplished by a careful functional analysis of client behavior and with a variety of behavioral techniques. The therapist pays very careful attention to the details of the client's day-to-day life and encourages the client to do the same. Let us be clear about our terminology. In BA, when we speak of a functional analysis, we obviously are using this term in a slightly metaphorical sense. When working with outpatients, one cannot do the kind of experimental manipulation of variables needed when conducting a formal functional analysis. We try to help people recognize the contingencies that maintain certain behaviors; we are not manipulating variables to observe what consequences are truly maintaining a particular behavior, which would be a truly scientific functional analysis. We have stated this already, but it bears repeating. In BA no assumptions are made about what activities will be reinforced or what reinforcers may be present in an individual's life.

The treatment of depression using BA, although relatively easily learned, is not simple. Increasing pleasant events alone has not been shown to effectively improve mood. Two studies conducted in the mid-1970s and mid-1980s demonstrated this. Hammen and Glass (1975) attempted to test the operant framework of Lewinsohn and colleagues. They noted that the behavioral model emphasizes environmental consequences of behavior at the expense of considerations of perceptions and evaluations of consequences. They assigned forty college undergraduates who had been previously screened and selected on the basis of presence of depressed mood to one of four groups. Each of the groups was given instructions. One group was instructed to increase pleasant activities that they engaged in daily from a list that each subject generated from the Pleasant Events Schedule (MacPhillamy & Lewinsohn, 1972). The second group was instructed to increase protein intake and to reduce carbohydrate intake each day. This group was considered an attention-placebo. The third group was a self-monitoring control and subjects were instructed to monitor their present pattern of activities and this was assumed to control for self-observation alone. The final group was a no-treatment control that was simply scheduled for retesting at the end of the experimental period. The results suggested that instructing depressed subjects to increase their activity did not alleviate dysphoria. The authors conducted a second experiment to replicate the finding, and achieved similar results.

One important observation made in the Hammen and Glass study, which is significant for BA, is that activity for the sake of activity is not the goal. This takes behavior out of context. The activities that a client needs to engage in so that life may become a more fulfilling, or simply a less traumatic, process are the kinds of activities that behavioral activation must target. The right activities to be targeted in therapy can only be discovered by understanding the client's life circumstances and the goals that may currently be impeded. Furthermore, prescribing a treatment without a treatment rationale is likely to be unsuccessful, a topic that we will return to in future chapters. Thus, simply telling clients to increase positive activities without providing them with an understanding of why this could be useful is contraindicated. Other studies have also shown that simple instruction to increase pleasant events is not as effective as trying to do something that increases the pleasantness of the event (Dobson & Joffe, 1986).

From a behavior analytic point of view, asking subjects to reflect on the pleasantness of the activities they engage in may serve as a verbally mediated reward. This is also similar to the self-control model of Rehm (Fuchs & Rehm, 1977; Rehm, 1977) in that the instructions may have assisted the clients in connecting the antecedents and consequences of their behavior. In behavioral activation the focus is not only on observable, overt behaviors. Nor is the focus only on the environment of the individual. Behavioral activation brings the focus back to the context in which depression occurs. Although specific cognitive interventions are proscribed in research on BA, and may not be necessary according to emerging data, practitioners who determine it would be useful to teach a client to find alternatives to negative automatic thoughts may do so. The difference here is that the emphasis is on a good behavioral analysis and on an understanding of depression that is contextual and not exclusively cognitive. The following clinical example demonstrates how a client may be very active and yet depressed. In other words, it is not the activity itself or, as we stated previously, the form of the activity, rather it is the function of the activity that is important.

Clinical Example of an Active, Yet Depressed Client

Anna was a 40-year-old artist who had recently left a full-time career to be a full-time mom. She had been feeling very depressed for six months prior to seeking therapy. She missed her friends at work, and she and her husband were having difficulties in their relationship. She spent a great deal of time with her children engaging them in creative projects and driving them to school and extracurricular activities. She also kept herself involved in her art by working part-time on various exhibitions. Although Anna kept herself very busy, and found her activities occasionally pleasant, she did not feel any better. She continued to experience a depressed mood and to have occasional thoughts of suicide.

Rather than simply increase activities, Anna needed to be able to recognize the consequences of her behavior. When she was able to recognize that she felt accomplishment as a result of activities but few activities gave her pleasure, she began to see that her near frenetic pace was a way of avoiding the distress in her life. Anna had been married twice, and she was unhappy in her current marriage. She also had difficulty with her oldest child, a ten-year-old son, who would have tantrums when his father disciplined him. Anna consistently responded to the son's tantrum with reassurance. Unfortunately, reassurance reinforced his tantrums and opposition to her husband, and the son's tantrums apparently reinforced Anna's discouragement about her marriage. She felt guilty that she had caused her son to suffer by marrying the kind of man she did and would then become angry at her husband. On closer examination of her activity, it became apparent that interactions such as the one described above occurred repeatedly when Anna was with her children. Any discussion of her husband with her children led to anger from the son, which triggered Anna's anger at her husband. So, within the context of her activity there were contingencies of reinforcement maintaining depressed mood. Although in relation to work, her activity was positively reinforced, the activity was negatively reinforcing her avoidance behaviors in regard to her husband and marriage responsibilities. Furthermore, her activity was apparently mood dependent. She was more likely to take her children to get ice cream if one of them (or she herself) had had a bad day than she was to plan the activity and follow through. So, the reward may have been reinforcing the bad days. Even if there was no reinforcement, however, Anna was perpetuating a habit of behaving according to her mood rather than a plan. She also spent time during most activities ruminating about whether or not she should stay in her marriage.

Anna provides an excellent example of complex schedules of reinforcement at work in an individual's life. Although one could initially recognize the professional satisfaction and other positive outcomes involved in Anna's activities, it took detective work to see that within that class of behavior there were components that may have blocked the reinforcement potential in the environment. Anna began an activity as a way to avoid pain, and she ruminated over her unhappy marriage or discussed her unhappiness with her son during an activity. Her three-year-old daughter was too young to understand the discussions, and Anna appeared less concerned about the daughter than the son.

FOCUSED ACTIVITY AND INCREASING POSSIBILITIES FOR CLIENT SUCCESS

In order for BA therapists to increase the likelihood of success, they need to fully recognize what their task is *not*. They are not to assume that activities are necessarily pleasurable, or that pleasurable activities are *the* way out of depression. Rather, increasing pleasurable activities is one intervention that may help some clients. When it appears that clients are not experiencing much pleasure, a functional analysis is conducted to reveal what sorts of activities are pleasurable and how these might be integrated into the client's repertoire in different contexts. In BA we promote directed activity that will lead to solutions of problems and increase the possibility of contacting natural reinforcers in the environment; we are not trying to get people to do nice things. In fact, from a BA perspective, we cannot say what a "nice thing" is until we have seen the effect of a certain behavior either in changing the client's environment or improving mood, or both.

The overall purpose of BA is to:

1. determine the patterns of coping that have exacerbated the depression, and

2. develop a treatment plan for improving the coping patterns and potentially providing access to more reinforcing life circumstances.

Clients in BA are encouraged to use their therapist as a personal trainer. The BA therapist does not pretend to understand all of the details of the client's problems. Formulations are presented tentatively and the client is asked to test any hypotheses about behaviors that may improve his or her mood, or activities that will be rewarding and ultimately may be reinforcing. The assumption that any activity will enable a client to contact positive reinforcement in the environment is never made until a change in mood or behavior is seen (indicating that it has been reinforced). The BA therapist must ask herself and her clients the following questions when trying to develop a treatment plan:

1. What is important to this individual?
2. What gives him or her a sense of purpose in life?
3. Within this context how can I help the client to do things differently that will capitalize on this?

In many cases the answers to these questions are embedded in the complaints that the client brings to the initial sessions. During an initial interview and history taking, if a client mentions that her depression began after the loss of a prestigious job, one can begin to hypothesize that prestige or money may be meaningful to this individual, or that interesting and challenging work is important to the person. Although the hypothesis would remain a theory until further information was gathered from the client, using activity charts and discussions in session, it begins to form the initial idea for change interventions.

DRAWING THERAPEUTIC
INTERVENTIONS FROM HYPOTHESES

The reliance on hypotheses in BA is no different from the same strategy in other forms of therapy. Many forms of therapy see therapist interpretations, conceptualizations, and theories about a client as hypothetical until confirmed by the client. The idea of collaborative empiricism between therapist and client is prevalent in both cognitive and behavior therapies. What distinguishes BA is the open admission that we may never arrive at the absolute truth. In the real world the consequences of behavior may be diffuse and neither the therapist nor the client may ever be able to accurately analyze a true connection. We are not concerned about uncovering the "real" beliefs of the client, which we think are suspect at best when a therapist is involved in an interaction with a client trying to help her to "catch" thoughts. The BA perspective suggests that therapy can help clients to get involved in their lives in such a way that they increase the likelihood that their behaviors will be positively reinforced. We know that their behaviors are currently being reinforced, but we hypothesize that they are on a negative reinforcement schedule that maintains their depression. Having the possibility of contacting positive reinforcement increases their chance of feeling better about their lives. It is not uncommon to hear depressed individuals complain that they "just don't know how to have fun." We would say exactly that. Rather than fish around for negative beliefs about the self, or uncovering clients' ideas about being unworthy or unlovable, we accept that they either have not learned to engage in such a way that "fun" is positively reinforced, or that life events have prevented them from engaging.

The BA perspective on thinking and behaving is different from the cognitive or biological perspectives. A BA analysis suggests that phenomena emphasized by these other theories are important parts of the picture. However the parts do not explain the whole or the etiology of depression, necessarily. In BA, for example, the process of thinking but not necessarily the content of thinking is an important focus of treatment. If a client states that he spends a great deal of time thinking about his incompetence while engaged in an activity, the BA therapist would not challenge the idea that he is incompetent but would instead look at the consequence of engaging in the rumination. The client may be less engaged in the activity, unable to recognize his mastery of it, out-of-touch with the pleasure of it, or may feel emotionally worse as a result of the ruminating. Since stopping ruminating is a very difficult task, the BA therapist would help the client find an alternate behavior, for example, being mindful of the minute details of an activity.

CHAPTER 3

The Contextual Approach

ACCORDING TO THE CONTEXTUALIST, the past and future of an act exist in the ongoing action (Hayes et al., 1988). There is an integration of the textural details of the event. Writing this sentence consists of many details: thinking of the words, moving the fingers on a keyboard, touching each individual letter, taking moments to gather thoughts, etc. However, the sentence is experienced as an integration of these details. Pepper (1942) calls this "fusion." Viewing people as "historical acts" allows one to see people as an integration of all of the past and current details of their lives. The past is still happening in the present, because it is only through the fusion of all of the details of life that one comes to know the world as she knows it. When conceptualizing a case to develop a treatment strategy, one looks for the environmental events that may serve as a cue for how the current context came to be. One can never be certain, however, and contextualists must be comfortable with uncertainty. We have many clues, but only in trying to help a person shift her behavior and change the context of the here and now can we really see if our clues have helped us to find a shift that will work. By making such a shift in context we can help the individual to live life without being enslaved to feelings.

When we view all human activity in context the world begins to look very thick and ever-changing (Geertz, 1973). Actions occur in layers of context which themselves are embedded in broader layers. For example, a recently divorced person might cry when she is alone. The action of crying is certainly embedded in the context of being alone. However, it is also embedded in the broader cultural context of what it means to be married, divorced, female, and so on. Labeling a set of behaviors as depressed, in turn, occurs in a context where the word "depression" is used to describe such behaviors. Pretty soon we realize that it is hard to say anything is "undoubtedly the case" because such assertions are themselves actions embedded in particular contexts.

From a contextual point of view, a way out of this confusion is to follow the idea that what is true is what works, what Pepper (1942) called the pragmatic truth criterion. In BA we follow the pragmatic truth criterion quite a bit. We don't, for example, assert that contextualism is *de facto* the right way to view depression. Rather, we find it useful to focus on changing actions and contexts. We don't tell clients that their thoughts, feelings, or biological processes are *not* causes of depression. Instead, we ask them how such a view might work for them in making the sort of changes they want to make. The pragmatic truth criterion always leads us to ask our clients and ourselves "what are the consequences of thinking/talking/acting in this particular way? Are these the consequences we desire?"

A good deal has been written about contextualism as a philosophical perspective (Hayes, 1994; Hayes et al., 1993; Hayes et al., 1988). Our use of the term in the context of BA is, in some ways, rather loose and, in other ways, fairly specific. It is important to remember that BA evolved from two fairly distinct interests. On the one hand, colleagues in Jacobson's lab were motivated by an unexpected empirical finding; namely, that depression could be effectively treated by simply encouraging people to change depressive behavior. On the other hand, there was a good deal of interest at the Center for Clinical Research in the current applications of modern behavior analytic and contextualist theories to adult outpatient problems and treatment (e.g., Hayes, Jacobson, Follette, & Dougher, 1994; Kohlenberg & Tsai, 1991; Linehan, 1993; Pepper, 1942). Thus, we had two fairly different agendas going; one was practical and empirical, and the other was theoretical. Practical interests have always reminded us to keep things pretty concrete. Ideally, we'd like every BA client to know what we mean by contextualism, without inundating them with incomprehensible jargon. Our theoretical interests at times lead us into philosophical considerations that may not directly affect the behavior of a BA therapist.

Our experiences in training therapists suggest that it is a balance of the practical and the theoretical that allows for good BA treatment. Thus, the BA therapist must know clearly what is meant by taking a contextual view of a client. He must know what to attend to and what not to attend to when looking at a client's depressive behavior contextually. Such clarity requires an understanding of the difference between contextual and noncontextual thinking and talking. At the same time, the BA therapist needs to have his two feet planted firmly on earth. In other words, he must be able to talk plainly to a client about the rationale for treatment and develop practical interventions to shift the context in which the client is operating. Thus, thinking and acting contextually itself varies from context to context. Below, we consider the philosophical context, the case conceptualization context, and the treatment context. We separate these for the sake of exposition but, again, when BA is working well the philosophy informs the case conceptualization, which in turn guides the treatment context.

THE PHILOSOPHICAL CONTEXT

Key Philosophical Ideas

There are three philosophical ways that the idea of context is used in BA.

1. *The meaning or function of a particular action cannot be understood apart from its historical and contemporary context.* No actions occur in a vacuum. In order to understand the meaning behind any current activity, both the past and the present must be considered. For example, Elaine may truly enjoy listening to Beethoven and may find great meaning in the music. She may turn to this music when she feels that she needs contemplation and comfort. Beethoven is only meaningful to Elaine in the present because listening to Beethoven has been meaningful to her in the past. Over the course of her life, as Elaine began to understand the various nuances of the compositions or felt a sense of being uplifted by the music, listening to Beethoven became a meaningful action for her.

Note also in Elaine's case that listening to Beethoven had a certain function. The function, however, changes according to the context. When Elaine has been in a contemplative mood, she has listened to Beethoven in the past, and she has found the music to be soothing and to assist the pleasant flow of thoughts and ideas that she wished to engage in. At other times, however, when Elaine needed to explain to a friend how a certain piece of music was built around a few notes, she may have spent hours listening to Beethoven in order to develop an example of such a composition. In the first context, listening to Beethoven served a function of providing solace and relaxation. In the second, the same activity — listening to Beethoven — served a purely academic and scholarly function. Elaine may have enjoyed the music in each instance, but the meaning of the music would change depending on the contemporary context based on the historical context of the same act.

The root metaphor of contextualism is the historical act. All activity is seen as complex, and not easily explained in terms of mechanics.

> It is doing, and enduring, and enjoying; making a boat, running a race, laughing at a joke, persuading an assembly, unraveling a mystery, solving a problem, removing an obstacle, exploring a country, communicating with a friend, creating a poem, re-creating a poem. These acts or events are all intrinsically complex, composed of interconnected activities with continuously changing patterns. They are like incidents in the plot of a novel or drama. They are literally the incidents of life.
> The contextualist finds that everything in the world consists of such incidents. (Pepper, 1942, pp. 232–233)

2. *Claims about the nature of things gain meaning from the context in which they occur.* The pragmatic truth criterion guides decisions about what sorts of knowledge claims might be considered "true" from a contextualist perspective. Pragmatism, as a key criterion for establishing what is true in contextualism suggests that there are no "real" truths apart from those that accomplish a particular goal (Hayes, Hayes, & Reese, 1988). An analysis of truth is always made for some purpose, and that analysis may consist of alternative views in different situations. "Truths" such as "all men are created equal" are only true because the concept was a benefit to many people. From a contextualist view it is not true because it is the discovery of some real "law" that exists apart from its being a useful construct. In fact, over time, the words have taken on different meanings. The word "men" once was interpreted as meaning white males, and the idea that men were created was accepted by all. Therefore this "truth" once meant that God had created all white male pilgrims equally. Given current understanding of evolution, the idea of people being created is less "truth" now than in the eighteenth century. The term "men" was usually interpreted as "mankind" or "humankind" in the nineteenth and twentieth centuries; today, however, there are still many who are offended at the use of the male pronoun to indicate all people. Thus, any "truth" can be rendered extinct given a shift in context that occasions a more useful understanding.

3. *The dependence of actions on context is similar to the behavior analytic emphasis on the relationship between behavior and its consequences.* Behavioral analysis (or radical behaviorism) has been described as a paradigm based on pragmatism rather than realism (Baum, 1994). To the pragmatist, ideas can be more or less true, but the criterion of truth is based on

the explanatory power of the idea. Ideas that have explanatory power lead to prediction and control as scientific goals. Control is, of course, a sticky word. In this context it simply means that ideas which have explanatory power lead to effective action in the world. Often, effective action depends on our ability to predict events and make choices in line with particular goals.

To the behavior analyst, or the pragmatist, the interest is in providing a description of behavior that is most useful. Therefore both public and private events can be taken into account, because both are natural and can be described in terms that are useful and economical (Baum, 1994). From a contextual, pragmatic, or behavior analytic perspective, one is not limited to the study of observable events only—the study of private events, which may or may not be related to what actually occurred, can also be studied.

The emphasis on pragmatism, and the reliance on the context of a behavior in order to explain it, places behavior analysis or radical behaviorism in a contextualist camp philosophically. Hayes, Hayes, and Reese (1988) argued that two radical behavioral concepts, the operant and the pragmatic truth criterion, make radical behaviorism a contextual system. An operant is defined as "a relation among behavior and stimulus events" (p. 101). Behavior cannot be explained apart from the antecedents that occasion it and the consequences that follow it. Behavior analysts have always rejected the vocabulary of mentalism. This rejection is based on the criterion that the terms were useless to an adequate explanation of behavior.

Considering mental events as causes relies on circular reasoning. For example, a mentalistic notion of a person "having a lot of anger" is not acceptable as an explanation for the behavior of the individual. The only way to know that someone (or oneself) is full of anger is if it is observed (publicly or privately) that the individual engages in certain behaviors that we have come to call "angry." Hence, if a man is observed to be raising his voice, to become flushed in the face, to have a heaving chest and clenched fists (all public events), the observer may conclude that the man is angry. Further, if the man himself observes that he is thinking of smashing an object and has a feeling of his "head swimming" (private events), he may conclude that he is angry. However, if someone were to ask him why he was acting the way he was, and he explained that he was doing so because he was angry or because he "had a lot of anger inside," that explanation would not make much sense. In effect, he would be saying that he is angry (engaging in "angry" behavior) because he's angry (engaging in "angry" behavior). The explanation is not practical, and would be rejected by the behavior analyst and the contextualist, because it cannot describe a truth since it does not successfully and adequately explain the event. Moreover, it does not lead to effective action and therefore does not meet the pragmatic truth criteria. If we accept the claim that a person behaves angrily because they are angry, we are forced to try and change some abstract internal thing called "anger." If, instead, we assume that someone behaves angrily because of the context they are in, and because of the history of reinforcement of the behavior in similar contexts, we can do things to shift the context and thereby shift angry behavior, which would be a more effective way to deal with the problem.

So, in the context of BA these three philosophical ideas are central regarding contextualism. When we work with clients in therapy, we cannot assume that we understand their behavior because of the topography of the behavior (see earlier discussion of form and function of behavior in chapter 2). We can only understand the meaning and function of the behavior within its historical context. Any claims that we make about a person or about a person's life are only true insofar as they lead us to a useful analysis, provided the claims are made considering the context of the person's life. Finally, we place a primary emphasis on the consequences of behavior in our understanding of the meaning and functions of behaviors for a given individual.

The Philosophical Context: What Context Doesn't Mean

In order to prevent misunderstanding of what is meant by contextualism in behavioral activation, we would like to clearly state what is *not* meant. We will then demonstrate how contextualism informs the thinking of a behavioral activation therapist. The following ideas should be kept in mind when discussing context within the framework of BA.

1. *Contextualism is not biological determinism.* Although biology certainly has its place in the overall context of people's lives, we reject the notion that biology alone determines behaviors. There are data to indicate that certain biological and physiological phenomena are related to certain behaviors and mood states, but they are not adequate explanations of causes. For example, although serotonin levels may be elevated in people in leadership positions (or primates in dominant positions), one cannot say that serotonin levels cause one to be dominant, although it may be a necessary biochemical shift that equips one for positions of dominance

or leadership (Wright, 1994). Certain patterns of behavior may have evolved through the process of natural selection, and certain biological or biochemical processes may be associated with these patterns, but all occur within a certain context. As we have explained in earlier chapters, with our current understanding of biology and environment, claiming that depressed mood or other emotional phenomena are caused by dysregulation of neurotransmitters is to make the logical error of assuming causation from correlation. The direct manipulation of dopamine levels, for example, has not consistently resulted in the onset of depressed mood, despite the hypothesis that depression is caused by dysregulation of the dopaminergic system (Valenstein, 1998).

2. *Contextualism is not cognitive determinism.* Thoughts can be said to affect behavior at times, but they cannot cause behavior. The origins of behavior lie in the historical and the contemporary environment (Baum, 1994). It is not a contradiction to recognize the accumulating data that demonstrate changes in mood following changes in thinking. A shift in one part of the context, for example, an individual's self-talk, can have an affect on other parts of the context, such as the individual's experienced emotion. However, one cannot conclude that the change in thinking caused the change in mood because one can never get beyond the self-report of the individual and the resulting circular reasoning that would result again from confusing correlation with causation. Moreover, citing a change in thinking as a cause of a change in mood begs the question, what caused the change in thinking? Ultimately, the pragmatic goals of a contextual approach always lead us back to environmental changes because these can be directly influenced.

3. *Context is not life events.* By context, we do not mean simply the situation that a person lives in. Certainly a person's life situation contributes to depression and this is a key assumption of BA. However, context is much more than, for example, "married, two kids, works in sales, 36 years old, etc." For us, context refers to the transactions between a person and the environment as both evolve over time. Recall that transactions occur between person and environment without defining them as two separate entities, such as the word "interaction" implies.

Although a person's situation certainly has important implications for that person's well-being, it is important that one not confuse the idea of context merely with external situations. Understanding that the distinction between things that are internal to the person and things that are external is an arbitrary one, the BA therapist will still assist the individual to act in a way that may change the situation in which he or she exists. Figure 3.1 illustrates the individual as part of ever-shifting contexts; the environment changes and the individual changes as well. The dotted lines in the inner section of the person and the environment illustrate that the boundaries blur and become arbitrary. Behavior and context merge into one unit that cannot be meaningfully understood by separating it. In BA, for example, if a client complained of repeated frustrations at home, the therapist may bring in a significant other to be a part of the therapy (this is discussed in detail in chapter 7), but most of the interventions are with the individual. This would be contradictory if we thought that the context simply consisted of the situations in which a person finds him- or herself. We would want to make sure that we were doing more prevention work, to change the context by changing the situations. The treatment would look more like case management or involve a social intervention such as providing a client with money to move out of a bad neighborhood. Although these contextual elements are important, in BA we work with the individual, whose behaviors and moods occur in a certain context, and help him or her to act in such a way as to begin to change external circumstances and shift the context of the occurrence of the depression.

Undeniably, there are certain life situations that a therapist should help a client to change. A woman living with an abusive spouse or partner should be provided with information about safe housing and be encouraged and helped by her therapist to make use of such resources. People who are underemployed should be coached to try to find proper employment. However, no therapist will be able to change the situations that people live in. What a therapist can do is help the client develop a new behavioral style. When the client activates rather than retreats, the chances of such proactive behavior being positively reinforced become greater. So, the context in which we view depression is not simply depression in the presence of life circumstances that would be called, in colloquial terms, a bummer. It is, rather, the context of the historical actor in a current situation. The individual has developed a repertoire of

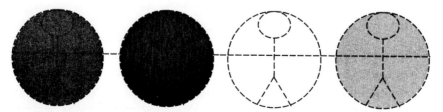

FIGURE 3.1 *Contextual variation in depression.*

behaviors that has allowed her or him to adapt to certain life circumstances, and have in turn, changed some of those life circumstances. In BA, it is important to try to look at the whole life of the person.

4. Context is not about people creating their own reality or constructing a narrative of their lives. The ideas of constructivism have been presented in several forms of psychotherapy including George Kelly's (1955) personal construct therapy, and more recent understandings of constructivism and narrative (Neimeyer & Mahoney, 1995). In essence, constructivism proposes that individuals receive feedback from their environments and simultaneously create their environments from their own thinking and experience. It denies an objective reality apart from the observer. Constructivism also sees truth as contextual.

In behavioral activation, like constructivism, the concern is not with an objective reality. What are of concern are the ways that people's behavior is shaped and maintained as it transacts with an ever-changing environment. For example, if Lisa describes her life as a series of failures, a BA therapist is not concerned with whether in fact Lisa "actually" failed. The BA therapist is interested in the contexts of failure — situations where Lisa behaves and is not rewarded for her efforts. If the therapist finds out that Lisa seems to receive rewards for her efforts, but continues to describe her life as a failure there are several possibilities. It may be that the behavior of describing herself as a failure has a particular function in certain contexts (e.g., it may be a request for help or sympathy), or it may be that the consequences that look like rewards to an observer are not effective reinforcers for Lisa. Either way, our interest is in the transactions between Lisa and her environment. Of course one cannot be absolutely certain about the exact nature of these transactions, but one can develop a hypothesis and understanding of the context of Lisa's life that either does or does not lead to effective action and to shifting the context in an antidepressive direction.

THE CASE
CONCEPTUALIZATION CONTEXT

It is impossible to understand all of the contingencies that have occasioned and maintained particular behaviors over time. It becomes too convoluted to try to do a functional analysis of behaviors that occur in a moment or to understand events that directly precede or follow each other. BA deals with what have been called molar behaviors (Baum, 1994; Rachlin, 1991), or broad classes of activities. Present activities have a history, and the many past events that have been associated with the present behavior are important, although it is impossible to know what those past events have been. When a client comes to us and states that he or she is a failure, we do not take the statement as an absolute, nor do we question the validity of the belief. Instead we try to look at the client's past behaviors and the consequences that have followed the broad class of behaviors that would be seen as "failures." If it is the case that every time this person tries to change her life situation by getting a new job, she is turned down from the new job, her history will contribute to her experience of being a failure. The BA therapist would look at the broad behavioral class and begin to think about trying to help the client in her job search to increase the likelihood that the consequences of her search would be different if the variables that may be contributing to the failure were better understood.

The above example illustrates one of the subtle differences between how one would conceptualize a case using a purely cognitive therapy versus a contextual approach. It would be unreasonable to say that cognitive therapy (or psychodynamic therapies for that matter) completely ignores context. Cognitive therapy discriminates past and present contexts. For example, in the client who believes that she is a failure, a CT therapist may discuss the past situations when the client began to learn that she was a failure. The therapist might recognize that such beliefs about failing at finding a particular job were understandable in the historical context—although the cognitive therapist would question the overgeneralized belief "I am a failure" in the historical and the present context. In the present context, however, the cognitive therapist would see that the client had developed a belief that has become stable and would work with the client to change that belief by looking for evidence that proves and disproves the belief "I am a failure."

A Behavioral Activation Approach
to Case Conceptualization

The case conceptualization is focused on variability and situatedness rather than stability. In behavioral activation we have given up the need for stability. Behavioral activation discriminates the present context. When the client says "I am a failure," the BA therapist would ask the client under what conditions she has failed and under what conditions she has not failed. In other words, the BA therapist is always considering variability of behavior. When a client says, "I am X," the BA therapist will readily ask herself and the client "How? When? Where? When are you not

X?" Characterological statements are seen as predictions about future behaviors. The statement "I am a failure" predicts a future behavior based on the client's experiences of the past. This shorthand prediction may be practical in common usage, but doesn't refer to anything concrete. Behavioral activation and other contextual approaches assume variability and situatedness. Behavior, public or private, is situated in a particular context, and therefore is likely to be variable over time. If a behavior appears stable it is likely that the context has remained relatively stable. Although the client who is depressed and sitting in the therapist's office may say "I am a failure," that verbal behavior is occasioned by the context of being in therapy, and the therapist need not assume that this is a stable belief that the client holds. Instead, the behavioral activation therapist wants to know when the client doesn't think she is a failure. The therapist would also want to know what function is served by thinking "I am a failure." Therapists tend to react to such statements and seek to change them. However, such verbal behavior may serve this client in some way such as keeping her working in a lower-level job where she feels secure and it may be allowing her to avoid further turmoil in seeking a different job. The therapist would then be less worried about conceptualizing a belief that needs changing, and would want to look at how to help the client take steps to approach the frightening activities that might occur if she attempts to take a higher-level job, and to assist her to make the actual change in her life circumstance through planning the steps to attainment with her.

The case conceptualization is hypothesis-driven. Much of the case conceptualization in BA is an hypothesis. The therapy is very practical. If the therapist and client have a certain hypothesis about the possibility that an increase or decrease in certain activities will be useful to the client, they will discuss implementation strategies. If the strategies and changes in behavior are not beneficial, the therapist and client will consider other possibilities. This emphasis on collaborative empiricism between client and therapist is shared with other treatment approaches such as cognitive therapy. In cognitive therapy the goal is to test beliefs, in BA the goal is to find out what shifts in behavior work for a client in alleviating her depression.

BA is a molar rather than a molecular approach. It is important to look at the broad class of behaviors, such things that could be labeled in some way, like "unassertive behaviors" for example, but it is also important to try to help the client to be specific about the general conditions in which the behavior occurs. As was stated earlier, it is impossible to do a complete functional analysis of all of the contingencies maintaining behaviors, or for that matter, of all the "building blocks" that comprise certain behaviors. Therefore, the BA therapist looks at large units of behavior, taking the molar approach to the observation of behavior (Rachlin, 1991). In other words, it is not important to understand every stimulus and every response, but rather to look at classes of behavior such as "getting ready for work" or "going to a ball game." There is always a shifting analysis, however, and the BA therapist is concerned not only with the broad problems in a client's life, but also with what the client did on Thursday at 3 P.M. and the consequences of that behavior. So the shift goes from broad classes or molar behaviors to specific examples and concrete details of the client's day.

The BA case conceptualization emphasizes the assessment of function, not form. From a contextual perspective the form of a behavior is less informative than the function of that behavior. Two clients may do exactly the same thing, but the behavior has very different contexts and consequences. For example, Mary comes home from work and heads directly to her bed and sleeps for two hours. When she awakens she feels refreshed and phones friends for a late dinner. The early evening nap serves the function of helping her wind down from work and energizes her for the rest of an evening that includes social engagements. Elizabeth, on the other hand, also comes home from work and heads directly to bed. She stays in bed for several hours and when she wakes up she feels just as tired as when she first laid down. Instead of feeling energized to call friends, she feels exhausted and eats a small bowl of microwave popcorn for dinner and spends the evening feeling lonely and watching television. So, it is important for the therapist to remain aware that two people may be doing the same behavior, or that one individual may do the same behavior in different situations, but that the behavior can serve very different functions depending on the consequences. It is imperative that therapists not judge a behavior according to its form, but should work with the client to uncover its function and make behavioral changes accordingly.

The BA therapist considers the relevant data from the client's self-report of personal history while attempting to formulate a case conceptualization that will guide the treatment. Taking the darkened circle from figure 3.1, which we could refer to as the "depressive context," we can further elaborate on a process that we hypothesize to occur in this context. As depicted in figure 3.2, life events may be associated with decreased levels of positive reinforcement, which then lead to certain reactions or "symptoms" (biological, cognitive, and behavioral) of the individual.

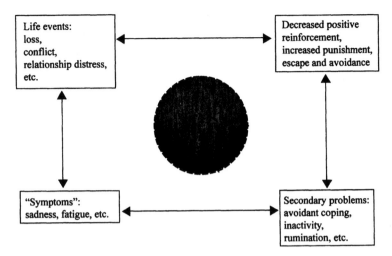

FIGURE 3.2 *The expanded context of depression: Bidirectional arrows highlight the interplays between different aspects of the context.*

These responses are often experienced as aversive to the individual who then tries to escape or avoid the aversive experience by engaging in behaviors that serve only to exacerbate the negative experience. The person's behavioral repertoire is narrowed to the point of keeping him stuck in the situations that may be contributing to the depression. Behaviors used to cope become problems in their own right, or "secondary" problems. All these processes influence each other and keep the individual stuck in the depressive context.

Variability and change. As people behave, they also shape the situations around them, which further shifts the context. The shifting situations occasion shifting behaviors, which shift the situations, and so on. We end up adding to our earlier depiction of context in figure 2.2 (page 15), and now have a larger context with the individual in ever-shifting contexts that occasion different behaviors that shift the situations (see figure 3.1). So, in BA, we believe that the context is ever-changing, and various behaviors will work differently in the shifting context (with the behaviors being, in fact, part of the context). While we are not so concerned with the individual's perception of reality, the notion of reality for the person is also likely to be shaped by changing contexts. Perceptions will continually change, as will levels of neurotransmitters, negative or positive thinking, proactive or avoidance behaviors.

Critical Elements of
the Case Conceptualization

Within the context of the case conceptualization, there are certain pieces of information that are essential for the therapist to know about the client. First, the therapist needs to know how the client's experience of depression is manifesting itself. Not all individuals who are depressed experience difficulty with sleep, for example. The only way that we know a person is depressed is if they evidence behaviors that we have come to associate with the term depression. Again, we are stuck in the circle of a tautology. Depression is not something apart from the symptoms experienced by the client, and these symptoms will vary from person to person. Thus, it behooves the therapist to understand what this particular client means by this particular episode of depression, and how he or she is attempting to cope with life in the midst of this particular context. Not everyone who reports being depressed will experience the same cluster of symptoms that have made their way into our current diagnostic systems. The therapist needs to know how a particular client experiences her depression. Does she lose sleep? If so, is it difficult to fall asleep, or does she wake in the middle of the night and find it difficult to return to sleep? Is anxiety mixed with the depression? From a BA perspective or a contextual perspective, the experience of the client, and the details of that experience, are much more important than the diagnostic labels that can be placed on that client because of those experiences.

SECONDARY PROBLEM BEHAVIORS AND AVOIDANCE

The symptoms of depression may have become problem behaviors in and of themselves. We refer to these as *secondary problems* because they are both a part of the symptomatology of depression and function to maintain or exacerbate the episode. Figure 3.2 demonstrates how secondary problem behaviors can increase the depressive reaction of the individual, maintaining a narrowed repertoire of behavior that continues to exacerbate depression. In behavioral activation, avoidance behaviors are particularly targeted as secondary problems, or secondary coping behaviors (Jacobson, Martell, & Dimidjian, in press). In short, avoidance can be explained as behaviors that prevent the client from contacting aversive stimuli. The stimuli may be private or public. In the case of private stimuli, a client who feels a great deal of sadness regarding the break-up of a relationship may engage in behaviors like drinking alcohol to excess in order to avoid the feelings of sadness or associated thoughts about the loss. An example of avoiding public stimuli would be a person who fears spiders and never enters dark closets in order to prevent an encounter with the arachnids. Ferster (1973) believed that depressed clients behave in ways that serve as avoidance behaviors. Some depressive behaviors, like sleeping excessively, may allow the client to avoid solving difficult problems, feeling or thinking particular things, or doing work that may be tedious or that is too challenging. Avoidance is a natural process, and should not be seen as a manipulation on the part of the client.

Just as anxious individuals tend to avoid the situations in which their feelings of fear and dread are aroused (Barlow, 1988; Beck, Emery, & Greenberg, 1985), depressed individuals tend to avoid situations that either make them feel more depressed or that require large amounts of energy, etc. However, avoidance behavior is not always bad, and it is very important that the therapist again consider context in conceptualizing a case and determining what avoidance strategies to target for change.

When an individual learns to drive a car he learns that putting pressure on the accelerator makes the car move faster and putting pressure on the brake will slow down and eventually stop the car. Quick, hard pressure will stop the car immediately. Driver education courses teach that certain signals direct the driver whether to brake or accelerate. At a red light one brakes, and at a green light one accelerates. Now, this is the rule, but it also is a contingency-shaped behavior (see Hineline & Wanchisen, 1989 for the distinction between rule-governed and contingency-shaped behavior). The driver has learned either in the driver's education lesson, from a bad personal experience, or from the experience of someone else that failure to brake at a red light can lead either to an expensive ticket or to an accident that damages machinery and bodies. So, the behavioral class of stopping at a red light is, functionally, an avoidance behavior. People brake at red lights in order to avoid negative consequences. They have learned to do so, the action is automatic, and it is a functional behavior that makes the streets safer for everyone. Surely nobody would want to change such avoidance behaviors.

Clients will sometimes talk about behaviors that are functionally avoidant, but are very adaptive. When Melanie says that she did not correct her boyfriend, Roger, when he used the word "me" when he should have used the word "I" during their dinner conversation because she didn't want him to get offended and angry at her, she is referring to an avoidance behavior. However, this behavior may have been very useful in that context; avoiding conflict with a boyfriend is often a very useful behavior. However, let's shift the context. Imagine that Roger and Melanie are not out to dinner, but rather that Roger is rehearsing an important presentation for work and has asked Melanie for feedback. If Melanie avoids telling him that he used the wrong word because she fears that he will be offended and angry she may have successfully avoided the short-term discomfort, but the long-term consequences could be troublesome for Roger when he uses poor grammar in his presentation.

The BA case conceptualization may change throughout therapy as new information is learned. This is true of most therapies. What is most important is that the BA therapist understands that she is to assume variability and not look for stable characteristics that may be useful descriptors but fail to explain anything meaningful about the client. The broad classes of behaviors and the life situations that are troublesome to the client need to be taken into account, as do specific activities that occur at specific times with very specific consequences. In general, it is practical for the therapist to have an idea of the life events that may have contributed to the depressive episode, the client's experience of depression, the behaviors that maintain the depression, and the consequences of those behaviors on the client's emotional well-being and on the ability to accomplish desired life goals.

THE TREATMENT CONTEXT

Behavioral activation, like all therapies, occurs primarily between two people, a therapist and a client. It is a treatment for individuals who are depressed. This is consistent with a contextual approach when one understands that context includes the person, her behavior, the situations that occasion it, past and present behaviors, past and present situations, the myriad consequences experienced by the individual, and all of the varieties of interactions with people in her life. Treatment itself is a context in which certain behaviors will occur. Some contextual therapies fully capitalize on the therapeutic context to try to create change in vivo that will transfer to the life of the client outside of therapy (Kohlenberg & Tsai, 1991). BA is not a therapeutic approach that is self-conscious about within-therapy interactions, but a good BA therapist will be aware that behaviors are occurring in the session that may or may not occur in other contexts in the client's life.

Within this context, however, the client is taught to look carefully at her life and to become an expert on her daily behaviors and the consequences of her behaviors. Treatment techniques that will be discussed at length later in this book are used to help the client monitor and analyze the behaviors and consequences of behavior and also to develop a plan for change. Thus, in many ways BA is simply about coaching people in becoming better observers and actors in the context of their lives. There is a popular notion that people should not "sweat the small stuff"; but in BA the adage "it's the little things that matter" would be more appropriate. The BA therapist tries to get clients to pay exquisitely close attention to the flow of their experience on a daily, hourly, and moment-by-moment basis. Which chunk of their life context they choose to look at varies from person to person and from time to time, but so few people will actually stop and look at what they are doing and what they are feeling and how they are related; it is this sort of coaching that predominates the therapeutic work in BA.

There are several empirically validated therapies (Chambless et al., 1998; Task Force on Promotion and Dissemination of Psychological Procedures, 1995) that have rather specific activities planned from session to session, and if the therapist does not do as instructed in a particular session she is not actually doing the treatment as it has been validated. BA is in the process of being validated, but the therapy does not consist of certain sets of behaviors to be accomplished in a stepwise fashion from session to session. There are certain activities that the therapist is expected to do, and certain activities that the therapist should avoid, but these occur according to the specific case and the context of a particular session. These behaviors will be elaborated in subsequent chapters and will be described in detail with case examples.

A typical session of behavioral activation will be structured; there will be one or two items on an agenda and the therapist is expected to keep the discussion on topic. The therapy is active; in other words, the client will be expected to be engaging in the generation of solutions and activities to try out. The therapist works in the role of an empathic coach rather than as a parental figure or advice giver. The therapist and client collaborate on establishing treatment goals, and the client should know the reasons that the therapist suggests certain activities or takes a particular therapeutic course. The therapist and client may agree that bringing in a significant other would be important in the treatment, and there are particular instructions for handling such a situation (see chapter 7). Discussions will usually consist of debriefing the client's weekly activities, examining how the client is conducting him- or herself in regard to life circumstances that have been identified as problematic, and progress on the client's life goals.

The philosophical idea of contextualism becomes extremely concrete in BA when the therapist continually helps the client turn nouns into verbs. Characterological statements (e.g., "I'm really a failure as a father and husband") are redirected toward historical acts in context (e.g., "Where are you when you think you're a failure? What do you do next when you think you're a failure?"). The BA therapist helps the client to focus on the relationships between actions and consequences, while viewing the "self" as an historical actor in a current context.

PART II
Describing Behavioral Activation as a Treatment

CHAPTER 4

The Principles and Essentials of Behavioral Activation

THE MOST IMPORTANT PRINCIPLE OF BA is that the therapist should know the model and be able to discuss it with the client. For this reason, we will refer to the model frequently in this chapter, based on the underlying theories that were discussed in part I. There are four principles for therapists to keep in mind to guide them in conducting BA:

1. Individuals are vulnerable to depression for a variety of reasons.
2. Secondary coping behaviors play a significant role in depression.
3. BA is not simply about increasing pleasant activities.
4. Clients should pay close attention to the context they are in and the impact of behaviors on the context of mood.

Since this is an idiographic, functional approach, it is better for therapists to have principles in mind and a basic philosophical idea rather than just a set of techniques. As will be seen later, the techniques are quite common, but the application of these techniques takes skill and a clear understanding of where therapy is going for a particular client.

Individuals are Vulnerable to Depression for a Variety of Reasons

Precursors to a depressive episode are often difficult to determine. The onset of depression for many individuals can be traced to a sudden loss, such as losing a job or the dissolution of a relationship; to the lack of attainment of a personal goal; or to difficulty coping with the daily hassles of life. There are others, however, who are not able to point to a particular life event that preceded the depression. In our contextual view of depression, the precipitants may have been present for many years and can still be found in the life of the individual even if the individual is not able to designate the particulars. One need not attribute the etiology of depression to a purely biochemical process even for those who cannot specify a life problem. Behavioral activation is based on the principle that individuals are vulnerable to depression for a variety of reasons. However, people who are depressed act in certain ways that maintain their depression. As was mentioned in part I, many behaviors function as avoidance and keep the person stuck in a vicious cycle of depression. We have called these types of behaviors "secondary problems" because they appear to be manifestations of the individual's attempt to cope with the negative experiences that have led to depression.

Secondary Coping Behaviors Play a Significant Role in Depression

Focusing on the secondary problems can be useful even when an individual is unaware of precipitants or states that depression has been a chronic experience with no obvious beginning. Typical patterns of behavior observed in depressed individuals exacerbate the depression, prevent them from addressing problems in their lives that could ultimately have a positive effect on them, and maintain a passive approach to living that creates a vicious cycle. Depression is diagnosed in the *DSM-IV* when a constellation of symptoms, such as blue mood, loss of pleasure in many or all activities, hypo- or hypersomnia, changes in appetite, and/ or ruminative negative thinking, are present. When BA therapists talk about the secondary problem behaviors seen in depression, we are often talking about the symptoms of depression. For heuristic reasons, in BA a separation is made between the feeling elements of depression (feeling the blues, loss of energy, etc.) and the action elements (e.g., decreased activity, sleeping long hours, anorexia or overeating). This distinction allows an easier approach to treatment and less complicated explanation provided to clients. Figure 3.2 (page 51) provided an example of the BA model in the context of depression. We can expand this figure as shown in figure 4.1, to show the model as it is presented to clients. Note that there is a distinction made between major life events or precursors to depression leading to a decreased or low level of positive reinforcement, the feeling components of depression that we simply label "depression"

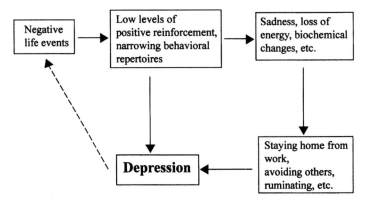

FIGURE 4.1 A BA *model of depression as presented to clients. Negative life events result in low levels of positive reinforcement and narrowing repertoires. The resulting symptoms trigger secondary maladaptive coping efforts, which maintain the depression. Much of BA is targeted at behavioral processes in the upper left and lower right boxes. The dashed arrow indicates that depressed behavior may exacerbate negative life events.*

or "feeling depressed," and the behavioral components of depression. The patterns of response to the environment are associated with either the development or maintenance of depression.

The model is more complicated than it appears in this figure. Context includes all aspects of the individual's environment, which is not easy to demonstrate in pictorial form since drawings tend to imply arbitrary distinctions between feelings, behaviors, life events, etc. In essence, the model states that given the context of the person's life, he or she has developed a particular pattern of responding to environmental events. These environmental events may be external, as in the loss of a lover. The environmental events may also be private experiences. For example, thinking "I am a bad salesperson" is occasioned by the individual's experience of having been turned down by a customer. This thinking is a cue for acting less aggressively toward the customer that has, in the past, led to retaliation and complaints made to a supervisor. Understanding this theory is a crucial aspect of the treatment. It comes alive in the therapeutic process because it guides the way the therapist interprets the client's behavior, and the way the therapist talks about the client's experiences. When doing BA the fundamental concept to keep in mind is that all behavior serves a particular function, whether those behaviors are observable to the therapist or are private events known only to the client and reported to the therapist.

BA is Not Simply About Increasing
Pleasant Activities

Many people engage in positive activity on a regular basis (e.g., they may exercise, go to movies, socialize with friends) and they are still depressed. Others have successful careers and have fulfilled life goals, and yet they report feeling like failures. Cognitive theory suggests that core beliefs or schemas are at work preventing the individual from accurately perceiving his or her world. Behavioral theory would suggest that the function of the positive activity or the successful career is not sufficient to affect the depression. A person who excels at her career but does not confront interpersonal relationship conflicts or fears may be subtly avoiding the very thing that will improve her life and/or mood. According to behavioral theory, "all that glitters is not gold" and pleasant events cannot be assumed to be antidepressive. If daily exercise continues, we can say that there is reinforcement involved in maintaining the behavior. We cannot say that the reinforcement is positive, however, unless we know the function of the behavior. If daily exercise decreases a morbid fear of obesity, then it is likely that it is being maintained via negative reinforcement (i.e., the function of exercise is to avoid anxiety and depression associated with gaining weight).

Behavioral activation treatment of depression is not about simple maneuvers that increase positive activity in a person's life. It is about trying to discover, through a functional analysis, what contingencies are maintaining the depression, and teaching the client about the functional aspects of behavior. We view the therapist as a consultant who helps the client to become an expert observer of the various relationships between different actions and different consequences in day-to-day life. If the metaphor seems appropriate, we sometimes tell clients that this treatment is designed to help them become scientific experts on their daily lives. The notion is similar to the idea of collaborative empiricism developed by Aaron Beck in the context of cognitive therapy (Beck et al., 1979). What's different is that we help clients observe how their behavior is or is not working for them, rather than focusing on how their thoughts affect their mood.

That BA is not about increasing positive or pleasant activities cannot be overstressed, as this is the mistake that is most likely to be made by therapists who are new to the approach. Recall from previous chapters that behaviors occur in a certain context, and that the BA therapist needs to be concerned more with the function than with the form of the behavior. From this perspective, it is difficult to name any behavior a "pleasant behavior" out of context. Eating chocolate cake is a very pleasant behavior in certain contexts, primarily when there has been some amount of deprivation from sweets or other foods. However, after the fifth cookie or the second glass of milk, eating a piece of chocolate cake may actually be an aversive experience. The behavior looks the same, and the piece of chocolate cake may look just as moist and chewy under both conditions, but whether the activity is pleasant depends on the context.

Clients Should Pay Close Attention to the Context They Are In and the Impact of Behaviors on the Context of Mood

A BA therapist continually questions the consequences of the client's behavior, and he or she accepts without judgment behaviors that the client describes as useful or mood enhancing that on the surface may seem rather dull or mundane. For example, one woman stated that she would like to increase the amount of time that she spent reading about stocks and investing. Her therapist would not have engaged in this activity to improve his mood; however, it functioned in this fashion for the client, and the therapist simply accepted that this was a behavior for the client to schedule during her week. Clients frequently ask, "Why do I feel this way?" BA therapists teach clients to observe their own lives so that they begin to answer this question and recognize the context of their moods.

DEPRESSION IN CONTEXT

It is necessary to understand the context and conditions that may have preceded the depressive episode and that are found to exacerbate the depression. Furthermore, from a contextualist perspective, it is important to assist the individual in freeing him- or herself from the tyranny of moods and the struggle against negative affect (Hayes, 1994). As Hayes noted:

> Often simply opening up the option of feeling what one feels, thinking what one thinks, and putting one foot in front of the other so as to do what needs to be done is a revelation to clients. Clients come in thinking that they have to win the war with their own psychology. (p. 31)

Acceptance and tolerance are implied in BA as the therapist coaches the client to make attempts at engaging in activities despite feelings of fear, sadness, low motivation, etc. The BA therapist encourages the client to work from the "outside-in," by changing behavior without waiting for any internal change. Clients often believe that they would improve if only they could feel motivated or empowered to act. From the perspective of BA, action can be independent of feeling. A client can choose to act despite motivation to do so, and by taking small steps that are scheduled to occur at specific times during the week, the likelihood of acting increases. Unlike other therapies involving acceptance, however, BA considers the experiences of people who are depressed as experiences worth changing, and it is hoped that mood will indeed improve as the client begins to act in ways that will prove to be antidepressant in nature.

Working with Thinking in BA

Behavioral activation is not psychotherapy from the neck down, however. In all aspects of the treatment, client thinking is acknowledged and assessed. No one would question that people think, and there is certainly mentation occurring at all parts of therapy. In some or many cases the client may change attributions and this may account for therapeutic effectiveness, but it need not necessarily occur in all cases. What can be observed is that assisting a client to approach rather than avoid, or to find better ways of coping, is therapeutically effective. Behavior analysts have begun to look at thinking and verbal behavior to try to explain how listeners understand rules (Hayes & Hayes, 1989), and what makes the listener follow or act upon the rule (Hayes, Zettle, & Rosenfarb, 1989). Detailing these theories is beyond the scope of this book; the main point, however, is that our understanding of what goes on inside the mind is still incomplete. Theorists and therapists from purely biological, cognitive, or behavioral camps see the same mountain from different sides.

The behavioral activation therapist accepts her clients' thinking, but encourages clients to look at the context of thinking rather than at the content of the thoughts. So, when clients present ruminative thinking about their depression or bad life circumstances, the BA therapist will help them look at the antecedents and consequences of this kind of thinking. The topics are not refuted, or addressed, but the process of ruminating is. It is important that the therapist not give the impression that the client's thoughts are unimportant, but that there are consequences to his thinking. Ruminating does not lead to constructive activity, so the client would be encouraged to do something different that would actually be constructive. This would also be true for thinking that was not ruminative. If a client said he thought that "everyone at work hates me," the therapist would ask what he does when he is thinking this way. If the consequence of the thinking is that he avoids his coworkers, the therapist would ask him if his goal is to avoid them. If he were then to say, for example, "No, I want them to like me," the therapist would say, "Well, how would you act if that was the goal?" The client would then be helped to describe actions that could lead to approaching coworkers, and the specific thought "everyone hates me" would not be directly addressed. The truth of that thought would not be evaluated, but rather the impact of the behavior "thinking that people hate me" would be assessed, and the client would be coached to act differently.

Essential Elements of Behavioral Activation

There are several essential elements to BA. First, client behaviors and the environmental context in which the behaviors occur are the primary focus. The primary question for the therapist to consider should be "What environmental factors are involved in how the client is feeling right now, and how is the client responding to these environmental factors that may be maintaining negative feelings?" (University of Washington, 1999).

The second essential element has been discussed earlier. The client is taught to become active in spite of feeling states — to act according to a goal or plan rather than according to an internal state. For example, one of our clients expressed dissatisfaction at work and said that she had a hard time "believing in" herself and thought that "others at work did not respect" her. She was asking herself if she should take a new job. Rather than addressing her internal state, the therapist asked her to list her goals for work. This list included things like "I'd like to work in my own office, rather than a cubicle; I want to have frequent interaction with coworkers; I want to be able to leave the office at 5:00; I want to make a lot of money." Obviously, some of these goals were incompatible. An important aspect of BA is that clients can be shown how to work toward goals even when those goals are incompatible and may occasion the distress the client experiences. Clients may need coaching in setting priorities, and in trying approaches to goals that may help them clarify which competing goals are most important to their emotional well-being. Also, clients can be encouraged to accept that they have competing goals and that some of those goals will be met at certain times while others go unmet.

BA is a therapy that works best when it is presented in a concrete fashion and when client problems are operationalized. So, if a client were to state that she "just feels unhappy," the BA therapist would help her to concretize that statement. The therapist may ask questions such as "Are there specific things that you are unhappy with?" "What do you think your life would look like if you were happy?" "What do you think leads to a happy life for others?"

The third essential element of BA is that therapists need to trace patterns of responding that may be maintaining depression. This is done by carefully reviewing the client's activities on a daily basis, using some form of activity log maintained by the client. In chapter 3 we explained that the BA therapist looks at broad classes of behaviors or that it is a molar rather than a molecular approach, but that she must also look at specifics. Patterns of responding are often difficult to recognize, so many examples of behavior must be discussed with the client. Since the therapist cannot follow the client around with a videotape recorder, it is important to help clients to be as detailed as they possibly can when discussing their behavior. The details of completing activity charts and looking at client behaviors will be examined in later chapters, but, basically the therapist wants to see what the client is doing, or not doing, during the day. This is achieved by simply having the client record general behaviors on an hourly basis. The next step is to look at the relationship between client activity and mood. Ultimately, the client and therapist will discuss specific situations that occurred, what the client desired to accomplish, what she actually did, the result, and other possibilities for behaving differently in the future if necessary.

Finally, it is essential that clients are taught how to do a functional analysis, by looking at antecedents and consequences to their behavior. This is not always easy to do, and most clients are certainly not used to thinking about their behavior in these terms. For most people behavior is attributed to internal causes. Although the antecedents can be "internal" or private, it is usually more helpful to look for public, observable antecedents in the environment. A person may say that he went to a horror movie because he "felt like having a good scare," attributing his behavior to a feeling or a desire. Another individual may say that she made a lewd gesture to another driver because he "made" her "angry," thus attributing her behavior both to an external cause, the other driver, and to an internal one, her anger.

Behavioral activation therapists need not be overly philosophical with clients or argue points of view. In other words, a BA therapist would be unwise to say, "Well, we need to look at other reasons for your going to that horror movie because we know that feelings do not cause behaviors." Likewise, the woman described above would most likely not respond well to being told that "nobody else can make you angry; that is not really what caused you to flip him off. Who cares if you were angry anyway?" Anger is on the chain but the therapist wants the client to look further back to environmental cues — anger may be the most proximal link to behavior, however, but anger may be aversive and then the behavior of flipping the bird is negatively reinforced by the reduction in anger. It is better to just accept the language of the client and to operationalize terms and help the client to see that behaviors are occasioned by certain situations and to be aware of the consequences. Leslie, for example, attributed much of her distress to "low self-esteem." The therapist did not argue with this concept other than to say "Well, people mean many things by that term, and I want to really know what you mean by it. Could you tell me what kinds of things are going on when you feel like you have low self-esteem? Are there times when you would say that your self-esteem is high? I'd be curious to know what is going on then." Once the therapist and client have workable terms with which to discuss the possible function of the behaviors that may maintain the vague feeling of "low self-esteem," they can begin to strategize how to activate Leslie in a way that will create, change, and improve her situation.

TREATMENT TARGETS

We have discussed theory, organizing principles, and essential elements of BA. We also stated that it is important for the therapist to keep the organizing principles in mind. It is equally important that therapists conduct a good case formulation (Persons, 1989; Turkat, 1985) and develop treatment goals with clients. We have found that there are several targets of treatment that are specific to BA. In this chapter we consider four specific targets: avoidance behavior, the context of client problems (both outside of therapy and within the therapeutic relationship), routine disruptions, and passive coping.

Avoidance Patterns: The Foremost Target
for Intervention

BA targets avoidance as a primary problem in depression. This is another difference between standard behavior therapy and BA as it has currently developed. The emphasis on avoidance has occurred in behavior therapy for other disorders, but not for depression. In fact, depression itself may be a form of avoidance. The individual does not have to deal directly with problems in life if social withdrawal, spending more time in bed, pushing people away with chronic negativity, etc., are used as a means of coping with painful feelings. Avoidance is like giving a man who is stranded in a desert, dying of thirst, a bottle of vodka. He may gratefully and greedily drink the vodka to escape from the aversive thirst, but the immediate solution ultimately keeps him avoiding the long-term solution. If he has an immediate decrease in thirst due to a substance that ultimately dehydrates him further, and he becomes intoxicated and neglects a further search for water, he will ultimately die. Depressed individuals are trying to resolve problems and to get themselves out of aversive situations. The short-term solutions often make the long-term consequences worse and maintain the depression. These *avoidance patterns* or *secondary problems* are the primary targets of BA treatment.

It is not always apparent that a client's behavior is avoidance or escape behavior. The client is doing what feels natural. It is only by looking at the consequences of the behavior that we can begin to understand its function.

Steve entered therapy after a series of life events had left him feeling depressed, suicidal, and discouraged. His depression had been intensifying over the past six months as he began to have increasing arguments at home with his girlfriend, to miss more days of work, and to get further behind financially. Steve described a sequence of events on days when he felt particularly despondent: He would awaken in a blue mood. Although he always felt better when he would keep busy at work and accomplish things, on these days he would stay in bed long after the alarm rang. As he would lay awake in bed he would begin to think about his children who lived with his ex-wife. He would then begin to ruminate about the losses in his life. As he began to sink deeper into the depression of the day, he would also have thoughts about his failures as a husband, a father, and now as an employee — after all, here he was staying at home when he was perfectly healthy, letting his employer down. He also would wonder whether his girlfriend was really committed to him. Although he was sullen and distant from her, and usually responded to her with irritation, he thought that she was behaving less affectionately toward him because she "no longer loved him."

The protocol for a cognitive therapist would be to address the faulty thinking in this client. In fact the thinking errors are quite obvious. Steve demonstrates several cognitive distortions, such as maximization, arbitrary inference, and overgeneralizations. A psychodynamic or interpersonal therapist might focus on his repressed anger, or the similar dynamics in various relationships in his life. What is interesting is that the behavior of staying in bed is typically assumed to be a consequence of some more fundamental cause, be it cognitive, dynamic, or even biological. In BA, however, the focus of treatment makes it clear that Steve's problem begins with staying in bed. Steve's responses to dysphoria are what we call secondary avoidance behaviors. Although Steve's stated intention is to stay in bed because he feels so badly and thinks that he cannot face the world or be productive at work, the end result is that it keeps him out of contact with possible reinforcers in his environment.

Steve is not necessarily intentionally avoiding anything. Intentionality is really not an issue for the BA therapist. Instead, we're interested in the function of various activities — regardless of whether clients are aware of the function or experience themselves as consciously controlling their behavior. Steve's painful feelings are a trigger for his staying in bed and the consequence is that the intensity of the experience of those feelings is decreased. Another consequence of this behavior is an additional decreased likelihood of experiencing situations that might bring a sense of pleasure or accomplishment to Steve's life. While recognizing that Steve does not experience himself as choosing to stay in bed, the therapist views his behavior as imbedded in an entire context of avoidance. The therapist focuses on the consequences of Steve's activity rather than some sort of internal cue. Steve also avoids situations that may be associated with anxiety or other distress. Instead of approaching his girlfriend in a loving, concerned manner, which may result in rejection of his affections, Steve responds in short, irritated sentences or ignores her altogether. Likewise, her response to his behavior confirms his belief that she does not wish to be with him. It is not necessary, however, to change or test the belief that she does not wish to stay in the relationship; it is simply necessary to change his own rejecting behavior. In BA the therapist and client hypothesize that it is Steve's rejecting actions that lead to his girlfriend's distance.

CONSIDERING THE CONTEXT

It is by now quite obvious that in BA the context is everything. This includes the context of the therapeutic encounter. The behavior of the client in therapy and the behavior of the therapist is very important. If the therapist is understanding, validating, and interested it is assumed that he or she will provide a relationship that will have some type of impact on the client. If somewhere in the client's history important people have appeared understanding, validating, and interested and have also been cruel these characteristics in the therapist may potentially be aversive to the client. So, the client may have a pleasant encounter with the therapist, but might actually become less self-disclosing as the conditioned response to the therapist's behavior is controlled by previous therapeutic encounters. It is important for the therapist to be vigilant to subtle changes in the client's response to him or her. Frequently checking in with the client to make sure that he or she is comfortable with what is happening in the session is a good way for therapists to stay attuned to behaviors that may be subtly punishing client responses. So, as in all forms of therapy, forming a positive therapeutic relationship with the client is important. Even when working like a coach, the therapist must quickly learn the types of interactions that may either reinforce or inadvertently punish the client's self-disclosure, and commitment to try change strategies.

Many clients like to talk about their problems. Ferster (1973, 1981) referred to some client complaints as magical or superstitious behaviors. In other words, a complaint such as "I'm cold" may have at one time been reinforced by the response of a caregiver to either provide a sweater or turn up the heat. For people who become depressed, the complaint may be occasioned by the individual's deprivation, but without a response from anyone who could minister to the deprivation. Complaining behavior was at one time reinforced, but the individual continues the behavior even when it is no longer reinforced by anyone in the external environment. The complaint, therefore, takes on the nature of being magical, in that the person engages in complaining apart from the presence of someone who could minister to the complaint. The statement "I'm lonely" may serve such a function. In a therapy session the statement "I'm lonely" may be a complaint that is made to escape from discomfort or it may be made in the presence of the therapist as someone who can address the feeling of social deprivation experienced by the client. It is important for therapists to consider the function of client verbalizations. In general, it is better to encourage conversation about productive behaviors rather than to allow the client to engage in repeated complaining about life.

It is important to try to understand the context of a client's behavior outside of the therapy session. Along with helping clients to break avoidance patterns, this is an essential target of BA. It is accomplished by using activity schedules (Beck et al., 1979) to review the complexity of a person's daily life and attempting to make situation-activity-behavior relations. This is how clients are initially taught to think in terms of functional analyses. Activity schedules, or activity charts, are simple forms that break the days of the week into 24-hour blocks of time (see appendix A). Therapists can experiment with various activity charts available that allow clients ample room for detailed writing. Therapists may also choose to develop their own. We have found several computer literate clients to make up charts that they find more pleasing to the eye or that allow them to include specific information.

Uses for an Activity Chart

While it makes sense to BA therapists that charting behaviors is an important part of therapy, it is not always so clear to clients. Therapists should present a good rationale for tracking behaviors on the activity chart, as in the following example:

"I'd like to get a good sense of what your life is like, and it is very difficult for me to do so without following you around on a daily basis. Since I cannot accompany you throughout your life, and can't get a sense of what kinds of things you do and how you feel when you are doing them, I'd like to have a visual presentation of the details of your life. Your daily experience is a rich source of information. I have a chart that can be used to help both of us to better understand all the intricacies of your life. It requires you to keep information as close to hourly as possible."

When the client understands that the activity chart is a vital tool to understanding behavior and that it helps the therapist to really understand the client's experience, resistance to using the chart is usually low. Keeping track of behaviors on an activity chart is a tedious endeavor, however. Any documentation is accepted as useful, even if a client returns with only a few hours of documentation from an entire week. The client would be encouraged to try to write something for an entire day, then two days, etc., until the client became more comfortable with keeping the charts in a detailed fashion. The therapist can use the charts with several different goals in mind. Here we discuss eight uses, but we assume that therapists will be creative and come up with additional uses.

Assessment of general activity level. In the very beginning of therapy it is important to gather an understanding of how active or inactive a client is. An activity chart should be the first and foremost self-monitoring tool that the BA client uses. At this point the chart is used in a very simple manner, and the client is asked to just write what they did during the hour blocks of time. Clients are encouraged to be as detailed as they can be, but they are also warned that they need not obsess over filling in every blank since any information they can give is better than none.

Assessment of activity and mood connections. This stage of the game becomes a little trickier for some clients because they have difficulty identifying how they feel. It is not uncommon for depressed people to say that they feel "blah" or "numb" when asked to describe their mood.

Nevertheless, they should be asked to add to that activity chart not only what they have done during the hours, but also how they felt when they were doing it. It can also be helpful to ask them to rate the intensity of their mood on a scale of 0–10 with 10 being most intense, but this should be done only after they have become familiar with recording activities and feelings.

Range of feelings. The activity chart is an excellent tool for evaluating the range of the client's feelings during the time between sessions. One of our clients completed an activity chart that was quite extensive. There were a wide variety of activities described and specifics about home and work activities. It was interesting to note that the client defined his mood as either "frustrated," "anxious," or "relieved." The therapist noted this and asked the client if he was aware of this, he replied that he was not. The therapist then began to explore how the client could engage in activities that might actually make him feel "happy," "calm," "peaceful," "content," and so on.

Mastery and pleasure ratings. This is relatively standard in cognitive therapy. Clients are asked to record whether they had a sense of mastery or pleasure or both when engaged in an activity. They can then rate the intensity of the feeling on a scale of 0–10. Mastery is defined as an activity that provides a sense of having accomplished something, having done a task that may have been difficult or that simply needed to be done. Cleaning out a desk drawer may give a client a sense of mastery, for example. Eating ice cream may give a client a sense of pleasure, but not much accomplishment. For some clients, washing the car could provide both a sense of mastery and pleasure. It is good to help clients to distinguish between the impact of certain behaviors on their feelings of having accomplished something, or just enjoyed the activity.

Observing the breadth or restriction of activity. The therapist can take a completed activity chart and begin to get a sense of the breadth of the client's activity. When there is a narrow repertoire of behavior it is important for the therapist to discuss this with the client. For example, a therapist may, while reviewing an activity chart with a client, recognize that the client has spent many hours in a week playing solitaire. It would be important for the therapist to point this out to the client. The therapist could hand the activity chart to the client and ask if he sees any patterns in behavior. If the client doesn't recognize the pattern, the therapist might simply ask, "Did you realize that you spent X hours playing solitaire? Do you think that is accurate?" If the client agrees that the total hours reflected in the chart is accurate, the therapist can then ask what impact he believes it had on his mood that week. If the client and therapist agree that this behavior may be contributing to the client's depression, they would work on guided activity (see below).

In the opposite case, the activity chart may reveal that the client is engaging in many varied behaviors. This is important for the functional analysis, because it is important to understand what is maintaining the depression if the client is, in fact, quite active. The therapist would acknowledge that the client seems to be very active and that therapy will not focus on simply "getting him moving" since he is already doing so, but on guiding his activity so that he will be engaging in activities that improve his mood and help him to attain life goals.

Guided activity. This is the heart of BA. Once the therapist and client have explored the overall activity level of the client, and what activities are connected with positive or negative feelings, they can begin to try to increase activities that have been associated with positive moods. Clients often get stuck at this point when they "don't feel like doing anything." The therapist must continue to coach and encourage the client to act from the "outside-in" and use the written chart to guide his behavior. Scheduling activities should initially be done in the session, with the client being given homework (see below) to add activities on his own.

Helping the client monitor avoidance behaviors. The difficulty that clients (and therapists) have in determining whether or not a behavior is avoidance will be discussed in greater detail below. However, it is useful to note that an excellent use of the activity chart is to help the client to monitor the function of various behaviors. The therapist can ask the client to take the activity chart and look back over the day, and ask himself if, given the specific goal at the time, he thinks what he actually did brought him closer or farther away from the goal. If the latter, then the behavior might have been avoidance. If the client knows he was actively avoiding an aversive event, he should mark that. He can also monitor when his behavior was an activation behavior, facing a situation he would typically avoid. This allows both the therapist and the client to begin to get a better idea of the functional analysis of the client's daily behaviors.

Evaluating progress toward overall life goals. Clients can also use their activity charts, once they have completed a week or more of them, to assess whether the activities they are engaging in are consistent with their overall life goals. Are the behaviors they see on the activity chart the kind of behaviors they want to engage in, given their goals in life? The therapist can ask, "As you look over this week's chart, do you get a sense that this is the life you want to be living? Do you feel content with most of the activities that you have engaged in?" If the answer is "yes," then the therapist and client can focus on specific situations that may cause difficulty for the client. If the answer is "no," then the therapist and client can focus on planning steps to help the client begin to reach desired goals or to engage in activities that would be more meaningful to the client.

It is hopefully clear that the activity chart should be carefully and thoroughly reviewed with the client every session. Sometimes therapists think that attending to this type of detail is obsessive or boring, but we believe that it is extremely important and that attending to the minute details of an activity chart helps the therapist to see into the complexities of the client's life. Therefore, rather than being boring or tedious, it is the tool that truly allows the therapist to get to know his or her client.

ROUTINE DISRUPTION
AND DEPRESSION

Avoidance patterns are important in the development and maintenance of depression. It is also important to look at the disruption in normal routines that may precede a depressive episode. Clients who experience major changes in their lives have had their routines disrupted. Many people actively establish new routines and get back on track after such a change. It is well known that changes in jobs, a move to a new home or new city, marriage or divorce, and the birth of a child are all major stressors in peoples' lives. Most people cope with the stressors and learn to adjust without becoming depressed. For those individuals who develop passive coping styles, however, and are otherwise vulnerable to depression, such changes in routine can be precursors to a depressive episode. The depression is exacerbated by the secondary problem behaviors that may increase the disruption in routine. The frequently observed depressive behaviors of sleeping until late in the day, skipping meals, and refraining from calling friends throw off the person's routine. The side effect of these behaviors is that negative moods are worsened.

Routine disruption has been recognized as an important component of bipolar disorders (Ehlers, Frank, & Kupfer, 1988). A German word that refers to contextual synchrony, *zeitgeber*, explains humans' dependence on social/environmental routines to maintain emotional stability. Light is a primary zeitgeber, as are schedules for meals and sleep-wake cycles; certain individuals in life (parents, spouses, etc.) can become zeitgebers as well (Ehlers et al., 1988; Wirz-Justice, 1995). It is quite possible that there is a connection between the regulation of routine and depression. Ehlers and colleagues (1993) also refer to *zeitstörers* as time disrupters. Transmeridian airflight, nightshift work, or the death of a loved one are examples of zeitstörers (Ehlers et al., 1993). The concept of zeitgebers and zeitstörers explains phenomena such as seasonal cycles in depression, diurnal variations in mood, and results of sleep deprivation (Wirz-Justice, 1995). In BA, change in behavior is not considered a one-shot deal. Therefore, another essential feature of BA is that the therapist helps the client to reestablish routines that may have been disrupted by depression or a major life change, or to establish routines that may never have been in place.

PASSIVE COPING

Needless to say, people who have developed a pattern of avoidance, trying to escape from aversive feelings or situations, becoming increasingly inactive and getting out of touch with their usual routines, often appear to be very passive. In fact, we have observed that many depressed people seem to simply react to life rather than act. In BA we coach clients to become proactive. This often begins to happen as they are breaking avoidance patterns, and trying to act according to goals rather than feelings. It is important that clients experience actively pursuing a goal so that they can begin to shift the patterns of passively waiting for life to happen to them. We want clients to make life happen as much as they can. Certainly, none of us have complete control over the joys or pains of our own or other's lives. Suffering is ubiquitous to human beings (cf. Hayes et al., 1999), but people who actively cope even during times of loss are more resilient to depression than those who react to suffering by giving up (Holahan et al., 1999).

CHAPTER 5

Beginning to Act Like a Behavioral Activator

B A IS AN IDIOGRAPHIC TREATMENT APPROACH. Unlike other manual-ized treatments, there are no session-by-session guidelines to follow. However, several general rules of thumb can be followed and there is a logical course to the treatment. In the research treatment manual (University of Washington, 1999) there are several treatment stages. However, it is important for the reader to know that this structure is usually a naturally occurring one and does not need to be forced to fit a protocol. It is provided to give the therapist a guideline for following the treatment from beginning to completion.

The first stage is the establishment of a good therapeutic relationship and presentation of the model to the client. At this point the goal is to create an environment where clients can feel that their problems are understood and that they are valued and respected. This can be accomplished in a number of ways. The most important thing for the therapist to do is to listen to the client. This does not require a passive stance on the part of the therapist, however. Therapists can demonstrate that they understand what the client is saying by reflecting back what they have heard. It is also important to ask questions that logically arise from the client's disclosures. Asking clients about their stories allows them to feel that the therapist cares about what is happening in their lives. The therapist can also begin to socialize clients to the type of treatment that they will be involved in by formulating questions about client behaviors and environments. The following dialogue is an example:

CLIENT: I just feel like I've fallen apart since Mark left me. I haven't been able to cope.

THERAPIST: So that must have been really difficult for you to have your partner leave after all those years. I'd like to understand what has made it even more difficult for you to cope since he left.

CLIENT: Well, I became so despondent. I just didn't care anymore.

THERAPIST: Often when people don't care, they begin to withdraw from friends and loved ones and stop doing the usual things that allow them to care for themselves like exercising, etc. Has that been so for you?

CLIENT: Exactly. You're pretty insightful. That's exactly what happened — I just shut down.

THERAPIST: Well, I've seen that happen with many people, and I thought from what you were telling me that it might be the case for you as well. That is a very sad process. Can we talk about the way that you have withdrawn? Are there particular things that you used to do or people you used to see that are no longer a part of your life?

The therapist demonstrates an understanding of the client's situation and asks questions that can lead to greater specificity of behavioral patterns that have become problematic for the client. The therapist then has the opportunity to present the model, as described in greater detail below.

The second stage is monitoring the relationship between situation/action and mood and doing a fine-grained analysis of day-to-day activity as it relates to mood. This will be the focus of treatment for most clients. The focus will be on both client behaviors and negative environmental factors that may be connected with depression.

The third stage is to apply new coping strategies to issues of life like existential anxieties, feelings of poor self-esteem, etc. This requires creativity in BA because the search for meanings in the lives of clients leads us almost automatically to other forms of therapy that are less behavioral. Further discussion of this difficulty will be provided later.

Finally, the last stage of treatment involves treatment review and relapse prevention. In the final sessions of therapy the therapist should attend to the following (University of Washington, 1999, pp. 17–18):

1. Review initial presenting problems.
2. List red flags and triggers within the TRAP framework (see chapter 6).
3. List the most helpful elements of treatment.
4. Formulate a relapse prevention/response plan.
5. Build activation strategies into routines.
6. Discuss client feelings about termination as indicated.

THE STRUCTURE OF A
TYPICAL BA SESSION

Although BA is a treatment tailored to the needs of individual clients, it is important to have identified goals within and across treatment sessions. We must strike a balance between attending to clients' concerns and adhering to treatment goals and techniques. An agenda is set for each session. In the first two or three sessions, the therapist may take a more active role in this endeavor, until the client is socialized to come into the session with one or two topics for the agenda. The therapist must take care to collaborate with the client to establish agendas that are manageable. Usually only one or two items can be discussed in any session. The therapist must allow time to discuss homework from the previous week, and to establish a new homework assignment for the upcoming period between therapy sessions. It is a good idea for either the therapist or the client to write out the agenda either on a white board in the office or on a pad of paper. This helps to keep the session on target.

Agenda setting can be somewhat informal, but the therapist should know that there are one or two things that are important to cover prior to jumping into any problem. Therapists often have difficulty when clients give too many details about a particular topic and the session is derailed; the client leaves unsatisfied because issues that she or he may have wanted to discuss have not been covered. Here is an example of an agenda gone awry:

THERAPIST: Carol, what would you like to talk about today?
CAROL: Well, I have a meeting at work that I am dreading.
THERAPIST: You'd like to put that on our agenda?
CAROL: Yes. I don't know how I am going to get through the meeting. I get so anxious and I just want to stay home in bed. In fact I stayed home in bed on Monday, and it made me feel really crummy. I was so depressed by Monday night that I just wanted to quit work.
THERAPIST: Hmm.

As you can see, the client suggested a topic but then moved too quickly onto other problems. A better approach is to slow the client down and write down each item to make sure that the client prioritizes what she wants to talk about. We would propose the following as a better way to set the agenda.

THERAPIST: Carol, what would you like to talk about today?
CAROL: Well, I have a meeting at work that I'm dreading.
THERAPIST: So, you'd like to put that on our agenda?

CAROL: Yes. I don't know how I am going to get through the meeting. I get so anxious and I just want to stay home in bed. In fact I stayed home in bed on Monday . . .

THERAPIST: Whoa, Carol, let me interrupt you for a moment. I want to make sure we use our time well. It sounds like you have several things to discuss—the meeting at work, the assignment from last week, your anxiety, and your staying in bed to avoid work. Do you think we should discuss all of these things?

CAROL: Well, I want to discuss the meeting, and I think I'm only anxious about that.

THERAPIST: Okay, let's write down "upcoming meeting."

CAROL: I also think I should talk about staying in bed—that really made me feel worse.

THERAPIST: Okay, "staying in bed." Can I also write "homework" here?

CAROL: Sure.

THERAPIST: Anything else you think we can discuss? Or do you think this will take the whole session?

CAROL: Well, I'm actually thinking about quitting work. But maybe that's just my anxiety. Let's stick with the things we have and if something else comes up we can talk about it.

THERAPIST: Well, if something else comes up, let me know, and we can either add it to today's agenda if there is time, or talk about it next time. But let's try to stay focused on these important issues. Where would you like to start?

Generally it makes sense to discuss the homework from the previous session as the first thing on the agenda. This begins the session with constructive talk and may help to avoid the danger of using the time for a "gripe session." The goal of BA is to get the client to act adaptively, so it is important that actions taken by the client outside of therapy be attended to. It is common knowledge among behavior therapists that the best way to guarantee that homework will not be completed is for the therapist to fail to address it in the following session. The tasks required of clients in BA can be difficult, and the therapist must respect all efforts that the client has made. Failure to discuss homework is disrespectful of the client's hard work.

HOMEWORK

Like most cognitive or behavioral therapies, BA makes extensive use of homework assignments. If a client's problematic behavior occurs outside of therapy, then he must practice a new behavior in his daily life. Phrases like "practice," "experiments," and "between-session exercises" are preferable because we all have a history with the word "homework"; it's something people in positions of authority have asked us to do and it eats into our free time. Although we use the word homework here, it is better to refer to it differently with clients. Whatever the therapist can do to set the stage for clients to follow through on homework is important. This is a crucial issue in BA. The client must see the value of homework and work collaboratively with the therapist to develop useful exercises. Thus, discussing the role of homework with clients is an essential part of treatment. The therapist might say this: "In this treatment I'll be working with you to develop some helpful things to work on between therapy sessions. How does that sound to you?" (Most clients will like the idea). The therapist might continue: "So, sometimes we might decide it would be helpful for you to practice certain behaviors or activities. Other times it might be a matter of paying attention and observing what's going on in your life. The important point is that you're much more likely to improve if you make changes between sessions in addition to coming to therapy. What do you think about that?" The therapist might also ask, "Can you imagine what sorts of things might get in the way of practicing between our sessions?"

There are several things to notice about this example. First, the therapist avoids saying things like "I will be asking you . . . " Instead the therapist says, "We'll be working to . . . " Our goal is to avoid power struggles with clients and create a more collaborative process. The other thing to notice is that the therapist frequently checks on what the client thinks about what the therapist is saying. This is an essential aspect of BA, and most likely of any relatively directive/active therapy. The therapist doesn't ask questions like, "Does this make sense?" or "Do you agree?" Rather, the therapist asks open-ended questions about the clients' reactions to the treatment model. We'll return to this point again when discussing the treatment rationale in BA.

It is important, however, that the therapist engage the client in developing homework assignments and activities. This increases the likelihood that assignments will be carried out. One also increases the chance that homework will be completed if there is a set time and place decided during which the client will do the task assigned. Developing a plan to implement the intended task has been shown to make actualizing intentions more likely (Gollwitzer, 1999). If homework assignments are not completed, it is important for the therapist to spend time with the client discussing what interfered with doing the assigned task.

Finally, as in CT, the BA therapist should ask the client for feedback regarding the session. This lets the therapist know the client's perspective on the pace of the session, the types of questions asked, the therapist's tone of voice, the focus on various behaviors, etc. Clients are more likely to participate in therapy if they know that they are respected and have input into the process. Even if the client were to say "I wish I had gotten to tell you more about how I am feeling," and the therapist thought that there was a danger of getting into the trap of complaining (see the previous discussion), the therapist can negotiate allotted time during the session for "just talk" as opposed to directed activity work. This allows the client to determine his or her own plan for treatment, which is, in itself, an activation technique.

THE INITIAL INTERVIEW AND EXPLANATION OF THE MODEL

Like all psychotherapeutic treatments, there are specific goals of the initial session. Since there is nothing unique in the BA model that would be used in the diagnosis of depression, the focus will be on establishing rapport, beginning to look at behavior patterns, and introducing the client to the BA model. The initial interview may actually take place over several sessions; however, in these days of managed care clinicians are encouraged to gather as much information as possible in one session in order to begin treatment. Assessment is an ongoing process throughout the treatment, and the therapist should treat all conceptualizations as hypotheses until there is ample evidence to confirm them. What may at first seem to be a positive, active behavior may turn out to be avoidance — for example, working diligently at the office can serve many purposes. The therapist must conceptualize the client's problems in order to develop a treatment plan, but also must be open to new information throughout the treatment that may change the original conceptualization.

Working with depressed individuals requires patience and empathy from the therapist. People who are not familiar with the therapeutic process can have difficulties as well as those who are familiar with the process. Many people have an idea that the therapeutic encounter provides them with a time to tell their story to a good listener. In order to establish rapport, it is essential that the BA therapist tell the client that she will attempt to gather information to help her understand the client's situation, but that she also will *give the client some information*. The client should also initially be instructed that more information is to be provided for examination at home. This disclosure allows the therapist to express concern for the client but also to claim the opportunity to structure the first session without invalidating the client's concerns.* Thus, the first session is an ideal time to practice setting an agenda in therapy. The therapist might say, "Well, this is our first meeting, and in each of our meetings we'll make an agenda for our session. Are there things that you would like to make sure we cover today? (The therapist writes them down to make sure they're covered.) Okay, I would certainly like to take some time to find out about you and your situation. I would also like to share with you some information about treatment. How does that sound?"

It is important that clients understand that BA involves helping them to change their behavior and that the therapist will make suggestions and provide homework assignments for them to complete between sessions. Also, since this is short-term therapy, it is important that the therapist include disclosure that this therapy is focused and time-limited. Such a written disclosure will begin to socialize the client regarding the therapeutic process and informs the client from the beginning that the goal of therapy is for therapy to end. This may decrease expectations that therapy will be an interminable process.

BA will be more difficult as a treatment for clients who strongly adhere to a medical model and believe that their depression is caused by a chemical imbalance. It makes sense that those individuals are more likely to seek medication. Therapists should not automatically assume that the client will tenaciously hold onto these ideas, and they should assess this in the first session. We have found that some clients will ask the therapist whether he or she thinks they have a chemical imbalance; this provides an opportunity to explain that there are several understandings of the nature of depression. The BA model of depression — being caused by a person-environment interaction with internal and external causes — should be carefully explained. BA therapists do not hold to one notion of the cause for depression since it is known that behavior is multiply

---

*Some states require psychologists to provide a written disclosure statement regarding their practice. Also, psychologists and other therapists are frequently required to prepare statements that provide informed consent for their clients. We recommend a written statement that explains that the client will be engaging in a directive therapy, that there are no guarantees that it will be successful, and that it may make the client feel worse before it makes him or her feel better. There should be a broad statement that this is a treatment supported by research. We do not believe that one needs to provide a long list of all possible and hypothetical side effects of psychotherapy. To follow these disclosure procedures is well within the current standard of care. We also believe that psychotherapy has far less negative potential than many other treatments for depression. However, this controversy is beyond the scope of this book.

determined. In most cases depression can be traced to some precipitating event in the life of the person, and it is naive to believe that depression develops in a vacuum caused solely by a change in biology.

The BA therapist should listen carefully for clues in the first session. It is not important to ferret out the exact cause of depression since causes can only be hypothesized. Furthermore, the past cannot be relived so correction can only come in the present. BA supports clients in their attempts to change things that can be changed and to try to establish better lives. However, BA therapists must recognize that many factors in a person's life are not changeable and they must help the client to learn to behave in productive ways in spite of negative feelings. As was noted earlier, initial interviews may take place over several sessions. It is not expected that a therapist will be able to get diagnostic information, hypothesize causes, begin to establish treatment goals, take a history, and introduce the model all in the first session. Making use of written descriptions of the treatment rationale (see "Beginning Activation Treatment for Depression: A Self-Help Manual" — appendix B) is most helpful for therapists functioning under the pressures of time. Assessment is an ongoing process, and the BA therapist need not become overly concerned with getting it all right from the very beginning. Contemplating one or two goals and getting an idea about the problems secondary to the depression may be all that the therapist can expect to do in the first session, after taking a history and making a diagnosis. The seeds of the model will be incorporated in the questions the therapist asks during the interview.

The following excerpt from a second session demonstrates how the model is discussed with a client. Henry was a 54-year-old executive who had been laid off from his job two years prior to entering therapy. After unsuccessfully trying to find work in his field, he took a job working in a warehouse checking incoming trucks. This was a job that he was highly overqualified for, but he needed to support his wife and son. Henry met criteria for Major Depressive Disorder in *DSM-IV* and on the Hamilton Rating Scale for Depression (HRSD; Hamilton, 1960). When he began therapy his Beck Depression Inventory (BDI; Beck, Ward, Mendelson, Mock, & Erbaugh, 1961) score was 37, which suggested severe depression. He was given a short pamphlet to read between sessions one and two that described the BA approach to depression. The therapist began the discussion of the model by discussing the pamphlet.

THERAPIST: Now that you've had a chance to read a little about our approach, I wondered if you had any questions or if you recognized your own situation in this?

HENRY: Well, it all made sense. I guess I can see that it fits my situation.
THERAPIST: In what way?

(Note that the therapist asks open-ended questions and tries to shape the client into concretizing his statements. It is important that clients see how the model fits with their life and their circumstances; if not, they will be less likely to do the hard work of activating themselves. The therapist didn't just say, "That's good, I'm glad," but asked the client to elaborate on his understanding of the model. It is good to find out what the client likes or dislikes about the model, what makes sense for them, and what doesn't.)

HENRY: Well, I can relate to the idea that I've gotten into a bad habit of not doing things that I should do and that may make me feel more depressed.
THERAPIST: Let's talk about those bad habits. What kinds of things do you notice that you used to do that you do not do now?

(Again, the therapist looks for specific detail as much as possible.)

HENRY: Well, I used to spend more time with my son, helping him with homework and things. Now I can't stand to be around him or his mother, because I know they will ask me to do something.
THERAPIST: So, what do you do?
HENRY: I just stay in bed, pretending to be asleep, or I get up and go directly to the couch and sit and watch television.
THERAPIST: And what happens then?
HENRY: My wife gets angry, my son leaves and goes into his room, and I just pay half-hearted attention to the television.
THERAPIST: Did you ever act like this before you were depressed?
HENRY: Well, I worked long hours. I'd come home and be pretty tired, but there wasn't the same trouble. My wife was happier then, now she gets depressed because we have so little money. We used to do things as a family. Not anymore.

(Here the therapist tries to establish the history of this pattern of behavior. If this is a way of behaving that has happened since the onset of depression then the client is more likely to have other behaviors in his repertoire that can be built upon through the treatment.)

THERAPIST: Henry, I'd like to show you the way I tend to think about depression and its consequences. From what you are saying, it seems to me that you first started to get depressed after losing your job as an executive. Is that correct?

HENRY: Yeah. Well, actually, I wasn't depressed at first. Many of us were laid off. It was only after I started seeing other people get jobs and I wasn't, that I started to get really depressed. We had to leave our house and move to a cheaper neighborhood into an old, tiny rental house. My wife hates it.

THERAPIST: Okay, so it seems that there were several events that led to your depression. Let me list them up here on my board. You were laid off, you were not hired, you had to leave your home and neighborhood, and you then moved into a small house. Did I get them all?

(Here the therapist uses a whiteboard [which we suggest all BA therapists use] or writing paper to illustrate. Figure 5.1 is an example of the therapist's illustration.)

HENRY: Well, I also had to take this crummy job. It was really tough watching other people get better jobs, and I was not getting hired.

THERAPIST: So let me add these things. I'm also going to put a big question mark down here also, because there may be other things that led to the depression that you aren't aware of right now. I am

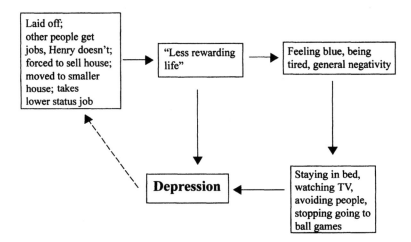

FIGURE 5.1 *The BA model as it related to Henry's case.*

also going to draw a larger arrow here, to indicate that all of these things have led to a decrease of rewards in your life. Would you agree that such a decrease has happened?

HENRY: Okay.

THERAPIST: So, I'll draw an arrow to the right of this list and just write "less rewarding life," which, of course, has left you feeling blue, being tired, and thinking negatively about things. Is that accurate?

HENRY: Yes, exactly. I just feel lousy about my life, and I'm tired all of the time.

THERAPIST: And what do you do when you feel lousy and tired?

(The therapist now attempts to get a sense of some of the secondary behaviors that may be targets for change.)

HENRY: Well, I usually just stay in bed. Then my wife starts to turn up the stereo, and I get the hint, so I get up and then watch TV.

THERAPIST: I'll write these things on the extreme right, and I'll draw an arrow connecting "depression" to these things, since they may be connected. Are there other things that you used to do before you began to feel depressed that you no longer do?

HENRY: Well, we used to go to ball games. Also, I used to be pretty busy at work, or shortly after the layoff, I would look for work. Now I do what I can to not run into the people I used to work with.

THERAPIST: Okay, Henry, I am going to add those things here on the right under the other things. So we have a list here: staying in bed, watching television, avoiding people at work, no longer going to ball games. I'm going to call these "secondary problems."

HENRY: Okay.

THERAPIST: I call these secondary problems because what happens to your feelings of depression when you stay in bed?

HENRY: It gets worse.

THERAPIST: Exactly. I am going to draw an arrow here that leads to a box called "depression." I'll also draw a dotted line here that circles back from depression to the initial problems we listed. Now, what happens when you get more depressed?

HENRY: I get even lazier.

THERAPIST: So these things on our list to the right get even more pronounced? Also, the initial problems don't get resolved, you don't go out and find a better job, you just watch TV, is that right?

HENRY: Yeah.

THERAPIST: Now, we have these life events that predated your depression, and I know you'd like to change some of these things, especially the work situation, right?

HENRY: Yes.

THERAPIST: But we have a dilemma here — we can't change these situations unless you are able to get out of this vicious cycle. So, I propose we start working here with the secondary problems and begin to help you get activated so that you can then tackle the other, bigger things that may have led to the depression in the first place. Does that make sense to you?

HENRY: Sure, but I don't know how we'll do that.

THERAPIST: Well, my job is to coach you through this. Can you tell me how this makes sense to you?

HENRY: Well, I know I can't fix the big problems in my life if I can't get the simple daily tasks of my life done.

THERAPIST: Yes, that is it in a nutshell. Also, the more depressed you feel, and the more you respond to those feelings by being inactive, the worse the entire situation gets.

HENRY: Well, that I understand, because it has just been getting worse and worse.

Henry's case presents an example of a client who had very obvious precursors to his depressive episode. When working with a client who has no obvious life events that may have led to the depression, the therapist can ask questions about early life history and put that in the box labeled "life events." Here is an example:

THERAPIST: So, you say you have always just felt depressed.

ANDREA: Well, not exactly. But lately I've just been feeling so blue, I can't stand it.

THERAPIST: Did something in particular happen to you recently?

ANDREA: No, things have been going well. I can't figure this out; I think it might be a chemical imbalance.

THERAPIST: Well, let me show you how I think about depression, and let's see if we can better understand how to work together.

ANDREA: Okay.

THERAPIST: Do you remember other times in your life when you've felt depressed?

ANDREA: Well, in high school, and maybe even before. I was a pretty sad kid.

THERAPIST: Were there things going on then?

ANDREA: No, just the usual.

THERAPIST: Such as?

ANDREA: You know, parents being strict, not really liking school, no big deal, I mostly had a good childhood.

THERAPIST: Well, I'm going to write down, "strict parents," "school," and maybe just "life hassles" — are you following me?

ANDREA: Well, so far. But I don't think that I'm depressed because my parents didn't let me stay out past 9:00 P.M. when I was 14.

(Figure 5.2 illustrates the first stages of graphically describing the model to Andrea.)

THERAPIST: Good, because I don't either. But I do think that there may have been an entire series of events and ways that you responded to the events that developed patterns of behaving that make you more vulnerable to depression. Sometimes there are family histories, so this vulnerability might be genetic or learned. Has anyone else in your family had depression?

ANDREA: Well, I found out later in life that my Dad was depressed. He usually just came home and ate dinner, watched TV, and went to bed.

THERAPIST (*Using a figure in the same fashion as Henry's case*): So, I'll add Dad's depression here, because maybe that had some effect. I'll then draw an arrow here leading to this other arrow that indicates that life may have been less rewarding for you, and this may then have made you more vulnerable to depression.

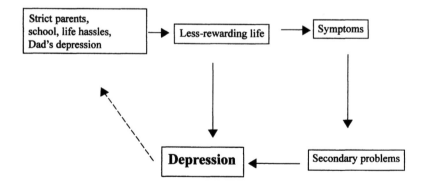

FIGURE 5.2 *The first stages of the BA model as it related to Andrea's case.*

The therapist can then complete the figure and try to discover the secondary problem behaviors that may be exacerbating the current episode.

During the initial interview, the therapist must begin to direct the client to focus her attention on her own responses to life events rather than the events themselves. We frequently observe that clients have a great need to talk about their lives and to tell their story. Many clients report that the process of telling someone about their pain and despair was initially helpful to them. We would propose that even in the initial sessions there is some reinforcement value to the caring understanding of the therapist. Perhaps it decreases the client's sense of isolation, or provides hope that they can get beyond their distress as they experience themselves telling a non-partisan observer about their pain. From a behavioral perspective, the therapist's attention and concern can be thought of as a verbal reinforcer that, as therapy progresses, can be used discriminantly to shape a client's behavior (Kohlenberg & Tsai, 1991). Therapists must be cautioned, however, not to be lulled only into listening without assisting the client to orient themselves toward an understanding of their own responses and the need to change. Therapists may even use talking about problems or complaining as a reinforcer for the client following concerted effort to change (such stimulus control procedures will be discussed later). Addis and Carpenter (2000) have suggested that therapists may allow clients to vent, but label it as such and place it on the agenda in order to maintain the structure of the cognitive-behavioral session. BA therapists may do a fair amount of empathic listening in sessions but must never make the mistake of thinking that this act alone will produce substantial relief or change for the client. We would assume that most clients who would be sufficiently helped by an empathic listener rarely make it into the psychotherapist's office since they are most likely helped by a caring friend, relative, or religious leader.

Therapists must be aware that their understanding of the client's depression may differ remarkably from the client's. Behavior therapists may find themselves in many difficult situations with clients who describe their problems in terms of mental illness, sexual or behavioral addictions, or chemical imbalances. Since those descriptions are often unhelpful from a therapeutic perspective, it is important to work carefully with clients to present an alternative rationale without invalidating their perspective. The way a client describes a problem may not be how the therapist would, but it's important only that they agree to work together and evaluate the outcome of treatment. If the client has difficulty accepting any behavioral rationale for his problem, treatment will be much more difficult. Keep in mind that clients may often interpret the therapist's rationale that depression is a result of person-environment interactions as blaming the client. This is particularly true when therapists try to explain that the way clients have tried to cope with their depression may lead to further problems and exacerbate the depression. Sometimes providing the client with an analogy like that of being offered vodka to drink in the desert may help to explain that the therapist sees the client's behaviors as understandable and perhaps unavoidable given their life circumstance.

As therapists and professionals we go through many years of training and learn to speak a professional language. We can expect other professionals to understand what we mean when we speak of reinforcement, consequences, context, and the like, but we must certainly not expect our clients to understand. Even well-educated clients are unlikely to appreciate explanations of their problems in jargon. Consider the following fictional interchange between a client and a therapist:

CLIENT: I don't know what is the matter, Doc. Ever since I was fired from my job I have been unable to get the motivation to do anything. It takes all I can do to get myself dressed in the morning. Even when I do get up and try to get moving, I just feel sad and useless.

THERAPIST: Well, it sounds like you are probably depressed as a result of being fired. Furthermore, your behavior since then has gotten you out of contact with reinforcers in your environment, and this heightens your depression. This is understandable in context and is certainly not your fault. We need to help you increase your repertoire of behaviors and also the likelihood of positive reinforcement in your life. How does that sound?

This exaggerated example may seem foolish, but it may not be all that far from the truth. It is easy for highly educated professionals to use jargon without recognizing it. A blank stare from the client may alert the therapist to this mistake; however, most clients do not wish to appear stupid and are likely to simply nod their heads in agreement. It is essential then, to present a therapeutic rationale in plain language and to make the rationale personally relevant to the client (Addis & Carpenter, 2000). By taking the previous interchange and turning it into a more functional description of the treatment, an interaction like this may ensue:

THERAPIST: So, it seems to me that it is difficult for you to get moving and that you feel so sad because you are depressed. Do you recall ever having this difficulty before you were fired?

CLIENT: Some days I'd feel kind of down, but never like this, never for days on end.

THERAPIST: What would you do during those times?

CLIENT: Well, I'd usually go see friends or just take a walk if it was nice outside. But life seemed better then, I guess I had more hope. I'd go to work each week and just deal with things.

THERAPIST: So having lost your job has really knocked you down. It seems like you aren't able to do the things that you once enjoyed or that once got you out of a funk. Do you think that being unable to do those simple things may make you even more depressed?

CLIENT: Well, it may be. But I just can't imagine doing anything that could make me feel better.

THERAPIST: You know, that doesn't surprise me because I often see it with people who are depressed. But, it will be good for us to look for ways to help you to begin to do those things again so that you can get a little more energy to deal with the bigger problems of your life. How does that sound?

CLIENT: Well, I'll give it a try.

The second interchange provides all of the same information as the first from a theoretical perspective, but does so in a way that is meaningful to the client. Asking questions also keeps a dialogue going rather than allowing the therapist to lecture.

The therapist also must explore the client's reactions to the rationale that is presented. Addis and Carpenter (2000) suggest that clients be asked their reaction to the rationale and what specifically they are reacting to. This prevents the therapist from accepting answers like "It's fine" or "You're right" which may function as the client's way of responding to something they don't totally understand or to terminate an aversive discourse. Asking the client what they think is "fine" or "right" keeps the conversation going. Therapists are usually highly motivated to maintain good rapport with their clients and to accept their clients for who they are. This is both a blessing and a bane. Being too willing to accept a client at face value may prevent the therapist from clearing up misunderstandings. Therefore, when clients say that they understand the treatment rationale, the therapist should ask them to explain what they understand. Gently asking the client to summarize important points from the session can be the best way of ascertaining the client's understanding. Most clients are painfully familiar with the ramifications of miscommunication and will respect the therapist for insisting on clarity and knowing that the client has understood what has been presented.

It is also essential to ask about a client's reaction to the treatment rationale throughout the course of therapy. It is a mistake to assume that because a client expresses agreement with the model when the therapist first presents it that the client will be "on board" throughout the course of treatment. Therapists should regularly ask questions like "How is this treatment sitting with you?" "What's making sense to you about what we're doing and what seems to fit less well?" "How would you describe what we're doing in treatment?"

ACCEPTANCE IN
BEHAVIORAL ACTIVATION

Many psychotherapies have been criticized by behavior analysts for promoting a struggle against negative thoughts and feelings and abetting experiential avoidance (Hayes, 1994). This criticism may be leveled against the BA emphasis on behavior change and activation, but there is also a strong acceptance component in BA. Research demonstrates that clients treated with BA improve on measures of depression (Jacobson et al., 1996). Also, transcripts from expert BA therapists reveal that therapists frequently ask the client how their behavior and feelings are connected — this is essential when a BA functional analysis is done. However, rather than promote the struggle to feel better, BA therapists try to help clients create an environment that promotes better living. This is similar to the approach to acceptance in integrative behavioral couple therapy (Jacobson & Christensen, 1996). The therapist tries to have the client engage in situations where different behaviors will be naturally reinforced. In other words, the BA therapist wants to help the client get activated to increase the likelihood that the natural reinforcers in the environment will maintain and increase behavior rather than instructing the client that "after you've worked hard at the gym, do something for yourself, have a nice cup of tea," which would be an arbitrary reinforcer. It is hoped that the benefits of going to a gym, to use that example, would come to control the behavior of working out at a gym. However, even if the client did not feel better or experience an improvement in mood, she would benefit from action that is independent of mood, accepting that bad feelings may be experienced in life but need not stop one from engaging in useful activities. Acceptance and change are combined throughout treatment.

So how can a client accept if they continue to want to receive treatment for their depression? According to some, they cannot (Hayes et al., 1999). Philosophically, this makes sense from the perspective of radical behaviorism. Thoughts and feelings are not causes of behavior but are only distressing in varying degrees. Western culture emphasizes an ideal of happiness that can cause people to see any form of suffering as pathological. The pharmaceutical industry will continue to support research to find a pill to "cure" all human discomfort. If you have an allergy, take a broad-spectrum allergy medicine (never mind the possible side effects), and even give it to your children (where side effects may be even worse). If you are anxious, take a pill to relax. If you have social anxiety, a recent television commercial promotes the use of Paxil as the "first proven treatment." If you are depressed, there is a large variety of medicines to choose from. The message is clear: Negative feelings are bad and must be changed. BA therapists take their clients' suffering seriously, but they do not engage in the clients' struggles to rid themselves of feelings at any cost. From a BA perspective, the point of acceptance is to divorce action from mood dependence. Clients benefit when they can act while acknowledging that they didn't feel like acting at that moment.

The secondary avoidance patterns that clients develop, as a result of fighting depression, are the targets of BA. As long as the client engages in the fight, they will most likely continue to feel depressed. Worse yet, clients often become more depressed because experiencing depression troubles them. When clients are screened for inclusion in depression studies it is common for them to have a mixed reaction to being accepted. On one hand they might feel relieved that they qualify to get free therapy, but on the other hand they might find it quite distressing that they meet criteria for clinical depression. Clients often worry about what the therapist believes is wrong with them and anxiously await the therapist's advice about a cure. Naturally, psychotherapy can never promise a cure. More radically, in BA we also try to teach clients that there is nothing wrong with them. Depression is a natural result of difficult life events. Therefore, if depression is a natural result, it doesn't make sense to try to fight it. It is the secondary problems that develop from the fight that cause the most difficulty for clients. However, if life events have led to unhappiness, it does make sense to try to change one's life from the present forward.

For the BA therapist, the worst words that a client can utter are "If I could just get myself motivated." As long as clients wait for feelings to change, they are not likely to improve their situation from the present onward. This is the BA concept of acceptance. Feelings are not something to change from the inside. One could take medication to help energize oneself (see chapter 9 for a discussion of medication used in conjunction with BA) or try to convince oneself that one feels differently than they really do. However, by definition, a depressed individual is going to feel depressed and consequently unmotivated, lethargic, negative, etc. The current zeitgeist of quick cures does very little for changing context, which has a more powerful impact on clients than changing feelings or thinking. The BA therapist can respond to the "dreaded words" in this way:

CLIENT: If I could just get myself motivated I'd be able to pull out of this depression.

THERAPIST: If you were motivated and up and about doing things, would you still consider yourself depressed?

CLIENT: I'm not sure what you mean.

THERAPIST: When you've felt motivated, what kinds of things have you done?

CLIENT: Everything. I get the kids extra goodies for their lunches, I call my friends. I can't begin to say — I just do everything.

THERAPIST: When you do all of those things do you feel depressed?

CLIENT: God no. I couldn't begin to do those things if I was depressed.

THERAPIST: Would you be willing to work with me on a little experiment? If you tried to schedule a few activities that are reasonably easy to do, even when you are feeling depressed and unmotivated, I wonder if that would have any impact on how you feel or if it would make life a little better for you and your family.

CLIENT: I think I understand what you're asking. But I couldn't do much.

THERAPIST: I'm not asking much, I'm asking for a commitment to something small. Try it out and see what happens. Any behaviors come to mind?

CLIENT: Well, what I mentioned earlier about goodies in the kids' lunches. I have to go shopping anyway, I have no choice. I try to get it over with and get the heck out of the store as quickly as possible. I could take a few extra minutes and look for something healthy that they'd enjoy.

THERAPIST: That sounds great. And then would you take an extra minute or two when making the kids' lunches to put the snack in?

CLIENT: Yeah, I could even write them a little love note, they'd like that.

THERAPIST: It is very interesting to me that you just thought of adding the note. It seems that activity breeds activity. Even though you feel depressed, as we talk about these simple actions, you have now come up with another idea. What do you think about that?

CLIENT: Well, I feel a little better when I actually plan something to do. I'm still afraid I can't do it though.

THERAPIST: Of course you're afraid you can't do it, and I bet that when you're about to do it you might be afraid. Keep thinking small. I've asked you for simple activities, so maybe just the snacks in the lunch without the notes. It would be great though if you did the notes as well, wouldn't it? Then we could see if you felt any differently through the week.

CLIENT: What if I don't?

THERAPIST: Will your kids enjoy their snacks?

CLIENT: They always like it when I do special things for them.

THERAPIST: Well, would that be a good outcome?

CLIENT: Yeah, and I think I'd enjoy seeing them happy even if I feel miserable.

BEING SPECIFIC AND CONCRETE

The BA therapist is typically very specific and concrete with clients. If clients say they want to be more assertive in a relationship, we ask them how, when, and under what conditions, what would that look like, and so on. If clients protest that they will only be more assertive when they believe they are worthwhile people, we tell them that acting like a worthwhile person is the quickest way to feeling like one. Then we get specific about how a worthwhile person acts in different contexts and, if appropriate, incorporate these behaviors into homework assignments.

Research supports the notion that will or willing some action into being is a fabrication created by perceiving a causal connection between thought and action (Wegner & Wheatley, 1999). In fact, it is possible to increase the probability of an individual acting on their intentions to work toward a goal if they are taught to form implementation intentions (Gollwitzer, 1999), which link the goal-directed response to anticipated situations. This is frequently done in BA when clients are required to specify when they will engage in a particular behavior. It is important to be as specific as possible. Therefore, although a client may have a goal to develop a vigorous exercise routine, simply wanting to do so is unlikely to lead to success. Depressed individuals have difficulties when they avoid activity until they feel better. Using their feelings as a link with behavior leads to staying in a downward spiral of inactivity and intensifying dysphoria.

When the BA therapist encourages clients to act from the outside in, they are essentially teaching clients to respond to environmental cues rather than to internal states. The client who wishes to increase exercise can develop a schedule that includes going to the gym every Monday,

Wednesday, and Friday at 9:00 A.M. Furthermore, if the client sets out a gym bag filled with appropriate clothing and even calls a friend to work out with, he or she will be more likely to follow through on the activity. The verbal commitment to the therapist may also be sufficient. The client would be required to monitor his or her mood before, during, and after the exercise but would be discouraged from basing actions on feelings. It is, however, important for clients to recognize that certain activities can regulate moods.

The emphasis on working from the outside-in, rather than the inside-out, allows therapists to encourage clients to set implementation goals for themselves that are short-term and could lead to a longer-term goal that is important to the client. The goal should not be that the client be free of depression, as this cannot be guaranteed. Regardless of how a person feels they can engage in activities that have been important to them. A person can feel quite sad and still derive pleasure from sitting with a beloved pet and stroking its fur. The same is true for interacting with others. Parents often desire to spend more time with their children but believe that they cannot do so unless they feel better. A frequent complaint for severely depressed people is that "nobody wants to be around me when I am so depressed, it just brings other people down." This may be true (Joiner & Coyne, 1999), but the client should not continue with behaviors that are self-defeating or that make others uncomfortable or repelled. It is important not only to specify that a client will interact during a given period of time but also how they will interact.

It is not surprising that emphasis has been placed on teaching social skills in the treatment of depression. A depressive episode causes a person to become focused excessively on their own misery and the problems of their own life. Remember Ferster's conceptualization of depression as resulting from the maintenance of behaviors through negative reinforcement.

> The control of behavior by its level of deprivation, more than by the audience or occasion that governs where and when it can be reinforced, is the important aspect of this inertia. (1981, p. 187)

The depressed person acts to reduce deprivation rather than acting in accord with the persons or situations that would positively reinforce appropriate behaviors. Therefore, if the individual engages with others and talks about how miserable life is as a way of reducing the misery, feelings of isolation may dissipate in the sharing of the negative experience. However, the interaction is likely to be nonreciprocal and the other person is less likely to continue contact with the depressed person. Even though the behavior is ultimately punished, the contingencies of the punishment may not be salient to the depressed individual because he feels relieved about getting things off his chest. The conclusion is then made that the other person has rejected him because he is depressed, rather than the more accurate conclusion that the rejection is of a particular behavior. So, it is important that depressed people attempt to act like they are not depressed.

Acting in that way is essential for allowing a person to contact all available reinforcers in the environment. The therapist should acknowledge the difficulty of acting according to a plan rather than a feeling and should empathize with the client's plight. This is where the therapeutic relationship is crucial. A cold or mechanical therapist is not likely to succeed in helping a client to do what is counterintuitive to begin with. BA therapists need to communicate to clients their understanding that changing behavior is not easy. If it were easy, why wouldn't the client have done it? Certainly clients themselves and their loved ones have encouraged, cajoled, and exhorted the client to change. What clients typically haven't tried is developing a specific and manageable change plan that has a high likelihood of success. This is where the therapist comes in. The general stance should be something like this: "I know that changing behavior is the most effective way to change your life situation. It makes intuitive sense and is supported by research. I also know that it can be difficult—if it were easy, you would have done it. I'm confident that by working together toward specific goals we can make a difference in your life." A compassionate therapist who has won the client's trust and presented a clear rationale for her techniques increases the likelihood of collaboration. When the therapist and client work in collaboration they can develop a strategy for the client's reengaging in their life so that antidepressant behaviors will be reinforced.

The interaction can begin in the therapy session or given as between-session homework. The therapist would ask the client to think about how she might interact if she were not depressed. The following questions may help the client to develop a strategy for their interaction:

1. Would there be any difference in your posture? Would you stand more upright when you are not depressed?
2. Do you think that you make better eye contact when you speak during times when you feel good about yourself and your life?
3. What types of things would you talk about? Do you focus on yourself more or less when you are not depressed?

When these questions are answered, the therapist and client can develop a strategy. For example, if Marian makes a plan to have coffee with her friend Sylvia she is more likely to do so if the plan is specific. Therefore it is better to have the homework assignment be to meet with Sylvia for coffee at 11:00 on Saturday morning instead of to call Sylvia for coffee. If Marian is to initiate the outing, she should also decide on a specific time when she will call Sylvia to set up the Saturday date. Once the date is set in Marian's schedule she should then have a list of things to keep in mind regarding how to behave in the situation. Her list may look something like the following:

- Sit up straight and make eye contact with Sylvia.
- Ask Sylvia about her week and activities that she is engaged in.
- If Sylvia asks how I am doing, tell her that I've been depressed, but that I am trying to move forward with my life, then try to turn the conversation back to Sylvia so that there is an equal balance between talk about myself and listening to Sylvia.
- Sylvia and I have a long history — think of the things we have in common and talk about them, especially recent movies as Sylvia is a real movie buff.

Marian will then have a plan for engaging in the activity with Sylvia that increases the likelihood that it will be pleasurable. She will also be acting in ways that are counter to her feelings of depression. If her mood improves after the coffee engagement, so much the better. If it does not, however, she should still be encouraged to schedule such interactions into her regular routine.

CHAPTER 6

Teaching Clients to View Depression Within the Context of Their Own Lives

B Y NOW IT SHOULD BE CLEAR that the BA model suggests to clients that depression is not a mysterious "thing" that must be dealt with. Depression is seen as a consequence of person-environment transactions. The client is encouraged to become curious about her own life process to find the roots and potential alleviation of depression. Through the use of activity charts to monitor mood-behavior connections and ABC analyses in session, the client is taught that there is a context in which their depression occurs.

THE ABC ANALYSIS

This is the simplest way to show a client how to do a functional analysis. In this formula the letter "A" stands for an antecedent, which is some situation, public or private, that occasions a behavior on the part of the client. "B," of course, stands for behavior. Finally, "C" stands for the consequence of the behavior. A simple analysis would be a client who heard a sad song that reminded her of the time her first husband left her (i.e., the "A" or antecedent), and who then proceeded to turn off the radio, close the drapes, and stay at home rather than visit friends (the "B" or behavior, in this case a class of behaviors), which left her feeling very depressed and discouraged (the "C" or consequence). Some clients may never need more than this level of analysis of behavior in order to begin to activate. When avoidance is the primary target, two other acronyms assist clients in breaking avoidance patterns.

THE TRAP AND ACTION TOOLS

During the sessions, specific situations are discussed which demonstrate patterns of behavior that may maintain the client's depression. In the beginning of therapy activity charts are used and any noted shifts in mood are focused on. If a client has noted that they had a shift to a more depressed mood, the situation would be discussed in a careful manner. Using the metaphor of a functional analysis BA therapists try to teach the client a general way of looking at situations. Three acronyms help the clients to remember how to analyze the situations and their reactions to situations. The first of the three acronyms is used to teach clients that there is often an environmental event that they respond to, which leads to some type of avoidance that ultimately maintains the response. We refer to the environmental event as the trigger. This may be an external or internal event. For example, the individual may be in the middle of the grocery store (an external event) or thinking about how many things have gone wrong in their lives (an internal event), and a change in mood is triggered. Individuals then usually have some type of response to the trigger. It is frequently an emotional response, but it may also be some type of overt behavior. There may be a repeating pattern of avoidance that the person engages in. We talk to clients about the TRAP they are in and what it stands for:

Trigger

Response

Avoidance-

Pattern

A hypothetical example of the TRAP can be seen in individuals who do not feel very confident in their ability to attract a lover. They may approach an attractive person and attempt to make conversation. For the sake of clarity we'll describe a heterosexual couple engaged in such an interaction. Larry is our depressed man, and he would like to ask Alice out. When Larry approaches Alice and begins to converse and asks her if she'd like to grab some lunch, she tells him that she needs to keep working. This is the *trigger*. Larry then feels foolish for asking her to lunch and also feels quite anxious about the uncomfortable situation. This is the *response*. Larry then walks quickly back to his desk where he continues to engage in the *avoidance-pattern* simply by ruminating about how he'll never get a date. Instead of checking out the situation with

Alice, he stopped the conversation and avoided any potential discomfort rather than to ask Alice if she'd like to go to lunch with him some other time. By avoiding the discomfort he also prevented himself from possibly getting the opportunity to enjoy lunch with Alice in the future. Figure 6.1 graphically illustrates this process. This example also provides an example of the difference between a cognitive approach and a BA approach. The cognitive therapist is likely to teach Larry how to question his thoughts regarding Alice and to test his beliefs and find alternatives. This may in fact include asking Alice out again. The BA therapist looks at the pattern of avoidance and sees the thinking as understandable given

FIGURE 6.1 *An Example of the TRAP.*

the context of Larry's learning history, the similarities of the situation with Alice to other situations, and helps him to recognize the ways that he avoids discomfort.

Another example of a "trap" is from a client who had been laid off from several jobs and never understood the reason for this. She would get called into her supervisor's office and told that there were problems with her work. This was the trigger. Her response was to feel anxious and despondent about her work situation. The avoidance-pattern for this client was a passive approach to life. Instead of getting details from her employer about why her work was unsatisfactory and pursuing a corrective plan of action, she would begin searching the papers for another job and just wait until the axe was dropped and she was laid off. This had occurred on several occasions at several different jobs.

The second acronym provides an antidote to the TRAP. The goal of BA is to help individuals to reengage in life. Once they have been able to identify the TRAP that they are in they need to learn a way out. In the same situations, with the same triggers and responses, they are encouraged to find *alternative coping*. So, TRAP becomes TRAC to easily help clients make the connection that they need to "get out of the trap and get back on trac[k]." In our hypothetical Larry and Alice example, Larry might identify questions he could ask Alice to find out the nature of her work. He might also take the chance to ask her if she would like to go to lunch on a day when she isn't as busy. If she is, in fact, not interested in having lunch with Larry, he may let her know that he appreciates her candor and would like to continue a collegial relationship.

Teaching a Functional Analysis

BA therapists try to help clients be more aware of their own behaviors and their consequences. This is similar to the goals of self-control therapy (Rehm, 1977). The third acronym used is as useful for the therapist as it is for the client as it entails the general process of BA. It is, appropriately, ACTION. The ACTION model is as follows.

Assess how this behavior serves you. Clients are taught to *assess* what they are doing and to try to gauge their current mood, the current context, if they are engaging in avoidance, and what's going on around them. It is like taking an emotional and functional temperature. For example, in Stan's case (first described in chapter 2), he would spend the morning in bed reading the newspaper. Stan had a great deal of work to do around his house that he found aversive. When he stayed in bed in the morning he was asked to assess whether he was avoiding or "taking a day off."

Admittedly, this may be difficult for people to discriminate. The cue we suggest is clients can accept that they are avoiding something if there is something waiting for them to do that they do not want to do. This can often be as diffuse as just not wanting to "face the day." Another cue that avoidance is operating is the concomitant anxiety and rumination that people experience when they avoid an anticipated aversive situation or task.

Clients often have difficulty knowing whether or not they are avoiding. This is the difficulty that results when the form of a behavior is not equal to its function. For example, David recognized that he spent a fair amount of time in the evenings playing computer games. He did this for different reasons, however, and his therapist worked with him to assess the function of his behavior. Many evenings, he had things to do such as talk with his wife about their budget or complete housework. When these things were ignored, and he spent his time on the computer, he recognized his behavior as avoidant. On the other hand, some days he was just extremely tired from work and needed to take a break from other tasks. When playing computer games served as relaxation, it could not be considered avoidant. It's obvious that the distinction is often murky, and the remainder of the acronym we use helps to clarify this all for the client (and the therapist).

Choose to either avoid or activate. It is not the task of the BA therapist to judge clients for their avoidant behavior. This is made clear to clients in the process of assessing whether or not they are avoiding. Even when clients know that engaging in their avoidance behavior may lead to further depression they have a right to *choose* if they want to continue to stay depressed or take time off from activating themselves. They are free to make whatever choice they want, and the therapist will stick with them as a coach regardless of their choice. An important aspect of this choice is that they need to make a choice via a target goal. If the client's goal is to feel better in a given situation, then they need to choose the behavior that will lead to feeling better. Often, if they have assessed their current behavior as avoidance relative to their target goal, it is best that they choose to feel better by not avoiding. However, clients have the right to choose to continue to feel lousy, provided that they recognize that "feeling lousy" then becomes their choice. When clients try to make a choice based on a goal it is important to keep in mind that their goals may be multiple and conflicting.

The idea that clients might choose to do activities that make them depressed is a potentially sticky one in the therapeutic process. All of us have a history with the idea that we can choose to be unhappy (how many parents have said, "It's up to you. You can sit there and be miserable or you can come out and join the party"?). Such statements are extremely aversive because, subjectively, we typically don't see ourselves as choosing to be unhappy, to lie in bed and become more depressed, and so on. When others suggest that we are choosing, we may feel that they are blaming or criticizing; after all, if it were simply a matter of choice you'd have to be an idiot to remain depressed. Thus, the therapist needs to be careful in discussing choice with clients.

Constructing the situation as one of choice is functional (whether it is true or not) because it shifts the context to one of activity and control rather than passivity and reaction. We try to present this to clients as something that they had no choice about prior to therapy. Now that they have an understanding of the connection between activity and mood, we have given them the tools by which they can make a choice. Any discussion of choice must always be discussed with the open acknowledgment that choice is difficult, that we will accept whatever choice the client makes, and that many choices we make are not conscious ones. On this third point, however, we want to make sure that clients understand that we want them to make as many conscious choices about their behavior as possible. As we will explain, the way we teach clients to choose without judgment is to choose, act, and then observe the outcome of the action. In looking at the outcome, clients begin to recognize that their behaviors have consequences and that they can choose an action focused on certain desired outcomes over others.

Try out whatever behavior has been chosen. Clients also need to *try* behaviors that will potentially improve their mood. Depressed clients are often discouraged when they try something new and do not get the desired results. We encourage them to try whatever activity they have chosen to do, even if it is an avoidance behavior, because we want them to become experts about their own lives and behaviors. In essence the message is "don't just think about it, do it." A related message is that even lying in bed ruminating about one's miserable life is an activity and not a state of being.

Integrate any new behaviors into a routine. What is most important is the establishment of routines. In fact the idea of zeitgebers suggests that it is the disruption of routine that may precipitate depression (see page 74). In BA clients are taught to follow a program of *integrating* any new behaviors into their daily routine. The old behaviors that they have engaged in are often already a part of their routine, so we don't encourage avoidance as a routine exercise. However, it is important for clients to know that changing behavior is never a "one-shot deal" and that behaviors change slowly.

Observe the outcome. Since we are trying to teach a modified functional analysis, it is important that clients *observe* the outcome of their new behavior or of a choice to remain in the avoidance pattern. Clients would be asked to write out what they did and what happened after they did the behavior. Activity charts are also good tools for systematic observation of the outcomes of new actions. Use of the activity chart can be encouraged throughout therapy. This is a way to help clients begin to make choices that are based on the function of the behavior rather than simply a choice about a behavior that "seems" to be good. For example, a client might assess that they are being avoidant by not giving themselves more positives in life, so they choose to go out to a grocery store and buy ingredients for a nice meal and a great dessert. They try this behavior and fix nice healthy meals (not always with the dessert) on several occasions, but while observing the outcome, they notice that eating the meal alone doesn't really make them feel any better. What looked on the surface like it would be a positive or pleasant event (the "form" of the behavior) turned out to have little effect on the overall mood or engagement of the client (the "function" of the behavior). So the client then decides to make another choice, perhaps to contact a friend and invite her to dinner.

Never give up. Finally, in good coaching fashion, the client is encouraged to "*never* give up." Like many such acronyms, there is encouragement to go back to the beginning and continue to engage in this process repeatedly. So the word ACTION is a brief description of BA.

Presenting the ACTION Model

It is a good idea to present the TRAP and ACTION ideas early in therapy. Once the therapist has a good idea of the client's general activity level and has used the activity chart to hypothesize mood-behavior relations, to identify avoidance behaviors, and to schedule activities, it is then a good time to introduce these acronyms to further specify the client's behavior and the function of his or her behavior. It is not necessary to introduce one before the other. The goal is to use whatever tools will best fit a particular client, and some level of clinical judgment is allowed. By clinical judgment we mean paying attention to the context of the therapeutic encounter with a particular client and making a choice based on what idea might work best. Clinical judgment, like the client's behavior, should always be informed by the outcome. If one tool doesn't work, use another. It is good for therapists to try to use both the TRAP and ACTION acronyms interchangeably and frequently to teach clients to engage in activity that will break avoidance patterns and to help them to see that their behavior has consequences that can be manipulated.

BEYOND INSIGHT INTO ACTION

Although we use acronyms and encourage clients to "take ACTION," "get out of a TRAP and get on TRAC," etc., we do not make any claim that insights about behavior will lead to any change. It is common for particularly bright and compliant clients to understand the ideas and relate them to their behavior. However, it is quite another thing to get those same clients to change their behavior so that they can be free from their depression. The BA therapist must constantly be vigilant about the client's behavior. When, for example, a client comes in and complains of having had a particularly bad day there are several questions that must be asked by any good BA therapist:

1. Did the bad mood last the entire day or was it episodic?
2. What situations occurred during the day?
3. What did you do when you were feeling badly?

Behavior matters. This is the primary motto of BA, and it is important that the therapist accept this concept wholeheartedly if they are to conduct competent BA. According to the BA model, clients do not have random feelings—the feelings occur in a context, so one must ask what the context was and how the client responded.

The behaviors of the therapist in the therapeutic process are similar in many forms of therapy. However, therapists conceptualize the cases differently and this will lead to fundamental differences in critical choice points throughout the therapeutic process. We recommend that therapists begin to think like BA therapists, and not just add a few techniques to a bag of tricks. How does a BA therapist think? The BA therapist always thinks functionally and contextually. The therapist, regardless of the technique being used for a specific intervention, should be asking him- or herself, "What are the conditions occasioning this behavior (the context) and what are the consequences of this behavior for the client (the function)?" We can't stress enough the importance of the therapist to constantly think of these ideas when working with clients in BA.

CHAPTER 7
Specific Techniques Used in Behavioral Activation

BA IS NOT A TREATMENT THAT CONSISTS of a series of techniques. The philosophical underpinnings of the treatment are more important than any technique that the therapist may choose. Given the roots in contextualist philosophy, and the pragmatic truth criterion, it could be argued that any technique that works to change a targeted behavior and improve the client's life is useful. However, that would make for a rather amorphous therapy that is difficult to teach and evaluate. It is difficult to conduct BA therapy elegantly with no behavioral understanding whatsoever because so much relies on the basic concept of behavior change as the primary target. When therapists see behavior as simple motor movements that they can observe, they run the risk of becoming automatons in sessions and making lots of mistakes in assessment. It is important therefore that BA therapists recognize the complexity of human behavior and use the simplicity of the BA model with care. The treatment is not designed to provide a grab bag of techniques to be applied willy-nilly, rather it is a comprehensive, empirically validated, theoretically based, model of depression that lends itself to certain basic tools for facilitating change.

The primary techniques used in BA are the TRAP and ACTION models. Since these models are useful in teaching clients about functional analyses, they will be used throughout therapy. Given the plethora of research on activity scheduling that has already been cited in previous chapters, activity logs are also primary tools that the BA therapist must use. Clients who are uncomfortable with worksheets provided by the therapist are encouraged to use an activity list or to write activities in their own personal date book. The object used for keeping track of activities is not important, but the monitoring of activity is essential. In fact, it is the most essential technique used in this treatment. Since focused activation is the overarching goal of treatment, therapists cannot go wrong by returning over and over again to activity logs and the review of avoidance patterns that block action on the part of the client.

ONGOING ASSESSMENT

One of the important aspects of any behavioral treatment is assessing the progress toward treatment goals. In BA clients are asked to complete the Beck Depression Inventory (BDI) weekly. Therapists can then monitor progress and discuss any significant items with the client. If the scores are not changing from week to week, but the client is endorsing different items, it is important for the therapist to gain an understanding of what the client does during the week to account for the changes. Therapists should be careful not to inadvertently pressure clients to improve their BDI scores. However, looking through the BDI each session and discussing with the client how he or she maintained the level of depression as indicated on the BDI can help the client to recognize mood behavior relationships and shifting contexts.

MASTERY-PLEASURE ACTIVITIES

We have discussed the confusion over what is reinforcing and what is not; this is relevant to the use of mastery and pleasure ratings. Some therapists find that having clients distinguish between activities that give them a sense of pure pleasure or of mastery or both is a useful way to help them to target activities to change. In BA it is not enough to simply increase these types of activities. That is the start. The goal is to provide the client with opportunities to engage in activities that will be positively reinforced in their environment. So, if a mastery activity meets with a compliment from the boss, or covertly from the client herself, it has been positively reinforced. If conducting an activity that provides a sense of mastery over a task helps the client to avoid facing another task that is perceived as aversive, it has been reinforced negatively. Mastery activities that are negatively reinforced should be discouraged in BA. The way to do this is to formulate goals with the client that she or he works toward. All activities are judged, in the final analysis, by how much closer they bring a client to a specified goal.

Some clients get confused about the difference between a sense of mastery or accomplishment and pleasure. Using a 0 to 10 rating scale and examples drawn from the client's life may help them to make the distinction (Beck, 1995). Although it is not essential, such a distinction to the client can be helpful in the learning process between the impact of activity on mood. Since marking down whether an activity provided a sense of mastery or pleasure is more specific and easier for many clients than recording a feeling, it is a useful first step. Clients can then be taught to record finer gradations of feelings and to use words to describe their feelings; this helps clients to recognize that depression is not a constant lingering fog. Depressed clients can have moments of feeling sad, giddy, shy, hopeful, afraid, nervous, etc. Specific activity ratings allow the client and therapist to analyze the types of behaviors that are connected with various changes in mood.

GRADED TASK ASSIGNMENTS

Asking clients who are depressed to activate themselves is an enormous request. When a client feels fatigued for most of the day, has lost interest in most activities and suffers from a loss of hope that anything will improve in her life, even the simplest activities may feel like tortuous chores. It is therefore necessary to help clients to break tasks down into small steps. Furthermore, this is a useful technique for breaking avoidance patterns, since activities that may be associated with anxiety can be broken down into safer chunks that allow the client to progressively face the anxiety. Breaking tasks down into smaller units has been referred to as a graded task assignment (Beck et al., 1979).

Stan, who was mentioned earlier, had a goal to fix up a dilapidated house that he lived in. He described his house as dark, damp, and depressing and avoided going home until very late at night because he felt very depressed at home. The house had also become cluttered and dirty, which made it even more depressing for Stan. In therapy Stan declared that cleaning his house would be a good goal. In his estimation this was a step toward larger goals like finding meaningful work. The therapist then asked him to break the task down. At first, Stan had great difficulty doing this, but then he and his therapist agreed that he could begin by simply tackling one pile of papers and mail on his kitchen countertop. Stan had become familiar with the notion that inactivity breeds inactivity, but he frequently found himself spending his time in front of the television set getting nothing done on his house. Stan came into sessions without having completed his assignments on several occasions.

Using the ACTION acronym, the therapist coached Stan about choosing to remain depressed and lethargic or choosing constructive action.

He was encouraged to try a new behavior despite his lack of motivation. The therapist strongly believed that if Stan were to simply start a task he would begin to feel better and the likelihood that he would complete other tasks would increase.

When Stan finally took the first step in the graded task assignment and cleaned one pile in his kitchen, he was able to continue to the next step and clean off the countertops, and dust the bric-a-brac sitting on the counters. Stan then began to notice other things that needed cleaning. He removed several dead potted plants from a window ledge, and then he noticed that his windows needed to be cleaned. His next step was to clean his windows. When the windows were cleaned, Stan noticed that the amount of sunlight coming into his house dramatically increased.

At the next therapy session, he stated that the house felt different since he had cleaned the windows. Starting from a small task, Stan was able to experience that activity could lead to further activity. Although he went further than had been assigned by the therapist, the outcome was positive. Therapists need to caution clients not to go too far beyond assigned tasks, however, because it is common for clients to take on too much at one time, conk out afterward, and then fall back into the cycle of inactivity.

Therapists frequently have difficulty following up on assigned tasks. Few of us enjoy being rigid or confrontational with clients. After all, aren't our depressed clients suffering enough? Well, yes, they are, and one way that we help them to suffer less is to assist them in activating. It is essential that therapists recognize the importance of the activities that clients agree to engage in. The task itself is of great importance, and it is frequently a good idea, when a particular client has difficulty with following through, to have the client call to leave a message with the therapist when a task is completed. This is good for the therapist's knowledge of the client's behavior between sessions, and it can be a good motivator for the client.

It is possible to follow up with clients on the intricate details of their lives and to be very concrete with clients without sounding condescending or parental. One way to do this is to be forthright with the client and tell them something like "I'm doing this because I think it's very difficult for people to become more active when they are depressed, but I firmly believe this is the road to recovery. I am going to help you by being, in effect, a reminder person, checking up with you about everything. I am not trying to be your parent, nor am I trying to be your boss—I am trying to be your coach." The therapist would then check on what the client's reaction to this is. It is important to give them an opportunity to describe how they feel about this sort of working relationship. It is also good to ask the client if they see themselves getting resistant to this kind of work at any point and to head this off by engaging the client in problem solving about how to prevent this resistance.

VERBAL REHEARSAL OF ASSIGNED TASKS

Verbal, or imagined, rehearsal in BA consists of the therapist asking the client to describe the task they are to perform, the setting that it is to be performed in, and the steps that will be taken to perform the task. The following is a mental rehearsal of the assigned task to prepare a resume.

THERAPIST: So, I would like you to imagine what you will be doing when you sit down to work on your resume. It might be helpful if you close your eyes and really try to get into the situation. First, where will you be?

CLIENT: Well, it makes sense that I'll be at my desk in the den sitting at the computer.

THERAPIST: When you sit down, is the computer on or off?

CLIENT: It's off. I never leave it on during the day when I'm not working on it.

THERAPIST: So, can you imagine turning your computer on?

CLIENT: Yes.

THERAPIST: Good, can you then tell me what you picture yourself doing as you go through the steps of preparing your resume. I'll jump in if I need you to clarify details.

CLIENT: Well, I'd have to go into my files, which are in a desk drawer, and find a copy of my old resume. I never got a chance to put it on the computer. I need the old resume to remind me of the dates for other positions I've held. So, I'd get that . . .

(The client then continues to describe what he is imagining he would do when he works on his resume. If the client describes a feeling the therapist can ask, "What would you do if you began to feel like that?" Note the following exchange.)

CLIENT: Well, I think I'd just get so damn mad that I got fired from that job.

THERAPIST: And then what would you do if you got mad?

CLIENT: Well, I'd want to turn the stinking computer off and forget the whole thing.

THERAPIST: Well, that is what you would want to do, but if you were to keep at your goal of completing your resume, what would you do?

CLIENT: I guess I'd have to just keep writing. Maybe I could take a few deep breaths and count to ten or something.

THERAPIST: Okay, if that is what you think you should do. Can you imagine yourself doing that right now?

Note that the therapist does not comment on whether taking a deep breath and counting to ten is a sufficient behavior for dealing with anger. It is the tactic that the client wishes to try and is worth experimenting with. The therapist simply accepts the client's idea and asks him to continue with the verbal rehearsal.

MANAGING SITUATIONAL CONTINGENCIES

Experimenting with new behaviors is an essential element of BA. If clients do not try new activities, the therapy will be of little use. Therefore, it is important to try to set homework assignments that the client is likely to accomplish. One of our guiding assumptions is that depressed clients need to have successful experiences with a new behavior in order for the behavior to be incorporated into their repertoire. There are several factors that come into play in setting appropriate homework assignments. They occur when the task is assigned and, when it is refined, when the client attempts to do it.

Whenever the client and therapist develop an assignment together, the client must make a commitment to the time and place that it will be done. Although some clients will simply use a list and commit to following the list of activities between sessions, it is most helpful to have the activity set in a schedule. This assists the client in relying on an external source rather than on a sense of motivation or desire.

The client should also be asked to hypothesize the contingencies that might increase the possibility of successfully completing the homework. Here are some examples that clients have provided of situational factors that increase the success of activating themselves:

- Telling a close friend, relative, or colleague about the activity. This provides a social commitment that holds very strong power for some clients. Given our notion that negative reinforcement schedules cause more harm than good for clients, it is good that the client complete the activity because a friend or relative will be pleased rather than because the client will save face if he or she does the task. It is not always possible to determine the reason that committing to another helps a client to follow through on a task in advance.

- Setting up physical surroundings that are conducive to doing the task. For example, a client who needs to clean an apartment can put favorite CDs in the CD player, open blinds or drapes to let sunshine in, write out steps to follow, set out cleaning implements so they are easy to reach. The client could also plan short breaks to have a snack or call a friend after significant portions of the task are completed.

One process of contingency management that can be complicated is having clients reinforce their behavior by doing something nice for themselves. We consider this complicated because it makes use of arbitrary reinforcers that may be unnecessary or interfere with the natural contingencies at work in the situation. When clients accomplish a task that they have been avoiding, the relief that they experience, or the other positive consequences of having done the task, will either reinforce the behavior or not. In BA we consider it more important that clients make contact with natural contingencies than that we assist clients in setting up arbitrary rewards for their actions. For the client who wants to send a sympathy card to an acquaintance whose mother has died, allowing herself to eat a cookie when the card is in the mail is unlikely to be as reinforcing as the response of gratitude from the acquaintance. Although we cannot control the response of the acquaintance, we have helped the client to set up a situation that increases the possibility that sending the sympathy card will gain a positive response.

However, there are some behaviors that have a low probability of being naturally reinforced in the environment. For example, when someone is trying to be more assertive in a really awful personal environment, the assertive behavior may not be reinforced. Some bosses, for example, have very difficult personalities and an employee's recommendations for change on the job may result in greater interpersonal problems at work. It might be fine to suggest that the person do something nice for him- or herself in this situation; this can be looked at as an arbitrary self-reward for trying a new behavior, or it can be considered good self-care. There is nothing wrong with having people do nice things to reward themselves as long as that does not become the primary or knee-jerk reaction of the therapist, thereby losing the notion that the goal is to bring the client into contact with natural reinforcers.

Examining Alternative Behaviors and Potential Outcomes of Different Behaviors

This process is similar to the problem-solving techniques described later on. The therapist can debrief alternative behaviors that the client has engaged in or discuss the potential outcome of planned behaviors. By "alternative behaviors," we mean behaviors that differ from those hypothesized to maintain depression. The TRAP and ACTION models can be useful in teaching alternative behaviors when avoidance is a problem. A client who spends much of his time watching television talk shows or reading the poetry of Sylvia Plath, becoming more depressed as a result, can implement alternative behaviors that may be more stimulating. The behaviors may be similar in topography, like watching a comedy channel or reading uplifting poetry. They could also compete with these types of behavior by participating in an on-line chess game on the computer, for example, or leaving the house altogether and going for a drive in the country. There is no guarantee that the alternative behaviors will have any effect on the client's mood. This is part of the process of collaborative empiricism that is a hallmark of BA and other therapies for depression.

ROLE-PLAYING BEHAVIORAL ASSIGNMENTS AND THERAPIST MODELING OF ACTIVATION STRATEGIES

Some clients are hesitant to engage in behaviors that involve other people because they fear the outcome. For example, a client may be afraid to ask someone out on a date because they fear that the person will reject them. BA therapists do not question the validity of such fears, but they do help the client to prepare for the situation by role-playing in session. The therapist should ask clients to describe what they plan to do and how they believe other people will respond. The therapist can then simply role-play the event as described by the client. The therapist would ask if the client would have done anything differently to change the outcome. They would then role-play that situation. It is best to let clients play the role of themselves. The therapist can give instructions or feedback on the impact of the interaction, and suggest aspects of the client's behavior that were connected with that impact.

CLIENT: I'd like to tell Sherry that I want to buy the new car, but I'm afraid that she'll blow her stack.

THERAPIST: How do you think the interaction will go? Can we play it out?

CLIENT: Well, I'd call her and say, "I am going to buy the car we looked at last week."

THERAPIST: Tell me how you think she'll respond so that I can play her part.

CLIENT: Well, she'll be sullen at first, and just go along with me, and then wham! she'll nail me.

THERAPIST: How will she nail you?

CLIENT: She'll tell me how selfish and irresponsible I am.

THERAPIST: Okay, let's try that, you say what you will and I'll play the role of Sherry, without trying to mimic her voice or anything, and we'll see how it goes.

CLIENT: Sherry, I want to get a new car and I am going to buy the one that we looked at last Saturday.

THERAPIST (*as Sherry*): Okay, fine, whatever, do what you want.

CLIENT: I just don't want to wait any longer. We have the money and we both liked the car.

THERAPIST: You liked the car, and you think we have enough money. I don't like to be told what you are going to do. You are so selfish and self-centered that you always do what you want regardless of my desires!

CLIENT: Look, I don't need your bull or guilt trips.

THERAPIST: Fine, why don't you just do everything without me then! (*as self*) So, shall we stop the role-play for a minute? Is there anything that you think you could have done differently to lead to a better result?

CLIENT: Well, I could have not told her she was playing a guilt trip.

THERAPIST: What about before that, anything that might have changed things?

CLIENT: Maybe I could have asked her opinion.

THERAPIST: Try it and see what happens.

CLIENT: Sherry, you know I've been wanting a new car for a while now. Last Saturday you saw how much I liked the Honda we looked at, and it seemed like you liked it too. I'd like to buy it, I know that I can swing it financially. What do you think?

THERAPIST: Well, I kind of liked it, but I am really concerned about spending that kind of money on a car right now. What if you lose your job? You've missed so much work lately.

CLIENT: I'm stuck.

THERAPIST: Do you understand her position? If so, let her know.

CLIENT: Well, I can see that you'd be worried about that, but therapy has been helping me, and I haven't missed work since I've started therapy. I think that having a car that doesn't break down all of the time will make me feel better and will be more reliable for getting me to work.

THERAPIST: Well, I guess it could work out. Can we talk about it a little later when you come home before you make a final decision?

CLIENT: I guess so, sure.

THERAPIST: Good, let's stop the role-play. Did that seem different to you?

CLIENT: Yes.

THERAPIST: What did you do differently?

CLIENT: I guess I gave her a chance to express her concerns.

THERAPIST: Yes, in the second role-play I felt like you were working with me rather than against me.

The therapist could model behavior for the client if the client gets confused or stuck in the process. It is good to allow clients to try out the new behavior on their own so that they get practice in session before trying it in real life.

ACTING TOWARD A GOAL

This technique is similar to techniques used in other therapies. It has some aspects in common with "committed action" in acceptance and commitment therapy (Hayes, Batten, Gifford, Wilson, Afairi, & McCurry, 1999; Hayes, Strosahl, & Wilson, 1999) as well as the fixed-role therapy of George Kelly (1955). Similar strategies are also used in dialectical behavior therapy (Linehan, 1993). Clients are instructed to act according to their goal, or to act in a manner that is consistent with how they would like to feel or would like to be perceived by others, etc. Using this technique can be particularly useful when done during the session. The therapist can use this idea of acting according to a goal rather than according to a feeling to demonstrate to clients that their behavior can have an impact on how they feel and how others interact with them.

In one case, William, was showing little improvement in depressive symptoms after weeks of treatment. He had followed through on assignments, and had begun to incorporate his friends in activities that he found engaging and uplifting. However, William still complained of "low self-esteem" and of generally feeling guilty and ashamed of his behaviors. He also complained that people did not respect him at work, where he frequently complained to his boss about poor productivity on the part of his team and of unhappiness with his work situation. William's feelings of being ashamed and guilty were particularly evident in one session after he had engaged in a flirtatious and sexually explicit conversation with a woman in an Internet chat room. The therapist asked if William was willing to conduct an experiment in the session. He agreed, and the following interaction took place.

THERAPIST: So, William, I'd like to see that "low self-esteem" and guilt. How do you act when you feel guilty?

WILLIAM: Well, I keep my head down and talk very slowly.

THERAPIST: I wonder if you'd be willing to act that out for me, show me how bad you really feel. I'll ask you to do that for just a few minutes and then I'll ask you to stop and act the opposite of that.

WILLIAM: I've got you. Well, first I'd look at my feet . . .

THERAPIST: Please show me — tell me the story about the chat room as if you feel really crummy and guilty about what you did.

WILLIAM (*talks in a monotonous voice, avoiding eye contact, head down*): Well, there was this chat room that I looked up on the Internet. I didn't even know if one really existed or not, but it did. I logged on as "Downtown Dan" and just watched the flow of conversation for a while. It's hard to call it conversation. It is not as if anyone is looking for true love on that thing. (*looks at his feet*) Then I got a private message from a woman who asked me what my real name was. I didn't feel comfortable giving that out.

THERAPIST: Okay, let's stop the role-play. How are you feeling right now?

WILLIAM: God, I just find myself feeling really down and I feel really guilty, thinking all sorts of negative things.

THERAPIST: I'm not convinced that you really showed me how truly miserable you can be, but let's change that now. I want you to act out the opposite. Act as if you had high self-esteem, felt really good about what you did, you had made a decision to enter that chat room and by gosh you did it and had a good time. Can you try that?

WILLIAM: This is hard, but I'll try. (*looks the therapist in the eyes, sits up straight and begins to talk, using hand gestures, and showing a full range of affect*) Well, I logged on to this chat room. Mostly there were men just wanting to ask if there were any women who wanted to have cybersex. I logged on as "Downtown Dan" and a woman e-mailed me privately to ask if I lived in the city. I said, "Yes, hence the name, Downtown Dan." At first I was a little uncomfortable with the nature of the conversation — it was pretty graphic. But, I got used to it after a few minutes and it just felt comfortable and innocent. I knew nothing was going to happen for real, so I was just playing a fantasy game.

THERAPIST: Okay let's stop. Now how are you feeling?

WILLIAM: Fine.

THERAPIST: Do you notice any change from the way you felt the first time when you were doing this?

WILLIAM: Yes, I actually feel better. I felt better as soon as I sat up and looked at you rather than at my feet.

THERAPIST: I can tell you from my perspective that there was also a big difference in how much I wanted to engage in the story. The first time I was, frankly, bored. I should have had some interest in a conversation that in some ways could be titillating, but instead, because of your demeanor and the sound of your voice, I just felt like disengaging. The second time, I felt like actually conversing with you. I was interested in the story; you were an engaging person. So, I wonder if this ever happens in your life? Do you sometimes act in ways that may make you feel terrible and make others disengage from you?

WILLIAM: I think I do that all the time at work. Well, if you were trying to make a point, you did. It felt better to simply act differently the second time.

The therapist can then assign a similar task to be done in a real situation between sessions. The therapist needs to be careful not to give the client the impression that the goal is to "just get over it." A good rationale for using this technique is that the therapist wants the client to experience greater control over his or her behavior, and not respond directly according to a mood as much as in accordance with his or her goal in a particular situation. In some interactions, for example, it is helpful to pay attention to mood especially if there is something important to communicate to others and they need to know how the person feels. In this case acting according to mood is necessary. In other interactions, if the client has a broader goal than expressing him or herself, then acting in accordance with a goal and not acting according to a mood is a better tactic.

In William's case, he had done such an assignment prior to this session, when he was instructed to enter a frightening job situation as if he felt very confident and assured. He found that people were asking him for advice rather than ignoring him, as he had perceived that they usually did. These exercises began to take effect, and within several weeks, by the time therapy was completed, William was scoring in the sub-clinical range on the Beck Depression Inventory, and he reported that he was coping better with several difficult areas in his life. He said that he felt happy for the first time in over two years.

TECHNIQUES THAT BRING
TEMPORARY RELIEF

Techniques that are basically escape or avoidance techniques may be used when other techniques do not supply immediate relief for dangerously depressed clients. They should be used sparingly, however, for obvious reasons given the above discussion of avoidance. Used in moderation, however, these techniques can allow the client time to feel better before facing situations that must ultimately be approached in order to prevent future exacerbation of depression or relapse.

Distraction From an Unpleasant Event

When clients use distraction techniques from unpleasant events they do a number of things. Some of the activities that therapists often encourage clients to engage in like going to the movies or taking walks function, at times, as distraction techniques. These activities are useful when they allow clients to engage in behaviors that were formerly enjoyed, but they should be used sparingly if they are means of distraction from unpleasant events. It is difficult to determine when distraction is functional for the client. A good rule of thumb is that some aversive events that cannot be changed may lead to the functional use of distraction. For example, if a client has been diagnosed with a life-threatening illness such as HIV, and the client is maintaining proper attention to good medical care, it would be functional for the BA therapist to encourage the client to engage in activities that shift the focus of attention from the disease to a more life-affirming activity. There are many things that clients can do to distract themselves from unpleasant events like singing to themselves or taking a road trip.

Limiting Contact With Unpleasant People

This can also be a functional technique. It will depend, of course, like everything else we have talked about— on the context. Limiting the amount of time one makes oneself available to an annoying, negative, disrespectful person at a church social is healthier from a BA perspective than limiting contact with an irascible boss which may lead to negative consequences. However, in cases where the choice is between the client staying in bed with the covers over her head (or some other drastic measure) rather than going to work where she can slip into her office and close the door, it is better to choose the latter and allow the avoidance behavior of ignoring the boss until the client has become more activated. Perhaps the determining factor of whether avoiding an unpleasant person is functional or not has to do with the long- and short-term consequences of the behavior and the goal of the client. If the long-term consequences could be negative for the client, distraction should be discouraged. It would be better to do a graded task assignment to help the client to face her surly boss rather than to have her ignore the person altogether.

Behavioral-Stopping

Behavioral-stopping is similar to thought-stopping techniques (Cautela & Wisocki, 1977) used in cognitive-behavior therapy. In behavioral-stopping the client does something to interrupt the behavior like snapping a rubber band on one's wrist whenever one engages in an undesirable behavior. Simply shouting the word "stop!" and engaging in a different behavior can also be used. One difference in behavioral-stopping from the thought-stopping techniques is that the client would not be encouraged to purposely engage in the behavior for practice. The client would be instructed to interrupt the behavior during its natural occurrence. In thought-stopping, the ruminative thoughts are elicited in session and the client is taught to shout "stop!" in order to interrupt the rumination. Behavior-stopping is most useful with discrete behaviors that a client wishes to gain control over. It is likely to be a relatively little-used technique in behavioral activation, where the emphasis is on the broader class of activation and approach behaviors.

DEALING WITH
RUMINATIVE THINKING

Depressed individuals frequently spend time ruminating about the misery of their lives. Both behavioral and cognitive-behavioral writers have commented on the tendency of depressed people to focus on the negative events in their lives or the complaints that they have about their lives (Beck et al., 1979; Ferster, 1981). In BA, we do not assume that negative thinking or cognitive distortions are necessary mediators of overt behavior. We look at the thinking as behavior. The work of Nolen-Hoeksema and colleagues, and others, (Just & Alloy, 1997; Nolen-Hoeksema, Morrow, & Fredrickson, 1993; Nolen-Hoeksema, Parker, & Larson, 1994) has shown that individuals who tend to respond to depression by ruminating about the symptoms of their depression, rather than engaging in distracting activities or active problem solving may have extended or exacerbated episodes of depression. BA therapists try to get clients to stop ruminating and activate themselves, not only to achieve a distraction, but to begin to engage in active coping strategies that will increase the likelihood of obtaining reinforcement. Therefore, the difference in the BA model from standard CT is that in BA the concern is with the process of thinking or the context in which the thinking occurs, whereas in CT the concern is with the content of the thoughts.

Activating clients often requires that the therapist help them engage in more productive behaviors. Furthermore, ruminating tends to keep people focused on themselves and can block opportunities for adaptive client behaviors to be positively reinforced. Like so many other behaviors, it appears that ruminating is also an escape or avoidance behavior. It keeps the individual separated from others and prevents true problem solving. In the same way that complaints have been reinforced in the past by preceding some type of ministration from someone in the environment (Ferster, 1973), so too the ruminating behavior has most likely been reinforced in the past of the individual. If it is escape or avoidance behavior, then it is reinforced by the removal of some type of aversive experience. Although the rumination may be experienced as aversive to the individual, it is possible that it is maintained by the avoidance of even more aversive conditions. Perhaps such rumination is a misguided attempt at resolving the problems that have led to the depression. However, a passive coping style is unlikely to resolve anything and may, in fact, amplify the problems. This is a speculation that should lead to further study.

BA therapists do not question the truth of the client's thoughts. It is not the content but the context that matters. In BA, the first question to be asked about client ruminations is "What were you doing when you began to start thinking this way?" This is an essential question because it is the way in which the therapist can begin to conduct a functional analysis of the ruminating behavior. For example, if a client engages in ruminating behavior in certain circumstances and not others, there is a clue as to the function of the behavior. What might the client be avoiding? The client who ruminates mostly at work may be avoiding the challenges of the job or the tedium of the daily grind. Yes, rumination is unpleasant but, according to our behavioral hypothesis, it is not as unpleasant as the circumstance avoided, otherwise it would not take place.

Why would such negative thinking be maintained if it is so aversive to the individual? An individual told by her parents that she is stupid will eventually begin to tell herself the same thing. But why? Surely it is not experienced as pleasant when one's parents criticize or demean. Since this issue is an important one in understanding why BA therapists deal with ruminations as we do, we'll take a brief excursion back to the theories underlying the treatment. Once again, Ferster (1981) had an explanation of why such a phenomenon might occur that is still viable today and deserves greater attention. He considered the covert statements that depressed persons make to themselves as a form of counter control of aggressive impulses engendered by others in the environment. In essence, since aggressive feelings are overtly demonstrated they are met with some type of punishment or loss of interaction. Therefore the individual begins to make the statements privately, to avoid public punishment. The behavior is negatively reinforced because the aversion to public punishment is avoided (remember, when a behavior increases after something is taken away it is negative reinforcement). So, why are the aggressive private statements harmful to the client? People have histories of aggressive or mean things being said about them. Regardless of who is saying these mean things (including the person himself), the history usually conditions the person to experience mean things being said as harmful and aversive.

The idea that the behavioral process of reinforcement has maintained ruminative negative thinking and conceptualizing rumination as behavior allows the therapist to tackle the behavior and not the thoughts. The therapist asks the client if spending time thinking and worrying was of any benefit. If not, the therapist will suggest more productive ways of spending time. The therapist will help the client to attend to environmental details, to turn the focus away from the ruminations, and block the ruminative behavior from continuing. The following dialogue is an example.

THERAPIST: So, I notice on your activity chart that on Tuesday evening you spent several hours sitting and thinking.

CLIENT: Yeah, it was strange. I was just sitting there thinking so much about my family and all the crap we've been dealing with, just trying to figure it out.

THERAPIST: Sounds like a lot. Did you figure anything out?

CLIENT: I'm not sure. Probably nothing new because I've known for a while that I'm unhappy with the way things have been and I wish it was different.

THERAPIST: So, you sat there thinking a lot about how much you wish it could be different.

CLIENT: Right.

THERAPIST: As you tell me about this I start thinking about the approach we've been talking about where we learn to observe what we're doing and examine whether the consequences are beneficial, and then work on making choices about what sorts of things to do in different situations. Do you see that applying here?

CLIENT: Yes.

THERAPIST: In what way?

CLIENT: Well, it's clear that sitting and worrying wasn't helpful. I just didn't know what else to do and it felt like I wanted so badly to figure it out.

THERAPIST: Exactly. It often works in our lives to think real intensely about problems until we figure out what to do. Of course, if we don't figure out what to change, or how to change it, then all we're doing is thinking very intensely and, in some cases, feeling more depressed.

CLIENT: I don't know what else I can do in those situations.

THERAPIST: I think that's really the issue and it raises a great question. How can you know when you're thinking very intensely, or ruminating, and it's not helpful to you? What other options do you have? What I'm wondering is whether it would be useful to you to practice observing when you're worrying, then ask yourself, "Is this useful right now?" and "What are my options?"

CLIENT: But that's it, what are my options? That's what makes me worry!

THERAPIST: Yes, that is true about the options regarding your family. I am actually thinking about the options regarding sitting and worrying or doing something else. Do you think, for example, that on Tuesday evening, if you had gone for a walk or called a friend, you would have felt better?

CLIENT: Had I gone for a walk I would have just been cold outside and still worrying.

THERAPIST: What if you were to really feel the cold? To pay attention to your legs as you walked, when they felt tired. Looked at all the houses and gardens along your way. Do you think that would have been more productive?

CLIENT: Well, I might have at least enjoyed the walk except for the cold part.

One of the alternative behaviors that clients can learn to substitute for ruminating is practicing what we refer to as "attending to experience" as in the above example. Attention to experience, as described in BA, is akin to "mindfulness" training (Linehan, 1993; Teasedale, Segal, & Williams, 1995; Thich Nhat Hanh, 1996). In attending to experience, it is important that the client be aware of all of the sensations involved. Clients should be instructed to notice the colors, shapes, and other sights that they see, the sounds they hear, odors smelled, and textures touched. It is more difficult to engage in repetitive self-talk when one is making an attempt to be fully present in a particular situation. When engaging with others, clients should be aware of their physical proximity to other people. Too often clients make attempts to follow through on recommendations to participate in social activities, but they remain physically distant from others and attend to the thoughts running through their own minds rather than engaging in conversation. This is particularly true for individuals who are both depressed and socially anxious. Social situations serve as a cue for the client to privately run through the list of self-inadequacies, comparisons with people who are wearing more expensive clothing or who appear to be calmer and friendlier, and other general self-critical thinking. It is impossible to interact meaningfully with others while simultaneously focusing on oneself. The process of thinking in this ruminative manner must be interrupted in order for the client to become activated and truly engaged in events that increase the possibility for positively reinforced encounters.

Consider Steve's case. Steve was a divorced, noncustodial parent of two children. As part of a homework assignment, Steve was to participate in an activity with his children and stepchildren over a visitation weekend. He planned to invite his children to join him in doing yard work, because he knew that they enjoyed helping him work around the house. During the following session, Steve reported that he had, in fact, completed the assignment and felt much more depressed afterward. The therapist then debriefed the incident with Steve.

It was approaching autumn and Steve's children liked the idea of being able to jump in the leaves once they were piled up. Steve gave his children rakes and set them about the task of raking leaves in a large pile. He did not take a rake, however, but took on the job of clearing away brush and debris from the outskirts of the yard. This set up a physical distance between Steve and his children. The children were together, laughing and enjoying raking leaves, while Steve was off to the side clearing branches. Steve then began to think about the sad fact that he could not spend every day with his children. The children gathered large piles of leaves and jumped and played in them. Steve, on the other hand, kept busily working, alone, in hearing range of the children, thinking about the miserable circumstance of needing to be separated from his kids most of the days of the month. The ruminating kept him from spending quality time with his children even during his short visitation period.

The therapist did not challenge Steve's belief that life would be better if his children could live with him full-time. Instead he asked Steve to describe the physical setting of the yard and where everyone was situated. Using a whiteboard, the therapist drew a circle to represent each of the children and a triangle to represent Steve. It became obvious that Steve did not actually interact with his children at all. He didn't know what the children were wearing or which child was the first to jump in the leaves or who got dirtiest. Steve and the therapist then developed another assignment that included an exercise to attend to his experience rather than ruminate. He was instructed to set up another outing with the children but to focus on all of the sensations of the experience, to converse with the children about school projects and vacation plans. He was to pay attention to the sound of each of their voices, any scent that they each had, and other sensory aspects of the encounter. Upon Steve's return, he reported having had a much more pleasant experience.

An important aspect of the therapeutic intervention in the case of Steve is that the physical distance between Steve and his children and the rumination would never have been evident to the therapist had he or she not pursued the specific details of the experience. Once again, the concrete and detailed focus of the BA therapist allows for a close functional examination of the client's experience. The BA therapist should probe and probe again every experience described by the client, especially when high affect has been reported or an unexpected result has occurred.

It is important that therapists empathize with the struggle of the client plagued with repetitive negative thinking. By advocating that therapists conducting BA therapy teach clients to engage in attention to experience rather than ruminate, we are not suggesting that it is ever as simple as just stopping rumination. When depressed clients tell themselves to stop certain behaviors it is often a set-up for further self-recrimination when the client fails. In BA, the therapist coaches the client to change entrenched patterns of behavior and this is very difficult—acknowledging this with the client is essential. Like all of the interventions suggested in BA, the therapist can ask the client to conduct an experiment and observe the results.

TRAINING TO OVERCOME
SKILL DEFICITS

In keeping with the general approach in BA, therapists focus on getting the client to take an active rather than passive stance to life, and problem solving is taught using current situations suggested either by the client's review of their week or an activity chart. Also, in the process of goal setting and problem solving, the therapist continues the work of teaching the client to be her own behavior analyst. Problem-solving training has a long history in behavior therapy (D'Zurilla & Goldfried, 1971; D'Zurilla & Nezu, 1982). In essence, problem-solving training according to the model developed by D'Zurilla and colleagues teaches the client to distract their attention from negative emotional states and focus on the environmental factors associated with the responses, find all of the relevant facts about a problem and set a realistic goal, "brain-storm" alternative solutions, select the best alternative, implement the solution in real-life situations, and verify the results. Only the stage of implementing the solution in real-life situations involves actual behavioral change, although the entire process could be a useful activating exercise for clients. We take a more idiographic approach than D'Zurilla and Nezu in that we do not try to teach a broad class of behaviors that fall under the category of problem solving. Instead, the BA therapist helps the client to clarify a specific goal, propose steps to attain that goal, try them out, and then observe the outcome and find alternative behaviors if necessary. Again, the ACTION idea can be useful in BA problem solving. There is less emphasis on teaching a set of rules; there is more emphasis on helping clients recognize the goals they wish to achieve, and the impact of their behavior on achieving those goals, and assisting them in delineating alternative steps to achieving the goal and trying them out.

Tisdelle and St. Lawrence (1986) stress the importance of recognizing that problems arising in the natural environment are often more ambiguous than those in experimental situations. They emphasize that problem solving in real life does not always proceed according to the stages characterized by the research literature. Problems in life are usually complex and it is difficult to account for a "best fit," even with careful, reasoned decision making. The BA approach attempts to avoid the difficulties of generalization inherent in problem-solving training by taking an idiographic approach. It follows Biglan and Dow's (1981) recommendation that depression treatment should be problem-specific. In BA, problem solving is used as a treatment method as it becomes apparent that the specific individual has a limited repertoire for solving problems. It is further individualized in that actual accounts of the client's attempts to resolve conflicts are used to gather assessment data about the areas of difficulty. Unless the behaviors come under the control of environmental variables that reinforce them, they will not increase or continue after treatment. Other behaviors which are inconsistent with problem solving may be reinforced and block the acquisition or maintenance of skills.

The following transcript provides an example of work with a client whose repertoire regarding problem solving was very narrow. The client, Bea, was a 35-year-old female who initially presented to the depression treatment project because she felt fatigued and irritable. She had never thought of herself as depressed until she read an advertisement in the paper describing symptoms of depression. The immediate, precipitating event was the loss of a job. At the time of the initial session, Bea was unemployed. She found work early on in therapy, however. Bea was not certain exactly why she had been fired, and this was suggestive for a functional analysis of her depression. Her boss had called her into a boardroom, told her that she had not performed up to standard, and that he was firing her. Bea had prior questions about the expectations her boss had, but she had not gone to her boss to discuss what was expected of her (we alluded to Bea's case earlier in the description of avoidance patterns). By the time Bea's boss called her in, there had been several months of attempting to do a good job without Bea ever really knowing what she was supposed to focus on or prioritize in her work. The significant information here was that *Bea did not inquire about the details of her poor performance.* This could be seen as a skill deficit or as a very limited repertoire and a lot of avoidance behavior.

This behavior generated several hypotheses concerning the maintenance of Bea's depression. First, it was important to begin to look for patterns of passivity across situations as Bea described her life. When the therapist had inquired about the circumstances of Bea's dismissal, Bea said that her boss called her into his office, told her she was fired, and Bea left and packed up her stuff. The therapist asked if Bea had asked for an explanation or if there was any way that she could change her behavior and save her job. Bea had not ever thought that she could have even asked to try to keep her job. She simply accepted what the boss said and left. When the therapist asked if there was anything to be gained in future employment if Bea were to understand what she had done wrong on this job, Bea said she had never considered that possibility. This pattern was clear. Second, it was important to understand whether the passivity was due to avoidance or to a skill deficit. Two possible skill deficits were poor assertion skills or inadequate problem-solving ability. Of course a third possibility was that there was some combination of avoidance and a very narrow repertoire of behavior.

After several sessions with Bea, the evidence became clear that she truly did not know how to resolve problems in a way that allowed her to attain desired consequences. Bea was a woman with very simple desires. She had been raised by parents who loved her and she had lived a mostly uncomplicated life. Disappointments had been regarding work, where she did not get the types of jobs she wished for, and her current marriage, which was fraught with difficulty. She wanted her marriage to be better— she wanted her husband to be more polite to her and to criticize her less. She wanted to go to the movies on Friday nights instead of just renting videos. Her BDI scores began to drop as she engaged in the very common activities of planting her favorite bushes in her garden, or doing simple repairs and decorating around her house. She enjoyed visiting friends and spending time with her parents. In other words, Bea preferred life to be uncomplicated. When things became complicated she was not equipped to deal with it. As in the situation with her boss, Bea wanted to take things at face value, so there was a combination of a limited repertoire as well as avoidance behavior that kept Bea safe from the complications of life but stuck in the negative patterns that were maintaining her depression.

Problem solving in BA is seen as teaching the client to choose action over passivity. In many cases, such as Bea's, teaching clients to observe the cause-and-effect relationship in their interactions is an important step that needs to be returned to again and again. As the client begins to recognize how her actions lead to undesirable consequences, she can take the first step in changing her behavior in the desired direction. Recognition alone is not enough, however, since the therapist needs to monitor the client's attempts at new behavior and observe the consequences as reported in session. It is not enough to *think* that certain behaviors will lead to certain consequences or that the choice of one solution over another will solve a problem, the client needs to try the new behavior. The therapist (and the client) may be surprised to learn what behaviors are reinforced and what behaviors are punished in the client's environment. The most logical solution to a problem may not work in the situation the client tries to apply it in. In Bea's case, for example, it would be logical to propose that she talk to her husband and express her understanding for his point of view even if she disagrees. This is where the behavioral activation rubber hits the road. We need to have clients test these things out to see what happens and then help them to modify the solution yet again. When Bea did in fact go home and try to talk to her husband in a validating way he quickly shouted at her "You sound like your therapist! Don't give me this crap." Again we find that what we believe are good methods of communication, pleasant activities, and important steps toward a desired goal will not always be supported in the context that our clients live in.

Teaching Bea a simple model of defining a long- or short-term goal and finding ways to get there was targeted as a necessary instruction. She had a pattern of responding in the moment to her husband and not sticking to a goal in conversation. She had difficulty telling him the things that she wanted to do. She and her therapist had worked many times at having Bea ask herself what she wanted to achieve in the moment and then trying to stick to a plan. Bea was also taught to apply this to her career situation.

Often clients are unhappy with their lives because they have had goals or dreams but have not been able to maneuver through the world in a way that led to their goals. In some cases, prior to therapy, clients are not aware that they had not been moving toward their goal. They go on with life as usual and find themselves feeling more and more dissatisfied but don't know why. Bea experienced this in her life. In order to help her to clarify goals, she was first taught to define a goal and then develop a plan. This was made specific to her own behavior when she was asked to review her jobs in the past and see what she had done to approach her goal.

BEA: So there are long-term goals and there are short-term goals.
THERAPIST: Yes, so you define both. Here you are talking about good long-term effects, so perhaps that means looking at a long-term goal. The first thing is to define the goal. So do you want to try that regarding work? What would be a good long-term goal regarding work?
BEA: Work as in career? Um, well let's see. For some reason that's always been hard. To be doing something in the creative field, I mean that's as close as I can define it so far.
THERAPIST: So that's your long-term goal. It's not real specific at this point but it's there, and that's okay, it doesn't have to be specific at this point. The goal is to be doing something creatively. So, the next

thing is to create a plan how to get there. But you are not starting now, you weren't just born today, you have a history. So look at what you have already done to get there and then what you have to do to continue. That is where your short-term goals come from. Include in the plan what you have already done and what you have left to do. What have you tried in the past, and what worked and what didn't?

(Following an assignment to write down all of the jobs she had held in the past, Bea realized that many of her jobs contributed to her feelings of depression at times. During a session she realized that very little that she had done had related in any way to her overall career goals.)

THERAPIST: So are there some things from the list you recall as being effective steps toward the goal of having a creative position?

BEA: No, as a matter of fact I've been going through this list and seeing that everything here had nothing to do with that creative goal. I decided that I wanted to be an illustrator because it was awfully vague to say doing something in the creative field, and I wanted to be able to focus on one thing. I have always enjoyed drawing and doodling, which is what an illustrator does. So I started with the list beginning with college and wrote in order all the positions I've held. I looked to see if any of them were involved in creativity and there's not been anything here really, it's all been secretarial or labor kinds of things.

THERAPIST: So they were jobs that paid the bills?

BEA: Precisely, they paid the bills or got me by eight hours a day, or just kept me moving forward.

THERAPIST: The purpose of the assignment was to see what you learned from the past that could have an impact on the future. If your goal is to be an illustrator, what are the steps to getting there? In looking at the past, are there any steps that you could continue to get there?

BEA: You mean steps I could repeat or steps I could take that I didn't take?

THERAPIST: Either.

BEA: I saw that I kind of picked the first thing that came along and went with it.

THERAPIST: So you didn't really stick to the goal for art—you just took anything that came by. Sticking with things is a familiar theme in here isn't it? Do you recall where we have talked about this before?

BEA: Yes, when we've talked about sticking to a goal in communication and not getting off track.

THERAPIST: Yes, so we are talking about behavior that has an immediate impact and behavior that has long-term consequences. Do you just respond to the moment or respond to a fixed goal?

Notice in this transaction that the therapist and client are not discussing specific isolated behaviors such as how to complete a resume (although they might in the future). Instead, they are discussing general classes of actions (such as taking the first thing that comes along and not sticking to a plan) that occur in a variety of contexts. Such an approach is, of course, not specific to BA since many different therapies focus on discovering patterns in clients' lives. What is perhaps more specific to BA is the intensive exploration of the client's current life situation and the focus on specific choices and patterns of coping of which clients may not be aware.

An important aspect of problem solving from this perspective is the accurate definition of a goal. If the client is confused about what he wishes to accomplish, he will have great difficulty planning appropriate steps to reach the goal. A client may describe a chain of events that leads to one outcome and state that he desired a different outcome. However, if, in fact, the only reason that he desired outcome B over outcome A was because the initial outcome was punishing there may have been goal-confusion present during the occurrence of the event. Clinicians often see clients who don't seem to know what they want, such as a young man who says that he wants a clean break from a relationship but finds himself driving back to his lover's house repeatedly, or a woman who states emphatically that she only wants her employees to respect her authority but continually undermines her own authority with angry outbursts at inappropriate times. These individuals may lack clarity in their own goals. From a behavior analytic perspective, we assume that the behaviors that actually occur are natural given the context despite the expressed desire of the client. Therefore, it is important to help clients clarify what outcome they truly desire in a given situation prior to helping them find ways to reach the goal. In our two hypothetical examples, BA goal setting would look something like this:

The young man states that he wants a clean break. However, the behavior that we see increasing is driving past his lover's house. It is important to understand what he gains by doing this. He may say that it makes him feel relaxed to know that she is home. We can then hypothesize that there is anxiety reduction involved in driving by. We then have a hint at the real goal, to avoid anxiety. If this is described to the young man, and he agrees, we have reached an important first step in helping him to define the goal and find reasonable solutions. Having learned that his goal is to be free of the anxiety about his lover seeing other men, we would then ask "How long does this freedom from anxiety last? If this is truly a solution, why must you do the same thing over and over again?" The client can then begin to generate alternative behaviors that may lead to a more permanent reduction in anxiety, such as going out with friends and meeting new people.

In the case of the manager who continues to undermine her authority by emotional outbursts, she has described her goal as "wanting her employees to respect her authority." What is the function of her outbursts? She might say that her employees begrudgingly do what she tells them to when she is angry. So, we have the true goal, "that my employees do what I say." This is different from respect since an employee can be compliant without respecting the employer. If it were compliance that the woman wants on a consistent basis, then the same process of questioning short- and long-term consequences of her behavior and generating alternatives would take place as in the former example.

People often have multiple conflicting goals, which makes problem solving difficult. The client who drives by his ex-lover's house may have all these goals: anxiety reduction, breaking free from the relationship, and maintaining the relationship. Any of these goals become more or less salient depending on the context in which the client is currently operating. Thus, the question is not what is the client's "true" goal, but rather what are the array of goals the client has and which ones would he or she like to commit to achieving since, of course, life rarely gives us everything we want. Thus, our approach shares elements in common with acceptance and commitment therapy (Hayes et al., 1999) — though the means to a similar end are quite different.

So the approach used here is person-specific rather than rule-specific. This approach also looks more closely at a client's report of what actually occurs in his or her life, than at what is merely a wish or desire. Whether current behaviors are maintained by something in the environment or by internal processes in the individual, the client is taught to look at what he or she is doing and ask him- or herself "What am I doing and what are the consequences of what I am doing?" They are then asked to choose whether they wish to keep things status quo or make a change. If they desire change, then they are given assistance at generating alternatives. They then try out the alternatives and observe the consequences. In other words, even during the goal-setting, problem-solving process they follow the ACTION.

Defining goals, and developing strategies to reach goals or solve problems, is important. However, it is even more important and consistent with the BA model for the client to act on this knowledge. In BA it is considered paramount that clients understand that insight is not good enough; they must develop new habits and incorporate them into their routine. Many clients know what they need to do but are not able to do it. There may be many reasons for this: (1) Clients may feel a great deal of anxiety about their ability to achieve a goal. It is frequently the case that people who suffer from depression have histories that conditioned them to doubt their own abilities. (2) There may also be obstacles to change in the client's environment. For example, clients that have a goal of being more assertive in their work and love relationships may fear rejection by others should the client's behavior become more assertive. The BA approach to such fears and the obstacles is to engage clients in a discussion about goals and means of achieving them. The therapist then works with the client to find ways to test new behaviors and assess their effects — again following the ACTION model.

Henry, who was described on pages 83–87, came to therapy two years after having been laid off from his job. He had initially looked for work, but gave up after several months of disappointment. Eventually he took a job checking freight on incoming trucks in a warehouse. His family income dropped significantly and he felt increasingly dissatisfied with his life. He knew that he wanted to get back into work that was meaningful to him. In fact, he had identified several jobs and had sent resumes. However, Henry also knew that face-to-face contact was essential in getting a job in his field. He also knew that he needed to let friends and acquaintances know that he was looking for work so that they could advise him about people that they knew in the profession.

Henry and his therapist had worked on his avoidance patterns for several sessions. They primarily discussed interactions at home with his family that left him irritable and withdrawn. However, he wanted to focus on finding a more satisfying job. The therapist decided in the eighth session that the time had arrived to address this directly and that any postponement would be colluding with Henry in his avoidance. An agenda for the session was established collaboratively. Henry agreed to put this on the agenda, and the therapist agreed to spend some time discussing an interaction in the home. When Henry had identified what he believed he needed to do, the therapist worked with him to turn it into a homework assignment that he would agree to do.

THERAPIST: So is the problem more just getting on the phone and calling some of these folks? Because you are saying that you know what you are supposed to do.

HENRY: Yeah. There're a couple of them that I talk to quite often but I never bring up the fact. "How's it going?" "Oh, it's going okay, keeping busy." Lie, lie, lie.

THERAPIST: And what makes you do that? Are you kind of afraid or ashamed to tell them about how things are at work? Do they even know what you are doing for work?

HENRY: Some of them. I do a little freelance work for some of them.

THERAPIST: So that seems to me that that is an example of trigger-response- and avoidance-pattern, isn't it?

HENRY: Yup.

THERAPIST: The trigger is they ask you how things are going, the response is you feel sheepish about telling them, and the avoidance-pattern is that you lie and tell them things are going well which in the short run gets you off the hook . . .

HENRY: I don't say things are going well, I say I'm keeping busy.

THERAPIST: Keeping busy, I didn't mean to misquote you. So you don't lie, but it's not the whole truth. So what is happening is you are off the hook in the short run, but in the long run you are shooting yourself in the foot.

HENRY: Basically I don't have to tell them what I'm doing, but just to tell them that I'm not happy with what I'm doing now and am looking for a regular job again.

THERAPIST: So could you call these people and say that? You say these things to me and I think that if you just said that to them it seems like there could be some potential for a positive outcome. Could you call some people?

HENRY: I haven't so far.

THERAPIST: So when I say "could you" I guess what I am asking you is can you commit to calling one or two of these people in the next week or so while you are out there looking to get the momentum going and breaking the avoidance pattern?

HENRY: One person.

THERAPIST: Yes. Can you identify one person?

HENRY: Yeah, I can.

THERAPIST: Who would that be?

HENRY: John, an executive in town.

THERAPIST: Okay, you will call John. When will you do that?

HENRY: I guess during the week.

THERAPIST: I think the best thing to do to break this avoidance pattern is to take an activity log and just schedule it in. It is like having a dentist appointment that you don't want to do, but it is there in the book so you just show up. I think that would be helpful. So is there a time that you can commit to doing it because it is there in the schedule?

HENRY: How about Wednesday, because we will meet before then and maybe I can work on some conversational ploys.

THERAPIST: Okay. Actually what I heard you just say was good, but I am happy to do that. We could even script it out so that if you feel a little nervous you'll have some things written out to fall back on. So the homework between now and then would be maybe for you to write out what you could say.

The style here is conversational. The therapist remains structured and follows the agenda and is very goal-focused with the client. However, the therapist is not particularly confrontational. Notice how the therapist simply redirects the client to greater specificity and commitment by asking questions or making suggestions such as "Could you call these people . . . " "I think the best thing to do is . . . ", and so on. BA therapists need not be, nor should they be, rigid, cold, or confrontational. Therapists should never confuse structure with rigidity. Like all good forms of cognitive and behavioral therapies, BA is simply a structured conversation between two people. Those people can follow an agenda, complete tasks, and make commitments to behavior change in a friendly and collaborative environment. These are the conditions under which good BA will occur.

ENLISTING SIGNIFICANT OTHERS IN THE TREATMENT

Skinner (1953) suggested that the social environment was the primary mediator of positive reinforcement (Follette & Jacobson, 1988). In the broad areas of both love and work, which occupy the majority of people's time, the social environment is a crucial factor. BA therapists do not assume that the interpersonal context is the most important one, but they often find themselves working there. Some of the research to date on bringing significant others into the therapy for a depressed client has focused on marital relationships. Marital/couple therapy has been evaluated as a treatment for depression, and there are guidelines suggested in the literature to help the therapist decide when individual or couple therapy may be the best recommendation for a depressed client. Because of our focus on context, and in so much as the significant people in any client's environment play an important part in the context of his or her life, we welcome significant others to come in for a session or two of therapy. To date, we have only seen spouses or life partners, although it is reasonable to think that a close friend, sibling, parent, child, coworker, etc., could be part of the treatment. It is useful for BA therapists to understand what the literature says about the interpersonal context of depression and to know when to recommend couple therapy or when to conduct BA and bring a significant other into the treatment of the individual.

Coyne (1976) recognized that people may find interactions with someone who is depressed to be aversive and may, therefore, withdraw from the depressed person. Recently, Coyne (1999) has expanded his earlier ideas about interactional patterns and depression. Depressed individuals may face a different social environment than nondepressed individuals (Coyne, 1999), with people who are less caring and supportive or interact in a way that reinforces depressed behavior (Lewinsohn, 1974). Many social factors either protect an individual from the severe impact of depression, or they make the individual more vulnerable to depression. We have noted marital distress as a primary social stressor, but there are also work pressures, childrearing, financial difficulties, and physical health problems that play roles in affective disorders. Studies comparing demographically matched controls have indicated that depressed clients report more stressful life circumstances and less family and work support than nondepressed controls (Billings & Moos, 1984; Holahan & Moos, 1987). It has been suggested that social context needs to be integrated into assessment procedures by clinicians for treatment planning (Holahan et al., 1999). The therapist should carefully consider the social environment when conceptualizing the case and deciding on treatment recommendations.

The Relational Context in Couple Therapy

People who have extensive social support are more likely to be emotionally healthy than those without such support (Cohen & Wills, 1985). Individuals with strong social support are less likely to become depressed during times of stress than those without it. The 2:1 gender difference in unipolar depression between women and men (McGrath, Keita, Strickland, & Russo, 1990; Weissman & Klerman, 1985) suggests that relational factors may have a greater impact on women than on men. In fact, some studies suggest that marriage serves as a "buffer" against depression for men, but has the opposite effect on women, and that relational distress may increase women's vulnerability to depression (Hammen, 1991; Koerner, Prince, & Jacobson, 1994). The literature indicates that there is a bidirectional link between relational distress and depression (Gollan, Gortner, & Jacobson, 1996).

Given the importance of the interpersonal context in the treatment of depression, researchers have evaluated the utility of combining marital therapy in the treatment of depressive disorders. In a review of the literature, Beach, Fincham, and Katz (1998) concluded that marital therapy is as effective a treatment for depression, as empirically supported individual therapies. The following reasons for considering marital therapy instead of individual therapy have been proposed by Beach and colleagues (1998):

> (1) the depressed partner is relatively more concerned about marital problems than about her depression, (2) marital problems are viewed by the depressed patient as having preceded and perhaps having caused the depressive symptoms, or (3) cognitive errors or "individual" symptoms are less salient to the depressed person than her marital problems. (p. 640)

Prince and Jacobson (1995) reviewed the literature on behavioral couple therapy and depression and concluded the following:

1. Behavioral couple therapy and individual cognitive therapy were equally effective in the treatment of depressed people who also complain of marital distress, but BCT was less effective when couples were not distressed.
2. Behavioral couple therapy results in greater improvement in the marital relationship than individual cognitive therapy, for both distressed and nondistressed couples.
3. Couple therapy did not improve relapse rates.
4. Couple therapy may be more effective for a depressed individual in a distressed relationship, but individual therapy is more effective when there is no relationship distress.

Taking these data into account, the BA therapist should evaluate whether recommending couple therapy may be a more useful course of action when conducting an initial interview with a depressed client. Often, the nondepressed partner is unwilling to accept his or her role in the problem and the depression of one partner may be identified as the cause for relationship distress. In some cases this may be true, but in others it is the relationship distress that precipitated a depressive episode. When a client reports significant relationship distress, the therapist should ask the client if he or she has considered couple therapy with his or her partner. In some cases, couple therapy may be conducted conjointly with individual therapy by a different therapist. Under such circumstances, it would be desirable for the BA therapist to obtain a release of information in order to coordinate care with the couple therapist.

A partner can initially be brought into the therapy process by discussing the interactional nature of depression and relational distress with him or her. In this way neither the relationship, the depressed client, nor the partner are blamed for the problems that are experienced by the individual or the couple. When individual therapy is either the treatment of choice or is the only option available (because either the client or her partner are unwilling to engage in couple therapy), the BA therapist can still suggest that a partner participate in one or two sessions with the client.

Working with Individuals with Distressed Social Relations

When we bring in a significant other, there is a very clear agenda. The client must be absolutely agreeable to this and see it as helpful and necessary, otherwise we would not do it or even suggest it more than casually. Enlisting the support of someone other than the client in the client's treatment is not the same as doing couple therapy or family therapy. The client remains the sole person being treated. In these days of increased liability therapists might find it a good idea to have a disclosure in writing about who is the client in any given case, and present this to the other person attending a therapy session. It should simply state something like the following:

"You have been asked to come in for a session to participate in Jennifer's therapy. The focus of these sessions will be on Jennifer and the treatment of her depression. Jennifer is my client and will remain the only client who is being treated. Your understanding and input is very important to both Jennifer and myself. This is not a couple or family therapy session. I appreciate your participation."

The distinction between couple or family therapy and a conjoint session including a partner or other significant person is not as clear as one would hope. There are no clear data to guide us in this area, and we are presenting ideas that are mostly speculative at this time, based on our experience in doing BA with a variety of clients. We know from the work of Jacobson and colleagues (1991) that it is difficult to determine the right balance of both conjoint therapy for relationship distress and individual therapy for depression. In a current study being conducted at our center we have tried to limit the number of sessions in which this occurs, although the treatment manual allows for "one or several" sessions of conjoint therapy (University of Washington, 1999).

Whereas couple therapy has a specific theoretical underpinning, whether it be traditional behavioral couple therapy (Jacobson & Margolin, 1979) or some other form of couple therapy, the inclusion of a significant other in BA is not based on a theory of relational interactions, but is utilized as one of many tools that can be useful in alleviating an individual's distress. Like other components of BA, it is used because the literature has suggested that it is useful. The BA therapist, therefore, needs to recognize that she is following the pragmatic truth criterion, i.e., looking to see if bringing in the other person works, before persisting in the intervention.

It is good to ask the client what he or she would like to accomplish by bringing in another person. The therapist should also keep the following goals in mind when bringing in a spouse or partner.

Opportunity to solidify the client's understanding of the model. When we invite another person into the treatment, we see this as a wonderful opportunity to both assess how well the client has understood the BA model and also to solidify that understanding. We ask clients to tell the other person about the model. Therapists should be ready to do a good bit of the explaining of the model, and this is not meant to be a test for the client. We find it useful to have discussions about depression in general by using the model presented earlier in figure 3.2. We particularly emphasize secondary problem behaviors, the TRAP model, and the ACTION acronym. The therapist may volunteer to write out on a whiteboard or notepad the general concepts or to draw a diagram and ask the client to fill in the details of the model. Ideally, the client will at least be able to say that depression is related to decreases in activity that provide some type of reward and that therapy is designed to help her to become more actively engaged in rewarding activities.

Shifting significant others' behavior toward therapy goals. It helps to enlist the significant other in supporting the activation process. Reactions in partners range from the negative, "She says she's depressed but everyone gets depressed, I don't know why she makes such a big deal of this," to the more positive, "I have been so lost as to how to help him — he just sits around all day — so I am very glad to get some advice about what I can do to help." The therapist can then either make suggestions, or better yet, ask the client to communicate how the partner can help him or her in terms of getting activated.

Bringing in other people also allows the therapist to see firsthand what the client can only describe in regards to the way others treat him or her. The reactions of those that join the sessions can give the therapist a glimpse of the support or lack thereof that a client has available. Keep in mind, however, that significant others often want to put on a good face to the therapist, especially if they are motivated to make the client look badly and themselves completely healthy. Nevertheless, the therapist and client can both benefit greatly from the therapist's understanding of what the client faces in his or her personal relationships. Even if it is an imperfect glimpse, seeing a significant other in person still provides additional understanding.

It helps to discuss the reciprocal nature of depression and relational conflict. For example, Julia was brought into a session because she worried about her friend Diane missing days of work. Julia helped the client avoid work by always covering for Diane when she called in sick. In this way, Julia unwittingly contributed to the avoidance pattern and interfered with the therapeutic work. Julia was asked to come in to learn how she could help by not covering up for Diane. Consider the following interaction.

DIANE: Well, Julia knows what I'm all about. She can tell you how I get when I'm really depressed.

JULIA: Yes, I've been really worried. Her job is in jeopardy. It has been three times now that she has not shown up for work and I have had to make up an excuse for her, saying that she had left a message with me, and I'm not even her supervisor.

THERAPIST: It seems that this really puts you in an awkward position. You want to help your friend, but you are forced to make up a story to cover for her not showing up.

JULIA: Yes. There are other things I have had to do as well, like go into her files and get a copy of a report that was due on Monday and give it to her boss so she wouldn't miss a deadline.

THERAPIST (*to Diane*): Julia is really trying to help you out. How do you think her covering for you has affected you?

DIANE: Well, it has gotten me out of some binds, and I appreciate it, but I wonder if it just allows me to screw up.

JULIA: Well, I don't want it to do that.

THERAPIST: Certainly you don't. It is really easy to get pulled into this process though, isn't it? You are covering because you are concerned and really want to help, and it does help in the short run, but it can lead to bad consequences in the long run if she continues to not show up for work. (*to Diane*) What have we been calling it when something is done to make a bad situation better in the short run, but doesn't solve the bigger problem?

DIANE: Avoidance.

THERAPIST: Yes, do you want to describe to Julia how your avoidance makes your depression worse, and how, inadvertently, you may have made her a co-conspirator in your avoidance pattern?

(In this exchange the therapist attempts to point out the reciprocal relationship between Diane not showing up for work and Julia covering for her without making Julia feel accused or responsible. It is also important that Diane not feel accused.)

DIANE: Well, I know that I have to get up and go about my day even when I don't feel like it. I've found that, on several occasions, going to work actually makes me feel better. But, some days I am so depressed that I just don't want to get out of bed and face the day. I've called you because I can't face calling the boss. That has put you in the position of covering, and then I stay stuck in my rut. I shouldn't call you.

(Note how Diane's interpretation is very contextual. It links her behavior to a specific context and set of consequences. So, even though she still is having problems getting herself to work, and Julia's behavior helps to maintain the avoidance behavior, Diane is not engaging in excessive self-blame. This is the beginning of good work on Diane's part to be able to shift the context and change her behavior to achieve different consequences. Julia, as part of the context, is enlisted to help to make the shift and change the contingencies that are currently maintaining the behavior of missing work.)

THERAPIST: Well, is calling Julia better than not calling anyone?

JULIA: Even if she didn't call me, I'd call her or go to her house if she didn't answer the phone.

THERAPIST: Right, how could you not, you care about her. (*to Diane*) It seems to me that your attempt to call Julia is a step in the right direction, but it is still a TRAP of avoiding calling your boss. How could she help you in a way that is not covering for you, and how could you not put her in a bind even when you are feeling at your very worst?

DIANE: Well, she could encourage me to call the boss.

JULIA: Yeah, right, like encouraging you to do that would help.

THERAPIST: Are you able to transfer calls in your office?

JULIA: Yes.

THERAPIST: What might happen if you transferred the call to the boss?

DIANE: Well, that would make me have to respond . . . or hang up.

THERAPIST: Is there a greater likelihood that you would approach your boss and actually speak to her if Julia connected you?

DIANE: I don't know . . . maybe.

THERAPIST: And if you took that step and talked to your boss, might you then take another step and get cleaned up and possibly go into work later?

DIANE: Possibly.

JULIA: Maybe another thing I could do is tell her that I am going to tell the boss that she called in and will be in late and then leave it up to her to get herself into the office by that time.

THERAPIST: Yes, you could do that or you could connect her to the boss.

DIANE: Ouch, both of those things would be really difficult.

THERAPIST: Yes, but they would help you in the long run, and they would also protect your friendship with Julia a bit, wouldn't they?

JULIA: I think the last thing you said was true, because I am starting to get a little resentful of being put in such a bad position.

The conversation is clearly centering on activation strategies, while also taking into account the reciprocal nature of both women's behaviors. If the two people were a client and her partner or spouse, the conversation would be similar, but might also include discussion of how the two can communicate with one another in a supportive manner. This discussion could utilize some of the communication skills ideas that have been derived from couple therapy (Gottman, 1979; Jacobson & Margolin, 1979), but the BA therapist would not use a formal training approach. Sometimes simply helping both individuals to state what they are feeling in a specific situation, based on specific behaviors, is a useful intervention in terms of allowing the client to feel more supported by his or her partner. The therapist would want the client to try this in the session and then to have the significant other to state his or her response. Consider the following exchange.

THERAPIST: One of the things that is difficult when a person is depressed is to interact with those closest by and to express a desire. I'd like to help in this process since we have your partner here.

MARY: Okay.

THERAPIST: I know that there have been times when John has said something that has made you feel really badly about yourself, and you then withdraw and feel sad. John, I know you probably aren't even aware of these things, because Mary withdraws and doesn't tell you. You then might even get upset with her because she withdraws. So, Mary, I'd like you to try telling John more directly how you feel.

MARY: It's hard because I don't think I have the right.

THERAPIST: I know it is hard, but this is the time to try hard things.

MARY: Well, I'll try.

JOHN: I'm here, you know, and I want to help.

MARY: Okay. John, sometimes I get upset about your work hours.

THERAPIST: Mary, I'd like you to be a little more specific with John. How about using a simple formula like "when you do X, in Y situation, I feel Z." Could you try that?

MARY: I'll try. John, when you stay late at the office and don't call me on Friday nights when we sometimes plan to go to a movie, I feel very sad and feel you don't love me.

THERAPIST: John, can you tell Mary how you are reacting right now to her taking the risk to tell you this?

JOHN: Well, Mary, I don't call because I don't want to take extra time . . .

THERAPIST: I'm sorry, let me interrupt for a moment. I am wondering if you could just tell Mary how it felt to have her say something so direct to you. Did you take offense?

JOHN: Well, no, I'm not offended. I feel like I should explain or defend myself, because I don't want you to think I don't love you. I want you to tell me these things, though, because I don't want to keep having misunderstandings.

THERAPIST: Mary, what are you observing right now about John's reaction?

MARY: Well, it is not angry, like I thought it would be. I don't want him to need to defend himself, though.

THERAPIST: Sure, neither of you want to hurt the other's feelings, and that is why it is so important that you talk to one another directly and not avoid these kinds of conversations.

The exchange may look very similar to one that may occur in a typical couple therapy session, but the difference is that the emphasis is on activating the client and getting her to approach rather than avoid a situation. The presence of the partner allows for immediate feedback on how her behavior is received. With a partner or spouse who is hostile, resistant, or extremely nonsupportive of the client, this type of intervention would be discouraged, since a full course of couple therapy may be necessary to alleviate the relationship distress.

Gain a better understanding of the client's behavior outside of sessions. The conjoint session provides an excellent opportunity to get another opinion about how the client is doing. Frequently, significant others are happy to discuss positive changes that they have seen in the client since the beginning of therapy. When significant others are critical or unsupportive of the client it is an important indicator of what the client has to deal with in his or her life. Although the BA therapist cannot really intervene with a "problem partner," he or she certainly can have more empathy for the client and help to develop realistic means for dealing with problems in the home. Significant others can also let the therapist know what may not be working well in the client's activation process.

CHAPTER 8

Clinical Examples of Behavioral Activation

T HE FOLLOWING CASE PRESENTATIONS ILLUSTRATE behavioral activation throughout the course of therapy. Because the therapy will be somewhat different for each case, depending on the functional analysis, there is no set intervention for the therapist to engage in from session to session. The logical course of therapy has been discussed previously, however, and it is assumed that the treatment will follow a similar progression. Two very different cases are presented to give a flavor for the similarity of the therapy from client to client and the differences based on the functional analysis.

In every session an assessment of the current severity of the client's depression is assessed using the Beck Depression Inventory (Beck et al., 1961). The reader may recall that scores on the BDI that are 9 or below suggest sub-clinical depression; scores in the teens are indicative of mild depression; the 20s represent moderate depression and scores 30 or above indicate severe depression; and scores above 40 would lead a clinician to seriously consider hospitalization after a careful assessment of the client's functioning and suicide potential. Certainly, no decisions about changes in treatment should be based solely on a paper and pencil inventory such as the BDI, but the scale is an excellent tool for monitoring progress.

Basically the treatment begins with an assessment of the symptomatic nature of the client's depression and history taking to begin to hypothesize about possible precursors. In the first two or three sessions the focus of treatment is on presenting the model and beginning to collect data from the client by teaching self-monitoring using an activity chart. Once the data has been collected and the therapist and client begin to see the behavior-mood relationships that are important for that particular client, assigned activity scheduling should take place. It is important to know what activities the client once participated in prior to the onset of depression or activities that the client had wished to engage in. At this point in therapy roadblocks to activation can be discovered and interventions made to help the client progress beyond them. As the client demonstrates improvement (usually measured by the Beck Depression Inventory), therapy will focus on relapse prevention and maintenance.

CASE EXAMPLE 1

Bill W.

Bill was a 50-year-old man who worked as a resident manager in a halfway house. He had been married for fifteen years but had divorced five years prior to coming to therapy, and he had moved in with a male partner. He had three children from his marriage: two sons who lived on their own and a young adult daughter who lived with him and his current partner. He described his relationship with his partner as "okay." He had difficulty describing the onset of his depression, stating that his blue mood seemed like it had been perpetual. The mood had worsened in the past seven years after leaving a prestigious job, where he had been hoping for a promotion that never came. He was a very religious and spiritual man and once took great pleasure in attending church and being part of a religious community, but he felt ostracized by the church after coming out as a gay man. He and his partner had tried to find a meditation group that they could fit into, but Bill thought most of them did not fit in with his spiritual beliefs, and he was unhappy with the groups they had tried. He felt like he lacked a spiritual community.

SESSION 1
BDI = 27

During the first interview, Bill described many symptoms of depression. He no longer took pleasure in going to church or being around church friends. This had changed following his coming out and getting divorced from his wife. He and his ex-wife remained friends, and she had married again one year ago. He had been unemployed for two years, and this left him feeling hopeless about his future. He eventually took a job as a resident manager in a halfway house, but was not particularly happy with his job; he believed that he had lost the status, position, and recognition he had from his former job. He felt guilt over many past behaviors, and he found himself procrastinating often, feeling "self-pity." Bill also stated that he and his partner were getting on better since he had been depressed, which led to a hypothesis that there were relationship factors that may have been maintaining the depression. Bill also had an adult daughter in her early twenties living with him, and there was conflict about her behavior of staying out late at night, going to work late, etc.

In session 1, the therapist asked Bill about his history and talked with him briefly about the connection between activity and mood. The therapist also began to formulate a problem list (Persons, 1989).* This list included the following:

- Dissatisfaction with work
- Relationship difficulties
- Limited social life/dissatisfaction with spiritual community
- Parent-child conflict

The problem list was briefly discussed with Bill, to determine whether he agreed that these were broad areas that could be targeted for change.

Homework assignment: Bill was given a pamphlet describing the behavioral approach to depression and behavioral activation therapy (appendix B) to read at home prior to the second session.

Figure 8.1 shows the model as it related to Bill's case. This model was explained to Bill in a similar fashion as described earlier in Henry's case.

SESSION 2
BDI = 30

In the second session, the main goal was describing the BA model to Bill and addressing any questions or reservations that he had about the treatment. The session began by establishing an agenda, with the therapist suggesting that there be discussion of the brochure and the treatment model, and introducing the activity chart. Bill added that he wanted to discuss "things that he had kept hidden for so long." The therapist explained to Bill that there would be two broad areas to work on:

---

*Using a problem list to generate target behaviors follows recommendations of the case formulation approach developed by Persons (1989), but the case formulation in BA differs due to the absence of assessment of cognitive restructuring, or evaluation of beliefs and assumptions as part of the case conceptualization. The BA case conceptualization consists of hypothesizing precursors to a depressive episode, developing a problem list for possible treatment targets, looking at avoidance patterns, and focusing on functional analysis of specific behaviors. The functional analysis is an ongoing process.

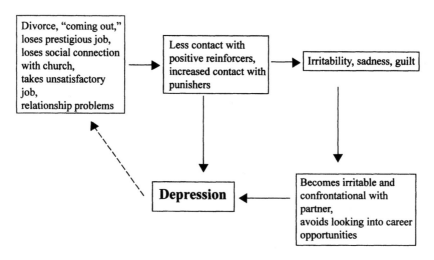

FIGURE 8.1 *The BA model as it related to Bill's case.*

1. Things in life that might need changing.
2. Things that Bill was doing to cope with his life or with his depression that resulted in the depression worsening.

During this session the therapist noticed that Bill continued to make self-derogatory statements. He did not state clearly what he believed or felt but began statements with either negative descriptions of himself or positive statements about the therapist. For example, when asked to repeat his understanding of the BA model to the therapist, Bill would say, "Think, Bill, don't be stupid," and then would summarize his understanding of the treatment. Or he would say to the therapist "You are good" or "I need to defer to you because you have the credentials." The therapist asked Bill to try to keep note of the times that he behaved in this way.

Homework assignment: Bill was asked to complete an activity chart and to record the things that he did and how he felt while doing the activity. This was the first step for the therapist in understanding what Bill's life was like outside of therapy. The activity chart documented behaviors in Bill's repertoire that were useful in managing his depression or limitations in his repertoire that could be modified through activation treatment.

SESSION 3
BDI = 29

In this session, Bill stated that he felt more hopeful. He and the therapist agreed to focus on the activity chart for most of the session. There was also a brief discussion of the way that Bill put his own ideas and desires aside. Looking at the activity chart demonstrated behaviors that Bill described as "maintenance activities": going to work, buying groceries, driving home, etc. Bill drew a blank when the therapist asked him if there were any activities that he engaged in just because he enjoyed them. Bill stated that he spent a great deal of time trying to avoid conflict with his partner and that he had done that with his ex-wife as well. Over time he "progressively shut down." He let his partner run things and wound up feeling inadequate and unhappy.

The therapist turned the attention to the activity chart. Bill was having difficulty writing down the emotions that he experienced during activities. He said that he was not feeling much and felt like he had lost spontaneity. In helping him to try to identify feeling states, the therapist discovered that Bill was more aware of changes in his body when he was sad than of any private experience of an emotion. He also noticed that he tended to avoid eye contact with people when he felt unhappy. The therapist helped the client to develop a scale to rate the intensity of any feeling that he did have the ability to describe. The therapist wanted to help Bill to identify differences in emotional severity at the same time that he was beginning to identify different emotional reactions. Using the activity chart, the therapist also helped the client to begin to identify triggers that may have influenced bad moods. Several interactions with his partner were associated with feeling worse, so the therapist focused on these interactions as possible triggers. The following is a brief exchange that occurred during session 3 after Bill complained that he and his partner had gotten into a fight because his partner, Ray, had packed Bill's suitcase for a trip and left out important articles.

THERAPIST: Were you upset about him packing, did you want Ray to pack for you?

BILL: It's always, well it always seems, incomplete. He'll pack part of my stuff and his stuff all into one bag. I can't visually look and see what I have or don't, what I need, it's out of order for me. I get our stuff mixed up.

THERAPIST: Would you like to pack for yourself?

BILL: Yes.

THERAPIST: This is important. This is the kind of information about the triggers that you're missing and you're just feeling a lot of the feeling that you can't articulate, the general sadness, but there might be specific things that are getting you upset or making you sadder. I am going to write some things down. 1. You'd like to pack for yourself, but Ray packs for you.

BILL: But he'll sure pack what he needs.

THERAPIST: Let me ask you, have you ever talked to him about this?

BILL: Yeah.

THERAPIST: So he's aware of it.

BILL: But it is something I'd have to remind him of every time and he would have his feelings hurt that I didn't want him to do those things.

(In this interchange one can begin to see the dilemma that Bill was in because he avoided hurting Ray's feelings but got angry and dissatisfied with his relationship because he felt that he had no control. Bill and his therapist discussed possible ways that he could actually do things like packing ahead of time before Ray did it for him. In this session there was also discussion of working from the "outside-in" rather than the "inside-out" after looking at Bill's activity log, and Bill pointed out a trigger for anger and discouragement—when his house is a mess.)

BILL: I am installing an entertainment center downstairs and it is at a certain stage of construction. It has to be done before we can move things out of this room and into another.

THERAPIST: How are you blocked? What's stopping you from doing it?

BILL: I don't want to do it, I don't have any energy and I don't care.

THERAPIST: We only have a little time left today, but I think that this will become a good focus for us. When you have tasks like this to do, especially when you are depressed, and you wait to feel like doing them, what's the likelihood of doing it?

BILL (*sarcastically*): I'm just waiting for the sun to come up.

THERAPIST: Well, I think a better expression might be waiting until hell freezes over. (*Bill laughs*) Sometimes when you don't want to do a task, waiting for a change from inside is not best. Here is a basic principle. What you are wanting is for things to change from the inside-out. When you are feeling depressed or don't feel like doing something, it is easier to make change happen from the outside-in.

BILL: I don't understand what you mean from the outside-in. Are you saying that you can act your way into a new way of feeling faster than you can feel your way into a new way of acting?

THERAPIST: Yes, that's exactly what I'm saying. Let me think of an example. . . . If I look at this messy desk I could keep saying "I hate this mess." I could walk into the office and avert my eyes from the desk. It would never get clean. If I look at the desk and pick up one pile to go through phone messages, little by little, as each pile is gone, the desk will look emptier. I may even get more momentum and, before I know it, I've got a clean desk. Maybe by the time you are done you will feel better. Maybe you'll feel the same as you did initially, but at least you got the task done. I'm not saying that if you act the feeling will always follow, but at least you'll act. Whereas, most often if you are waiting to feel something before you act, you are not going to act.

BILL: Exactly. These feelings always seemed so temporary in the past. They'd just kind of come and go.

THERAPIST: And this time it sounds like it is lasting.

BILL: Yes.

Homework assignment: Bill was asked to write down his activities and associated feelings and rate the intensity of each feeling on a 0–10 scale on his activity chart. He was also asked to write a short list of things that he believed brought him pleasure and "joy" (Bill's word). He was also encouraged to engage in those activities that he believed would bring joy into his life as well as to spend 15–30 minutes a day working on setting up the entertainment center. He was to report back to the therapist in the next session as to what helped him to feel better.

SESSION 4
BDI = 17

The agenda was to discuss the activity chart and dealing with things from the outside-in. Bill brought in a story that he enjoyed about someone's struggle to get to an ultimate destination. He stated that he also had never made it to his ultimate destination. The therapist asked what that might be, in order to understand clearly the goals that Bill might want to attain. Bill stated that he wanted acceptance and recognition. He could not specify by whom he wanted these things. He felt badly because some people at his work would walk by him and not exchange greetings. He thought that he was recognized at home. Bill added his "fear of rejection" to the session agenda because he avoided conflict whenever he could. As part of working on things from the outside-in, Bill had been asked to write a list of things that he found meaningful and that he enjoyed, that made him feel happy. He was reluctant to read the list because several of the items had to do with religion, and he feared the therapist's rejection. This provided an opportunity to show in-situ how his avoidance operated and blocked attainment of his goals. The therapist took this opportunity to introduce the TRAP model. Bill also had followed through and worked each day on the entertainment center. The project, though not done, was further along and Bill felt more hopeful that he would be able to complete it. He said that he never really felt motivated while doing it, and he watched the clock and stopped exactly after 30 minutes each day, but by the end of the week he thought that he had accomplished more than he had previously been able to do.

Homework assignment: Continue to relate activity and feelings on activity chart. Bill was also asked to add activities to his chart, particularly religious activities like meditation that he had stated had made him feel happy. He was to decide on times of the day that he would engage in these activities whether or not he felt like engaging in them. Continue progress on entertainment center.

SESSION 5
BDI = 17

Bill wanted to review the former sessions so that he could make sure that he fully understood the process. He stated that he felt like he had been making progress but could not define exactly what had contributed to it. The therapist asked him to explain the use of the activity chart, which he did. Bill was also asked to explain the TRAP and TRAC ideas and relate them to situations in his life. In this way a review of the previously learned material was undertaken, and it allowed the therapist to assess the extent to which Bill had understood the model. The therapist also explained the acronym ACTION to Bill to help him to recognize that he could choose different behaviors in similar situations in order to not feel depressed.

Homework assignment: Note any "traps" that he found himself in, and write down the trigger, response, and any pattern of avoidance that he recognized.

SESSIONS 6–11
BDI SCORES WERE 17, 13, 13, 11, 11, AND 13 RESPECTIVELY

In the following six sessions, Bill and the therapist continued to work on activity charts and to look at the avoidance patterns that Bill engaged in at work and at home. One of the most distressing patterns noted was that Bill had begun to hang out at a pub where he would take verbal abuse from a few of the patrons for not drinking with them, since he would only stay for a short time and have a Coke. He wanted greater intimacy with his partner, and to have a more exciting relationship at home, but he escaped from conflicts with his partner by going to the pub. He felt like he was inferior and not "one of the guys" at the pub, but continued to stop in after work. There was one man there who seemed to take an interest in him, which frightened Bill, since he believed this could interfere with his relationship. As Bill and the therapist continued to work through these issues, think of ways to approach the clutter of the house, state opinions to his partner, and stop contact with the people at the pub, Bill's BDI scores continued to drop. The therapist and Bill also addressed his dissatisfaction at work, and Bill began to look at other opportunities for professional development.

SESSION 12
BDI = 8

This session provides a very good example of how broad classes of pleasant events may not activate a particular client. The activation strategies need to be based on the functional analysis of the particular client's situation. The therapist would not have guessed that the kind of activities that Bill reported had been extremely helpful if the therapist relied on a broad class of pleasant events to predict decreases in depression. Bill was over 30 minutes late for his appointment. His BDI score was the lowest it had been. The lower score was correlated with Bill having had an extremely busy and difficult day at work. However, he had been able to help a client who was in serious need (hence the tardiness). He felt so gratified that he had helped the client and was energized by the intensity of his work that day.

Homework assignment: Collect information about health care facilities that offered training programs in the area of specialized study that Bill wanted to begin to focus on in his career.

SESSION 13
BDI = 9

Once again, Bill was highly reinforced by success at work and the intensity of his job. He had been cursed at by a client prior to the session, but still felt very good. The therapist and Bill discussed how important the energy "charge" was to Bill and that this came into play at work and at home. In fact this was an example of his conflicting goals. He liked the charge of an intense day at work, and it actually improved his mood, yet he had a tendency to avoid conflict. Therefore, the need for approach behaviors was stressed and homework given to increase his proactive behaviors.

Homework assignment: Bill had found the names of health care facilities where he could get training in HIV counseling and hospice work. He and the therapist agreed that a good task for him was to contact those facilities and gather further information about their training programs. He gave himself a deadline to contact five of them.

SESSIONS 14–19
BDI SCORES WERE 11, 14, 8, 5, AND 5 RESPECTIVELY

During these sessions the therapy continued to address Bill's approach behaviors. He began to make more effort to address people at work by looking them in the eye and saying hello rather than waiting for them to address him. He was being more forthright at home with his partner and stating his opinions. He also was getting projects done around the house that he had put on hold for many months. Bill also continued his pursuit of training opportunities to expand his career options. He was somewhat discouraged to discover that the training would require at least a year of sacrifice because the training opportunities required full-time attention since he lacked proper certification, but it did not pay a stipend that would allow him to support himself.

SESSION 20
BDI = 3

A colleague of Bill's died suddenly just a few days prior to this session. She had been someone whom Bill felt close to at work. Interestingly, his BDI score remained low. Bill attributed this to the fact that he was sought out by other colleagues for comfort and guidance. As the respect he received at work increased, his job satisfaction improved. A problem discussed in this session was Bill's continual search for feedback in order to "know where to go in his life." The therapist compared this search to Bill's earlier military and religious experiences, where everything was orderly and there was a routine and he was comfortable following orders. He could expect people to salute him and to respond in a certain fashion. Without that he doubted what others thought of him and would hesitate before acting in many situations. The therapist noticed that Bill tended to act in a deferential manner in the session and queried Bill as to how this might affect others in his life and if it had an effect on the amount of respect he received at work. The therapist also tried to help him explore the function of his behavior so that he could look at alternative ways of achieving the goal that would not lead to the same patterns of avoidance.

THERAPIST: What is the goal you are trying to achieve?

BILL: I can answer that. The first word I'll play with if I have the latitude to do that is seduction. To . . .

THERAPIST: Can you explain what you mean by seduction?

BILL: I don't know where other people are; I don't claim to be intuitive. I'm a fair reader of people. . . . My thought is that I don't necessarily know where people are so I go in low, humble and self-effacing. For me there's beauty in that. Not a heap where everybody is scrambling to get to the top.

THERAPIST: So the goal is to be equal to people or ultimately to be what?

BILL: The goal is to be friends with people.

THERAPIST: But you say you "go in low, go in at the bottom." That makes me think, hopefully you'll appreciate this since you have been a religious man, of the saying that "the person who would be first should be last." If you are invited to dinner, you sit at the back until the host invites you to the head of the table.

BILL: Yeah.

THERAPIST: That whole thinking in western Christian thinking to put yourself last so that you can become first. Is that part of your goal, to ultimately have a place at the head of the table?

BILL: I'd have to qualify the symbolism. To me being at the head of the table means to talk to someone, to be able to share and be open. I don't usually find that, especially with men.

THERAPIST: I wonder if the reason you don't find it with men is because you come in low, you are being obsequious. The goal is like you are trying to come in with an olive branch and they are saying "come on up" but you don't see them, and this may backfire on you, and they may see you as someone who is not very challenging. So, how do people who come to you to engage with you, how do they tend to act?

BILL: There is openness and candor.

THERAPIST: Let me ask you this. How would you have reacted if I came in and said "Hey Bill, I'd like us to set our agenda, but I'm not sure because I don't really know what we're doing here. I'd like you to set the agenda, because I don't think I'm smart enough to do it. I think we should talk about this, but I'm not really sure because sometimes I'm wrong about these things." How would you have reacted? Would you have felt secure having me as your psychologist or would you have thought "This guy is a little bit flaky"?

BILL: I would have wondered.

THERAPIST: I was sort of exaggerating the self-doubt. I wonder at times if you come across that way a little.

BILL: I used to do that more in the past, but I can identify with that. There is a flavor of it.

THERAPIST: Maybe just being very passive. You are passive and people don't do what you want and you get angry or feel sad. You may be stuck in one of these avoidance-pattern traps we've talked about.

BILL: What am I avoiding?

THERAPIST: Being seen as arrogant perhaps? Avoiding being up front with someone, giving a good firm handshake, and having them say "get lost"?

BILL: I am not good going toe to toe with someone. I tend to freeze up. Unless I have absolute confidence that I have the answer, then that's it. I also want to hear the other person's perspective; I just don't know what to do about it.

THERAPIST: Well that's what we are about here, figuring out how to activate and change some of these behaviors.

Bill and his therapist then developed a plan for monitoring when he was acting in a manner that "came in low" as he had described and to use this as a cue to shift his behavior and be more up front and forthright.

There was a two-week break between this session and the following session. Due to the limitation of sixteen weeks in the research protocol, the next two sessions were to be Bill's last. The focus needed to shift to maintenance and relapse prevention strategies. The therapist was only able to follow up briefly on the topic of Bill's passive behaviors and the way he dealt with people by being self-effacing and trying to ingratiate himself.

Homework assignment: Bill was asked to give some thought to what he still wanted to get from therapy and to what he had learned to date. He was asked to write down his responses.

SESSION 21
BDI = 4

When asked what had been most helpful in the treatment, Bill stated that the word "activation" came to mind and that he would become more active in addressing situations rather than just waiting for a response from others. Bill continued to want insight into the causes and nature of his problems. The therapist tried to encourage Bill to act rather than philosophize.

THERAPIST: When you talk about the depression, you basically say "If I could just figure out what is causing this." How useful is that behavior? That behavior is going to possibly maintain the depression rather than saying "who cares what's causing this, let me just do something." If you think of the word activate, then ask yourself what you can do now to feel better. If you are acting, and begin to feel less depressed, you may be better able to deal with the situations that may have been triggers to begin with. What good does it do to sit around worrying and waiting?

BILL: I'm not worrying.

THERAPIST: Not worrying, just thinking. You've said a number of things like you are waiting for insight. Now, insight is really nice . . .

BILL: I'm curious, that's part of it. I don't want to say something that is not true. Like I don't want to call 911 if I don't know what is causing a chest pain.

THERAPIST: Well, talking metaphorically, a pain in the chest could be gas. So, do you need to know before you act?

BILL: I need to know something!

THERAPIST: Sure, you need to know if you should call 911 or take a warm bath or take an antacid. So, can you act even if you don't have all of the information, especially with complicated emotions?

BILL: How do you take faster action?

THERAPIST: I don't mean faster action but action to figure something out rather than passively thinking about it.

Bill said that this was a pattern that led to a trap of self-doubt because he continued to question all of the explanations he proposed for things. At this point in therapy, Bill had learned that the way out of this trap was to act, but he was still not fully able to recognize when his curiosity was functioning more as avoidance or inaction rather than true knowledge gathering.

SESSION 22
BDI = 4

In this final session, Bill and his therapist discussed Bill's feelings about ending therapy, developed a short list of situations where Bill felt particularly vulnerable, and discussed a plan for coping. Bill's trigger situations mainly had to do with feeling interpersonally sensitive. He would react when others were perceived as demeaning or rude. Bill committed to trying to either confront people in those situations or simply turn to others who treated him kindly, rather than allow the behavior of others to trigger a depressive slump. Bill stated that he felt prepared to be on his own, although he was sad to leave therapy. He was encouraged to continue with self-therapy sessions (Beck, 1995), using his activity chart and the TRAP/TRAC and ACTION models to continue looking at the function and outcome of his behaviors. Basically in a "self-therapy" session the client decides on certain issues to consider, sets an agenda, and spends 30–60 minutes planning activities and using the tools learned in BA to help commit to action during the week. He said that he had continued to do that throughout therapy and felt prepared to do so without the help of the therapist.

Case Summary

Bill was chosen because his case presents an example of the complexity of clients' problems. BA is a treatment that can be used even when the initial goals of therapy are broad or vague. Bill was a client who felt very guilty about his past. He was functioning well at work, but was not in a job that completely satisfied him. It appeared that he was relatively active from the beginning, but only during a careful analysis was it discovered that he actually withdrew emotionally when he approached his home, and the domestic activities he engaged in were nothing more than going through the motions. As he began to recognize how much avoidance played a role in his daily interactions and understood the importance of breaking those patterns, he was able to take a more proactive approach to his daily encounters. This required gentle coaching from the therapist, and the therapist made use of opportunities to question avoidance that occurred in session and to help Bill to practice facing possible conflicts. This occurred when Bill wanted to discuss religious issues but feared rejection by the therapist. The therapist encouraged Bill to use alternative coping and observe the results of actually stating his beliefs and enjoyment of spiritual things. Bill began to experience the natural reinforcement available in forthright human verbal exchange. Whether or not the other person agreed, Bill's attempts to state his own thoughts were reinforced by the pleasure it gave him to take an equal position rather than placing himself in an inferior role.

CASE EXAMPLE 2

Carrie J.

Carrie was a 21-year-old woman. She had a long history of family distress and had been estranged from her parents during her teenage years. Carrie worked as a technician and had had recent difficulties with her boss and coworkers. Carrie lived in an apartment with another woman and a man and was involved in a love relationship with the man, but neither of their families knew the nature of their relationship. Carrie admitted that this caused a great deal of stress for her and placed stress on the relationship. Carrie's boyfriend had suggested that she seek therapy for depression. She became a part of a research study because of the prospect of receiving free therapy since she did not make a great deal of money.

SESSION 1
BDI = 32

As usual, the therapist shared that the agenda in the first session is somewhat set for gathering information about Carrie and explaining the type of treatment they will be engaging in. The therapist also told her that therapy would be a team effort and that he'd seek feedback from her. The therapist explained that therapy makes use of homework assignments and that in this first session he would give her a pamphlet to read about the therapy for her first assignment.

Carrie said that she first started to feel depressed about four years prior to therapy, and she had periods of remission but that there had been nearly constant change in her life, which complicated things. She reported getting depressed and irritable throughout the day; she either slept too much or had difficulty sleeping. She had limited contact with her parents but enough to continue to get embroiled in her parents' conflicts. Her parents were very young when Carrie was born, and they fought frequently when she was growing up. She currently lived with a woman friend whom she had known for six years and a boyfriend, Ron, whom she had known for about a year and a half. They had all lived together for six months. When asked how she thought her life would be different if she was not depressed, she said that she would be more active and have more friends. She and Ron had also recently thought about separating but had decided to stay together. They both acted in ways that escalated arguments and triggered each other's moods. Carrie had stopped seeing friends whom she knew from high school. The problem list for Carrie included the following:

- Sleep disturbance
- Relationship difficulties
- Financial stressors

- Dissatisfaction with employment
- Social isolation

The first session agenda also included a brief explanation of BA and an assessment of what Carrie's goals might be.

THERAPIST: What are some of your personal goals for your life? What would you like to be doing in two or three years?

CARRIE: I don't know. This has always been a problem. Other kids in school knew what they were doing, and I wasn't interested in that. I wanted to complete my diploma, but I didn't really know what I wanted to do. I hated my first job, and after I left it I just wanted to get back here in town where I had friends. I'd like to get a job in a smaller company. It is something that I want to do, but I have a couple of other things I need to go through before getting there.

THERAPIST: What are some of those things?

CARRIE: Getting a car that doesn't break down every month.

THERAPIST: What steps have you taken so far toward that?

(The therapist then begins to introduce the BA method of focusing on activation rather than feelings and tries to establish some preliminary ideas of Carrie's goals and assess her ability to move in the direction of her goals. Carrie also said that she enjoyed playing music, writing songs, drawing, and painting. She found her job allowed creativity, but there were deadlines that made it very stressful for her. The therapist presented Carrie with the brief manual [see appendix B] that explained guided activity and the activation model of depression treatment.)

Carrie said that she found the session to be easier than she had imagined it to be. She had been reluctant about coming into therapy, but by the end of the session she had said that she wanted to continue. She said that it had been helpful to talk, even though she had been initially skeptical.

Homework assignment: Read client pamphlet on behavioral activation for depression.

SESSION 2
BDI = 21

Carrie said that she had had a good weekend. She did not worry about things and "putzed" around the house and went shopping. When asked what was different, Carrie could not say what had made her worry less.

She did not have any topic to put on the agenda. The therapist suggested that they talk about her reaction to the manual, that he would introduce an activity chart, and that he'd try to continue to get to know her. The therapist demonstrated the BA theory of the cycle of depression, showing how the ways that clients try to cope with depression also become problems. In Carrie's case, some of the ways she tried to cope was to withdraw from friends, to sleep in, to express her irritability to others. Carrie was distressed by her parents' problems; her father was at risk of being fired from his job. She was tearful and worried that she would end up being forced to take care of the family if her father was fired. Figure 8.2 shows the initial model as it related to Carrie's problems. She and her therapist also discussed general sleep hygiene skills because Carrie would awaken two or three times a night and toss in bed until she fell back to sleep. Carrie also talked about her dissatisfaction with some of the people that she had to work with. There was one individual that she became particularly irritated with, and her boss would talk to other coworkers as well as Carrie if something was wrong with one of Carrie's projects. The therapist presented the activity chart to Carrie and started with the therapy as an example of writing what she was doing and how she was feeling. She said she moved from feeling sad when talking about her family to feeling content during the end of the session. She had felt sad at an intensity of 5 on a scale of 1–10, and contented at an intensity of 6.

Homework assignment: Activity chart including mood and rating of intensity of mood.

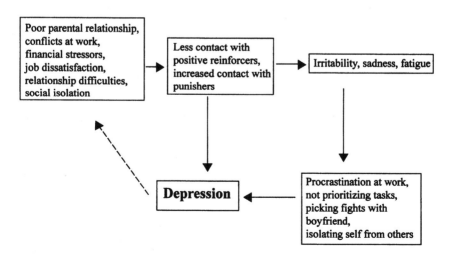

FIGURE 8.2 *The BA model as it related to Carrie's case.*

SESSION 3
BDI = 30

Carrie was feeling more depressed because she had been in an argument with Ron, but she did not want to put that on the agenda. The therapist asked to put the activity chart on the agenda. Carrie said that she had just had a "blah" day and couldn't think of anything specific to discuss, other than that she thought her depression might be "chemical." They agreed to look at the activity chart and see if there were issues that could be looked at and to talk about the biology of depression. The therapist asked if the argument with Ron had been resolved but respected that Carrie did not want to discuss details. Carrie had completed her activity chart very carefully. Like many clients, she had difficulty being specific in her description of moods, and she stated at times that she felt "indifferent," "irritated," or "happy." Her sleeplessness was noted on the activity chart. She had tried the therapist's recommendations to get out of bed and engage in a repetitious activity until she felt like her eyes were heavy, but she only had marginal success with this.

One of the difficulties noted on the activity chart was an interpersonal problem with some of the people at work. She did not address the problem, however, but just felt irritated with her coworkers. The therapist explored this with Carrie.

THERAPIST: When you get angry at home or at work, or when you used to get angry at your mom and dad, do you try to do things to resolve it, or has trying to do something in the past never gotten you anywhere?

CARRIE: It's never gotten me anywhere.

THERAPIST: So, what do you tend to do?

CARRIE: Depends how angry I am.

THERAPIST: Let's say anger at a 5 or 6 on a scale of 10.

CARRIE: Just try to ignore it and go on . . .

THERAPIST: I wonder if your experience has been that trying to resolve these things doesn't get you anywhere and you give up, and you then try to avoid the situation altogether when you are angry. That may partly be what makes you feel depressed because you feel kind of hopeless. Does that sound like your experience?

CARRIE: Yes.

THERAPIST: That gets us back into those secondary problems that we talked about. If you are avoiding feeling, and it is understandable that you would, if you have tried to deal with things in the past and it didn't work . . .

CARRIE: Right.

THERAPIST: So maybe what you and I can talk about while you are coming here is to find a different way to deal with these situations that might help you to resolve things. As time goes on in this therapy, we might also have Ron come in for one or two times so he can get on board with what is going on, but that would be totally up to you and up to him.

The therapist discussed the interpersonal context of Carrie's depression that occurred in her home and suggested that Ron could join them for one or two sessions. Carrie and her therapist talked about when leaving a situation might prevent any type of physical altercation. This had happened between Carrie and Ron on one occasion when Carrie slapped him in the face and he pushed her. They also reviewed when ignoring problems might make them worse. Carrie provides a good example of the sensitivity needed when activating clients. The therapist must always think about the specific case and the possible outcome of behaviors. It was not always good for Carrie to confront Ron, because arguments would escalate into fights. On the other hand, there were also times when Carrie would ignore Ron, and he would ask to continue to talk out a problem, and Carrie's ignoring would actually be an avoidance maneuver. He would get angrier at these times too, and Carrie would sometimes become physically aggressive in order to force him to let her be. It is good to consider past history when trying to predict what the outcome of certain behaviors might be. The best guess of what behaviors to try would come from the client's observations of the outcome of similar behaviors in the past.

Carrie and the therapist discussed the idea of biological changes that happen when a person is depressed. Carrie worried about having inherited depression from her parents. The therapist said that there may have been a genetic vulnerability to depression in her family but that just as there were biochemical changes there were behavioral changes. She had dealt with depression for a very long time, and the therapist said that it made sense that it would feel "biological" at this point. He asked if Carrie had difficulty engaging in the type of therapy that they were doing, and she said that she actually thought it would be good for her.

This session occurred two days before Christmas. Knowing that family distress was a component in Carrie's depression, the therapist asked if they could briefly add a discussion of some of the possible problems that might develop to the agenda. He also wanted to work with Carrie to propose a plan for her to deal more appropriately with situations rather than ignoring them or becoming angry and nasty. She was afraid that she would be left out of conversations or made fun of by a particular cousin. Because Carrie's relationship had not been disclosed to either family, she felt that this added stressors to the holiday gatherings. Carrie and Ron had a small set of friends who were supportive of their relationship.

SESSION 4
BDI = 36

Carrie stated that she had been too busy to complete an activity chart over the holidays, and she realized that she wasted a great deal of time at work. The therapist suggested that they spend time, therefore, talking about the activities that kept her busy and the things that she did to waste time at work. Carrie said that Christmas had gone badly. She said that she "thought too much," so that was put on the agenda, as well as trying to recreate the activity chart in the session. In this session the therapist introduced the TRAP model to Carrie and suggested a variation on attending to experience as a way of dealing with Carrie's "thinking too much." At Ron's holiday gathering, Carrie observed that the family was happy, and she started to think about how unhappy her own family was, which made her feel sad and lonely. Carrie's therapist acknowledged that when people leave their family homes they sometimes need to grieve the ideal family that they did not have, and sometimes feeling sad about family problems may be appropriate. Carrie and her therapist began to look at avoidance patterns that made her sadness worse and actually contributed to her feeling depressed. The therapist brings the topics together to introduce the notion of the TRAP.

THERAPIST: When you were with Ron's family and you started to think about how nice his family is and how not-so-nice your own is, do you think you started to disengage a little bit? (*Carrie nods in agreement*)

THERAPIST: Did thinking a lot about your own family ultimately end up with you missing out on enjoying a good time with your current, well sort of, family.

CARRIE: They are like family, yes.

THERAPIST: So, maybe we could write here . . . (*points to the whiteboard*)

CARRIE: I'll sit back and not talk.

THERAPIST: I'll write "sit back and not talk."

CARRIE: And I'll want to leave.

THERAPIST: I'll write here "think about your family . . . " I'll use the dirty word "dysfunction."

CARRIE: That's okay.

THERAPIST: And I'll write "want to leave." Did you leave?

CARRIE: Yes, because of that, and because we were both tired.

THERAPIST: What about when you get pulled into your family struggles, do you just think about it or do you try to be a peacemaker?

CARRIE: I try to be a peacemaker, and it never works. I am always told that I am taking sides.

(Carrie explains how she spent much of her life trying to get out of situations where her mother made a public spectacle of herself. Her mother had a quick temper and cursed loudly at the rest of the family in public when she was irritated. Carrie always tried to prevent her mother's irritation, but nothing she did worked. If her mother did not swear at Carrie, she would swear at service people or tell loud stories in restaurants with little concern about being overheard. Carrie had always been embarrassed by this behavior.)

CARRIE: This has happened all my life.

THERAPIST: You've become very good at avoiding negative things or getting out of negative situations — you may not be as good at getting into more positive situations. You've begun to do that since you got out of your parents' house. Sitting back and not talking at Ron's parents' house sounds a little like that avoidance thing. Thinking about your family's problems also sounds like it. Seeing the comparison between his family and yours was a negative experience for you, and the way you try to get out of it is to work out your own family issues in your head. You also left the party early, which is escaping the negative situation. This understandably blocked you from enjoying yourself. A lot of our guided activity is about increasing the chances that you will do things that result in a positive experience. We use a little abbreviation. You get into a TRAP. This stands for Trigger, which, in this case, is your partner's nice family; Response, which, in this case, is feeling lousy and lousy about your own family; and Avoidance-Pattern, which is when you say you start wanting to leave the situation. So this is a simple way to think about it — boom, you're in the trap again. So the way to get out of the trap is to use alternate coping, do something different. Maybe staying a little longer even though you feel like leaving, looking around the room to see who wore red on Christmas, or better yet, trying to engage someone in an interesting conversation; anything other than sitting and dwelling. Does trying to be the peacemaker in your family get you in a trap?

CARRIE: I think it does. But if I don't try to be a peacemaker I will be accused of not caring, or of still taking sides. So I am damned if I do and damned if I don't.

THERAPIST: Well, that sounds like the kind of situation that you would definitely want to get out of. In our work, I'll usually talk about avoidance as a negative thing, but there are people who are so annoying that the best way to handle them is to avoid them altogether. Then you need to find other people who may be more . . .

CARRIE: Like my family than my real family is. I have always felt like my friends were more like my family.

THERAPIST: Do you think this is important to have those same kinds of close friends in your life now?

CARRIE: Yes.

THERAPIST: Could that be a way to try to find alternative coping?

CARRIE: Yes.

THERAPIST: Great. Let me give you some paper and you can write this down as a reminder for yourself, okay?

CARRIE: Okay.

By the end of the session Carrie was able to say how she would get upset and not do things, then get upset with herself for not getting things done, and get caught in a cycle. She said that she knows that when she does certain activities, changes her environment or does something that she enjoys, she feels better quickly.

Homework assignment: Write tasks that need to be done on activity chart, check them off when completed.

SESSION 5
BDI = 27

Carrie said she had tried to schedule activities and had difficulty. She wanted to put that on the agenda. When Carrie and her therapist reviewed her activity chart, it was noticed that she had a number of daily meetings at work, so she was frequently reacting to problems that she experienced with coworkers during those meetings. She then would go back to her desk and try to escape by checking e-mail or making phone calls. She and her therapist worked out a modification of her activity chart where she set certain times of the day to check e-mail or return phone calls. During other times of the day, she would schedule in work on her projects.

Homework Assignment: Activity chart with modifications.

SESSION 6
BDI = 43

The therapist was concerned about the marked increase in Carrie's BDI score. She was not reporting suicidal ideation on question number 9 on the BDI, but the sudden jump was a possible indication that something was not working for Carrie. She was particularly upset because she had pain in her tooth and could not afford to go to a dentist. The therapist asked Carrie if she wanted to put the difficulties finding dental care on the agenda. As usual, Carrie was very passive about agenda setting. She would come into a session, bring up a few problems, but was never willing to target one or two for the agenda. The therapist always had to suggest that they put the problems she brought up on the agenda for discussion. This needed to be dealt with, but the immediate session was not an appropriate time given the level of distress Carrie was feeling about being out of work and suffering from tooth pain.

The agenda that followed was discussion of finding dental care in local clinics. Carrie had not looked in the telephone book for low-cost dental clinics. She assumed that she made too much money to go to some clinics, and too little to go to others. The therapist went through the telephone book with Carrie and helped her to find the names of several clinics near her home.

Homework assignment: She was to call these places and set up an appointment at her earliest convenience.

SESSIONS 7–10
BDI SCORES = 15, 24, 18, AND 28 RESPECTIVELY

Over the next four sessions, Carrie continued to deal with her physical problems. She had been given antibiotics for a bad tooth infection following her visit in session 6. Carrie's BDI scores varied mostly as a result of her shifting physical condition, it seemed. She was not very active and was upset that she needed to miss work because of her illness.

During these sessions Carrie and her therapist continued to work on activity charts and to look at avoidance patterns that she engaged in. Ron came in for session 8 and Carrie explained what she and her therapist were doing in therapy. She also talked about how she recognized that she had a tendency to avoid doing things and that she thought that activation was necessary. Ron noted that he had seen an improvement in Carrie's mood over the time that she had been in therapy. He talked about how worried he had been about Carrie. The two of them still got into arguments frequently, but Ron said that he felt very close to Carrie and that they both tried to work things out. The therapist talked with both Carrie and Ron about using "time-out" as a strategy for cooling down prior to trying to resolve arguments. Ron reported that Carrie had made greater efforts to organize work at home, which improved their relationship. Carrie said that this made her feel better as well as she didn't feel ashamed to have friends over because she contributed to keeping the house clean. They both got along well with their roommate, who only stayed in the apartment on weekends.

Homework assignment: Activity charts, assignments of specific tasks, and use of the TRAP and ACTION models to look at avoidance patterns.

SESSION 11
BDI = 13

Carrie reported that she felt particularly good during the previous week. She wanted to talk about how to tell when her behavior was avoidant. She said that she and Ron had made a conscious effort to activate themselves over the preceding weekend because they had both felt depressed. They actually activated themselves by talking about plans for the future, which included the possibility of moving out of state. Carrie and Ron thought that it might be a good idea to live a little further from both of their families. She felt good that she and Ron had a civil talk about this, because in the past one of them would get anxious about the possibility of moving and they would end up arguing. Carrie also felt that he had been supportive of her wanting a different job. Carrie wanted to talk about making a decision to leave her job. She and her therapist discussed the things that she liked and disliked about her job; she disliked more things than she liked and believed that if she was to find a different job she would be happier.

Homework assignment: Write a list of goals and fantasies about the type of work place, income, home, etc., that she would like in order to begin to refine a goal to work toward.

SESSION 12
BDI = 19

Although Carrie's BDI score had increased a little, she still felt much better than when she first came in for therapy. She had had a more difficult week at work. She wanted to discuss her "life goals" during the session. She admitted to not charting things very well on her activity chart, and she said that she had noticed a lot more avoidance during the week. She had written two days' worth of information on the activity chart and she and the therapist looked through it and marked activities that were either avoidance or approach activities. Carrie had made a list of goals she had:

- Wanting to leave her company
- Wanting to work in a place where her manager believed in open communication
- Working where there was no finger pointing
- Having opportunity for advancement
- Working for a company that provided health benefits and would pay for further schooling
- Having an opportunity for relocation — preferably to a sunnier climate

When Carrie and her therapist read the list, the therapist asked Carrie how she would know some of these things without actually working for the company. She said she would look at companies where she knew someone who already worked there. The therapist asked her, in the event that there was a potentially good company where she didn't know anyone, if she could ask certain questions in an interview or get certain information that would let her know if there was open communication, etc. Carrie said she would need to think about that.

Homework assignment: Write out all the information she would ask about in an interview and other possible ways she could get information about the management styles of a company before accepting a job.

SESSIONS 13–16
BDI = 12, 24, 14, AND 12 RESPECTIVELY

Carrie's mood continued to improve through the next four sessions with the exception of the week prior to session 14, when she had had another flare-up of her dental problems. During these sessions the therapist noted that Carrie was generating some ideas in the sessions for how to find a new job and how to take care of her physical problems, but she was not very active in implementing the strategies. The therapist used Carrie's behavior in sessions, especially her ongoing passivity with agenda setting despite instructions to prepare one prior to the session, as an example of her general avoidant style.

THERAPIST: Carrie, I know you feel criticized by a lot of people, so I want to address something with you that is a little sensitive. Can I do that?
CARRIE: I guess so.
THERAPIST: Well, we have talked now for many weeks, and we discuss

how important it is for you to be active. You've noticed how when you are active, you feel much better.

CARRIE: As long as I'm not sick. It just isn't fair how much I get sick and that I can't even afford a good dentist.

THERAPIST: I agree with you, Carrie, it isn't fair. However, a few weeks ago, you actually found your way to a dentist and got proper treatment. Your mood improved during that time to some degree, didn't it?

CARRIE: Yes, but when is life going to get a little easier?

THERAPIST: Well, I can't say. As you get more involved in a better job, there might be more opportunity for things to ease up. The problem is, as you get down and depressed, you stop trying to go for those things that will help you out. You seem to get very passive and just react to the problem of the moment. Does it seem that way to you?

CARRIE: I don't know what you mean.

THERAPIST: Well, instead of continuing to look for new jobs, you just wait until something comes along. Because you aren't looking, you aren't aware of what will come along. So you stay stuck.

CARRIE: Well, I've been in so much pain. I've also sent my resume out via e-mail to several companies but I haven't heard back.

THERAPIST: Yes, I know you have done a few things. How do you think that people really set themselves up to get what they want, though?

CARRIE: I don't know — some people just have luck.

THERAPIST: See, I think that is being passive again. Even in here with me you wait until I set an agenda based on a current problem you are having. It is all reactive to problems rather than proactive in trying to solve problems. Relying on luck is just a way to continue to avoid action. So, how do people who aren't just lucky get what they want?

CARRIE: I suppose they just keep trying.

THERAPIST: Yes, I suppose you are right. They keep trying no matter how they feel, and they don't let setbacks discourage them from continuing to try. They become proactive, in spite of setbacks.

CARRIE *(crying)*: But I feel like I have to work so much harder than anyone else.

THERAPIST: Yes, you had some disadvantages in your life. It is really hard, and it really doesn't seem fair, does it?

CARRIE: No.

THERAPIST: But you know, if you get yourself out of the TRAP of being passive, you might be able to turn those disadvantages around. Can we talk about that?

CARRIE: I suppose we can.

THERAPIST: It seems to me that we can look at any of these life situations as a "trigger." Even coming to therapy and needing to set an agenda is a trigger. Your response is . . . what would you say your response is?

CARRIE: I don't know . . . hopeless.

THERAPIST: Okay, so you feel hopeless. What do you do?

CARRIE: Well, you're telling me I don't do anything.

THERAPIST: I'm not exactly saying that you don't do anything, I've seen you work pretty hard during our therapy. What I am saying is that your general style is to get very passive and just complain about the problems but wait until something happens apart from you that will fix the situation. Would you agree?

CARRIE: Yes, I guess so.

THERAPIST: So that is your "avoidance-pattern" when it comes to these things. So what could get you back on TRAC, with an alternative way to cope?

CARRIE: Do it no matter how I feel.

THERAPIST: I think that may be worth a try, so how can you plan that for this upcoming week?

CARRIE: Well, I need to keep looking for a job, and I need to get back to see a dentist.

THERAPIST: And you might try to talk to your boss about some type of help with the costs, right?

CARRIE: Yeah, that's a long shot though.

THERAPIST: Well, maybe. Can you write some of these things on an activity chart and commit to times in the next few days when you'll do them?

CARRIE: Yes, I guess so.

Homework assignment: Return to clinic to talk with a dentist about the tooth pain. Look for job over the Internet during lunch break. Find an appropriate break in boss's schedule to discuss health care needs.

SESSION 17

BDI = 10

At this session, Carrie's BDI was the lowest that it had been. She had followed through on her homework assignment, and, in the meantime, she had received an offer for an interview for one of the jobs that she had applied for. Carrie continued to struggle with the dental problems, but her own family doctor had placed her on a different antibiotic that she believed would resolve the problem.

SESSIONS 18 & 19
BDI = 14 AND 15 RESPECTIVELY

Carrie's BDI scores had increased slightly while she continued to finish the dose of antibiotics and went to her job interview. She had been offered the job, but she was somewhat fearful of her ability to do the work. It was a larger company, and the job required computer skills that she was not fluent in. Her BDI scores reflected difficulty concentrating, appetite changes, and sleep problems due to her nervousness about starting the new job. She also worried about hurting her boss's feelings by quitting her current job.

Carrie had missed several sessions due to her illness and was only seen for 20 sessions. The therapist began to discuss relapse prevention with Carrie during sessions 18 and 19. He reviewed the ACTION and TRAP ideas with Carrie. Carrie thought that she was ready to complete therapy. She and her therapist discussed situations that could occur in which she would be vulnerable to avoidance and, thereby, more depression.

SESSION 20
BDI = 7

Carrie stated that she was glad that therapy was ending because she thought she would be very busy with her new job and needed extra time. Carrie was able to provide a summary of what had been helpful in treatment; she said that the main thing that had helped her was to learn to become active no matter what.

CARRIE: I know that I need to schedule things and just stick to the schedule, and I'll feel better, even when I am feeling lousy.
THERAPIST: So, activity charts have been helpful?
CARRIE: Yes, and recognizing when I avoid things. I know that I just need to keep facing things, because when I avoid them they just get worse.
THERAPIST: It isn't easy, though, is it?
CARRIE: No, and there may be times in the future when I don't do it.
THERAPIST: So, what could you do?
CARRIE: Well, probably get depressed, but not freak out about that either, and just go ahead and try even though the activity is hard.

Case Summary

Carrie was a challenging client to work with for several reasons: she had very difficult life situations; she made very little money on her job, although she worked many hours; and she had a relationship that was undisclosed to family and friends which made her feel isolated. Carrie had not wanted to address this issue in therapy, so the therapist respected her wishes. Carrie also had a remarkably passive style. She fit the description of the type of client who has had much of her behavior maintained by a schedule of negative reinforcement. Most of her activity was done in order to escape or avoid negative consequences. Teaching her to be more proactive in order to increase the likelihood that her behavior could be positively reinforced was a primary goal of therapy.

PART III
Challenges and Future Directions

CHAPTER 9

Difficulties that May Arise in Behavioral Activation and Future Directions for Use of the Treatment

I N THIS CHAPTER WE WILL DISCUSS several problems that potentially arise within the context of conducting behavioral activation, particularly when dealing with suicidal clients. BA is not the right approach for all clients. Clinical experience suggests that clients who have a strong commitment to biological understandings of their depression or who search for the right insight in order to treat their problems are difficult to treat within a BA framework, unless they truly buy into the rationale. We will also discuss future directions for the use of BA, as a treatment on its own, or through reinstating it, in the current format, within other treatments.

CHALLENGES ARISING IN BEHAVIORAL ACTIVATION

No therapeutic technique provides a panacea for all clients or client problems. In the previous and current clinical trials in Jacobson's laboratory, BA has been shown to be an effective treatment for depression. However, that does not mean that there have not been nonresponders, people who have relapsed, or treatment failures. It would be tempting to begin to add other treatment components to the therapy in order to make it more effective. This may do the trick, but there are as of yet no data to suggest that cognitive techniques or other interpersonal strategies add to the efficacy of BA alone. The standard of care requires that therapists be willing to consider options and discuss options with their clients should treatment not be successful. Ethical therapists will not persist in a technique that does not alleviate a client's distress once there has been a sufficient trial of the technique. Furthermore, BA is not simply about technique — it provides tools for a caring therapist to utilize to the benefit of the client.

The Suicidal Client*

One of the most difficult and challenging situations for therapists working with depressed individuals is the possibility of suicide. BA therapists need to properly assess for suicidal ideation and intent and properly intervene if a client is expressing suicidal ideas or is imminently suicidal. The BA therapist is expected to follow the standard of care which involves assessing whether or not the client has a plan for committing suicide, the things that might deter the client from following through on such a plan, history of past suicidal behaviors, social support available to the client, and immanence of the client's intent to hurt her- or himself. The therapist should make sure that he or she is available to answer emergency calls from suicidal clients and must follow proper procedures according to the laws of the state in which he or she practices.

Linehan (1993, 1997) conducts a functional analysis of the suicidal behavior. In this approach, the therapist assesses triggers for the behavior of thinking about suicide, the setting in which the behavior occurs, the consequences of the behavior, and the function that it may have for the client. This functional analytic strategy used in dialectical behavior therapy is also consistent with BA and is a useful approach for the BA therapist when working with a client who is thinking about suicide. The treatment goals would then follow from the functional analysis. If the client can identify triggers to suicidal thinking and the setting in which it occurs, the therapist can help the client develop a plan to avoid these settings. If the consequences of the behavior are desirable for the client, then the therapist can help the client to develop alternative behaviors to suicidal thinking and planning that can achieve similar consequences.

For many people, suicide is seen as a method to solve problems. Because they have limited repertoires for dealing with the difficulties of life, ending life altogether may be an attractive option for them. Since

---

*Detailing all of the precautions needed for competent work with suicidal clients is beyond the scope of this manuscript. Readers are referred to two excellent resources on this topic: Bonger (1992), which deals with all aspects of the topic of suicide; and Linehan (1993), which presents important information for working with chronically suicidal clients.

hopelessness is highly correlated with suicidal gestures (Beck, Resnick, & Lettieri, 1986), it is important for BA therapists to assess the hopeless cognitions of their clients. From a BA point of view, increasing hopefulness comes from helping clients to engage in behaviors that optimize the potential for positive reinforcement. The BA therapist helps the client to develop plans that undercut the hopelessness, and he or she would also help the client look at what their goals had been. If the goal had been to have more love in life, the therapist would then ask the client to assess whether being dead would be consistent with that goal or would be avoidance. The client and therapist would then develop some type of action plan, taking care to be sensitive to the client's despair and belief that nothing will work. If the client can be encouraged to experiment, and the action plan can be set to consist of small units of behavior (e.g., say "How is your day?" to a check-out clerk and observe the response), there will be more chance of the client having a successful experience.

Cognitive therapists deal with suicidal thinking in a variety of ways. One way is to have clients list all of the reasons they can think of for living, list all of the reasons they can think of for dying, and then write a rebuttal to the latter (Ellis & Newman, 1996). The first tactic of having the client list all of the reasons to live is consistent with the BA model. The second component would be a truly cognitive intervention and would be an addition to BA. However, in the case of suicide, the most important work is the work that saves the client, not the work that is true to a particular model. Linehan (1993) also questions clients' beliefs about suicide alleviating suffering. This, again, would be a cognitive intervention. In our laboratory, we have tried to develop a protocol that is consistent with the BA model. Again, a warning to therapists is necessary; no adherence to a treatment protocol is worth the risk of losing a client to suicide! Therapists ultimately may not be able to prevent a client from making such a choice, but the therapist should do everything in their power to provide alternatives to the client.

It is the provision of alternatives that is the mainstay of the BA approach to suicidal behavior. The client is not only asked to list as many reasons for living as they can possibly think of, but the therapist works with the client to develop a plan for dealing with problems instead of suicide. Suicidal clients usually cannot list many reasons to live. It may be necessary to make detailed and simple suggestions. Examples could be:

- Holding my cat
- Watching a sunset

- Feeling warm water on my face in the shower
- Reading a good book

Some clients may come up with idiosyncratic ideas that can be capitalized on. An example of this would be a client who said that they could wait for Stevie Nicks to record another solo album, and that would be worth living for.

Clients also need alternative methods for solving their problems. Hopefully, throughout the course of BA therapy, the client will become proactive in facing problems and breaking avoidance patterns, and this should strengthen the client's ability to engage in alternatives to suicide. Also, the TRAP model can give the client a template for considering suicide another avoidance-pattern and set the stage for finding alternate-coping behaviors. The therapist may need to be very directive and suggest alternatives for a client who is in such despair that the only viable option seems to be death.

Using the TRAP model the therapist should discuss with the client their triggers for suicidal feelings and thoughts. First, find out if a significant event has occurred in the client's life that has increased a sense of hopelessness. If so, debrief the event with the client. Encourage the client to talk about his or her feelings about the event. It is often useful to validate the despair of the client, offering hopeful statements. For example, the following dialogue deals with the suicidal thinking of a client who has just terminated a long-term relationship.

CLIENT: I have been so depressed for so long, just waiting for the other shoe to drop — bang, here it is. I don't know how to cope with this. At least I had Jon in my life. Now I have nothing. Life just isn't worth it.

THERAPIST: This has been a really hard blow, hasn't it? It *does* seem like it is yet one more thing. Understandably you are sad and confused by all of this. Remember when you thought that there was no way to deal with your boss threatening to fire you for making one mistake at work? We talked about ways to face him. Could we talk about ways to face this?

CLIENT: I can't face this. He was all I had.

THERAPIST: It sounds to me like the breakup is a trigger for you to really sink into despair, and you just want to get rid of this pain. Who wouldn't? This looks like another avoidance pattern though, just wanting to end your life. It looks to me as if you have stopped taking action and just want to escape.

CLIENT: Why shouldn't I? Everything goes wrong. I was trying so hard.
THERAPIST: Yes, you have been trying very hard, and this is a set back. I'd like us to talk about ways that you can cope with this even when you feel as terrible as you do. Most people feel terrible about ending relationships, especially when it was not their choice. Let's talk about the choices you do have. Suicide is one, can we talk about the others?
CLIENT: I can't see any others.
THERAPIST: I know you can't. Can I help you? Will you work with me on this?
CLIENT: I guess I'll try.

The therapist does not question the client's feelings but encourages action despite the powerfully negative feelings the client is experiencing. It must be done with great care and understanding, however. BA should never become an "oh, just get over it" therapy, especially when a client's life is on the line.

The therapist should work out an agreement with the client not to commit suicide. "No suicide contracts" are not guaranteed to help, but it is a good idea to have an explicit verbal agreement with the client that he or she will work toward behaviors that do not include suicide or other self-harm while in therapy (Linehan, 1993). However, the client must be set up with other resources. Therapists walk an especially wobbly tightrope in these situations. Responding to crisis calls may reinforce the crisis behavior, but rejecting the suicidal client may increase the degree of hopelessness.

The therapist may use the following techniques to help the suicidal client find alternatives to death as a way of escape.

- Say to the client, "Yes, that [suicide] is a choice you can make but what are some other choices you can make?" The therapist can then work with the client to develop a list of all of the reasons for living.
- Ask the client, "What are you gaining from engaging in this kind of thinking?" The therapist would then examine antecedents and consequences to suicidal thinking with the client.
- Instruct the client not to commit suicide.
- Encourage the client by saying, "While you are alive there is a second chance, and we can capitalize on this opportunity."

No matter what type of therapy a therapist provides, the suicidal client's life is of utmost importance. There is no other situation in therapy where the pragmatic truth criterion makes more sense. In other words, the right thing to do when a client is suicidal is whatever works to keep him or her safe. Strict rules or protocols for specific therapy techniques are less important than finding the strategy that will help a client to choose to continue trying to make things better for him- or herself. Therapists may question their own values about preventing suicide, but such questioning must take place outside of the therapy session, and our current standard of care requires us to prevent a successful suicide or a damaging suicide attempt.

BA and Medication

In the first part of this book, we critiqued the circular reasoning of biological psychiatry in searching for biochemical causes of depression. We also noted that the research on efficacy of antidepressant medications is far from convincing that they are always safe. Nevertheless, there are data that show that antidepressant medications used for limited periods of time, with certain clients, can be highly effective. There is nothing inconsistent with using BA in conjunction with medications, but the therapist will need to pay special attention to helping the client to persist in activities regardless of mood changes. Although taking a pill may improve the client's mood to some degree, it is not a permanent solution and clients may still face difficult life contexts that require active coping approaches. Medication may be even less helpful if it is not accompanied by increased activation and approach rather than avoidance on a client's part. If the medication helps to facilitate reactivation and engagement in life, that's a positive outcome. If, on the other hand, the medication inhibits clients from taking an active stance, then it is an obstacle. This is likely to happen when clients believe that depression is a biological process that is out of their control simply because medications are helpful. This raises, of course, the importance of developing an integrated treatment rationale that supports the use of medication without undermining the goals of BA. Thus, we suggest that therapists combining BA and pharmacotherapy discuss with clients how medication may assist in helping clients to become activated and reengage in active problem solving. Therapists should avoid suggesting that medication is remedying a biological deficit that is the primary cause of depressed behavior. It may even be useful to discuss with some clients the reciprocal interactions between biochemistry, behavior, and environment.

There is an inherent tension between the BA model and the use of psychotropic medications. Medication suggests illness, which suggests that there is something wrong inside the person — this is antithetical to the BA position that the person needs to be viewed in the entire context of life. Another way of seeing medication is as an environmental manipulation that changes the internal context in a fashion that has been shown to have antidepressant effects for some people. It is not necessary to understand depression as resulting from a deficiency or dysregulation of neurotransmitters, rather these can be seen as biological markers and antidepressant medication can be used as one more part of the arsenal to assist clients in getting activated. If taking medication suggests to clients that they have some sort of internal illness, then medication may work against the goals of BA. If, on the other hand, medication is seen as an asset in assuming an active approach to life, and the latter is understood as the primary change mechanism, then medication may help to facilitate change in BA. In BA it is essential to keep the focus on change despite internal states. Therefore, if taking medication suggests to clients that they are incapable of changing behavior until their serotonin levels increase, taking medication is not facilitating BA. A careful discussion with clients about how medication can facilitate action may ameliorate this dilemma.

At this time there is no clear protocol for BA therapists regarding referral for medication. BA has been used as a treatment in comparison to CT and Paxil. In our laboratory, no clients treated with BA have taken antidepressant medications. Therefore the following suggestions are speculative and tentative. We believe that it is important that clients understand and buy into the model, as we have said earlier. Should a client state that he or she thinks his or her depression may be caused by a chemical imbalance and wishes to have a referral for medication, the BA therapist should respect the client's request but suggest an alternative understanding. We could foresee a dialogue like the following.

CLIENT: I wonder whether some type of medication may help me. My depression feels like it's medical, like it is caused by a chemical imbalance.

THERAPIST: For many people, depression does seem almost biological. We know that there is a good deal of research to show that there may be changes in certain chemicals in the body when people become depressed. We think that it is possible that the chemicals in our bodies change when we think and act differently. If I move my arm up and down, there is electrical and chemical activity in my brain. So, if our approach doesn't work, you think your depression is biological?

CLIENT: Well, I don't know. If I could just feel better, I think that I'd be better off.

THERAPIST: Some, although not all, people do feel better when they take medication. I see no problem with you trying that, but taking medication is just one way of getting yourself activated. I'd like to continue to work on other things as well. We want to get you engaged in your life again, no matter how you feel.

CLIENT: But some people say that medication changed their lives. I don't think that I can get engaged without some kind of help. I'm desperate.

THERAPIST: I can understand how much you want to feel better. I think that is fair. I'd also like to help you live in a way that can prevent you from becoming depressed in the future. Medication may bring some relief, and by all means I'll support you in getting some relief from your distress, but immediate relief from distress is only part of the goal. Changing the patterns and ways of coping that keep you stuck might provide a longer lasting change. Are you willing to do both? We'll work from the outside in, and you can take the medication to see if it gives you a little boost along the way.

There would be no need to try to convince clients that they don't need medication or to make promises that BA alone will be just as good. It has been our experience that many clients are not interested in taking medication, and these clients are ideally suited for psychosocial treatments. However, although the data are not unequivocal, the combination of medication and therapy may be indicated for many depressed clients. BA therapists should not become obstructionist in order to be true to some kind of behavioral party line.

COMBINING BA WITH OTHER FUNCTIONAL APPROACHES

In earlier chapters, we emphasized the impact of Charles Ferster's work on the development of the BA model of depression. Ferster was also concerned with the process of psychotherapy and tried to apply functional analysis to the therapy encounter. We have not highlighted that aspect of his work in our present manuscript. The significance of Ferster's analysis of the therapeutic encounter has been emphasized by other clinicians. Kohlenberg and Tsai (1991) have recognized Ferster's emphasis on the performance of the therapist and client in the psychotherapeutic environment. They developed functional analytic psychotherapy (FAP) as a treatment that allows the therapist to attend to in-session behaviors and the therapeutic relationship as the primary treatment focus. Ferster (1981) emphasized three aspects of the process of therapy:

(1) the behavioral changes occurring in the context of the session; (2) the client and therapists' verbal descriptions of their immediate interactions; and (3) the way that these discussions and descriptions enhance observation on the part of the client elsewhere. In FAP, the therapeutic relationship is seen as the major focus and the catalyst for change. The therapist looks for in-session behaviors that may be examples of problems that the client experiences in other contexts, especially relationships in her or his life. The therapist then tries to reinforce any changes in this behavior that occur during the session.

FAP requires therapists to be keenly aware of the impact that the client has upon them during the therapy hour. They consider the possibility that others are responding to the client in the same manner (becoming irritated, bored, anxious) as they are. The FAP therapist highlights his or her own feelings toward the client, particularly the positive feelings that occur when a client engages in a behavior that has been a target of change. For example, a client, who is very unassertive and compliant to the point that it is disruptive in his life, may come in eight minutes late for a session and say, "I know I'm late, but I had to make sure I got a bite to eat on my way or I would have been distracted throughout the session, sorry." The therapist, believing this to be a positive change for the client to be so direct, may say something like: "I am pleased that you took the time to take care of yourself, and that you trust our relationship enough to risk being a few minutes late. Do you think this is different from the way you usually engage with people in authority?"

In BA, the therapeutic relationship is seen as an important aspect of treatment as well. The therapist with a strong connection to the client will find it much easier to coach the client to conduct difficult tasks than the therapist whom the client dislikes or feels disengaged from. However, BA does not emphasize the therapeutic relationship in the way that it is emphasized in FAP. As the use of activation strategies alone in the treatment of depression takes greater hold in the therapeutic community, a combination with FAP may result in a stronger contextual treatment. The activation would take place in the session, and the therapist would attend to his or her reactions to the client to point out clinically relevant behaviors (Kohlenberg & Tsai, 1991) that may affect clients in their lives outside of therapy. In essence, a combination of FAP and BA would simply bring more of the therapeutic work into the session as well as in the homework assigned. The therapist would serve a more intimate role with the client. Currently research is being done in Kohlenberg's lab to evaluate the use of combining FAP with a standard CT protocol for depression. A similar combination of FAP and BA may be looked at in the future, especially for clients who have multiple psychological problems or Axis II characteristics as well as major depressive disorder.

BA also shares some of the characteristics of acceptance and commitment therapy (Hayes et al., 1999), another functional approach that has been mentioned earlier. The primary similarity that BA shares with ACT is that in BA the therapist coaches clients to work toward goals and change behavior despite how the client feels. Both approaches try to break the dependence on mood. ACT differs from BA in its assumption of the necessity to break the context of literality before acting independent of mood. In BA that assumption is not made and it is assumed that some people can proceed to change behavior directly, without needing to break the literality of verbal behavior. An integration of BA with ACT may prove helpful if BA is not effective because the client cannot seem to give up the need for reason giving and insight or the need for changing thinking and private things before changing overt behavior.

GIVING BA GREATER EMPHASIS DURING COGNITIVE THERAPY

Behavioral activation has always been a part of cognitive therapy. Many of the studies to which we referred in this book suggest that the activation or behavioral components of cognitive therapy may be sufficient treatments on their own. The research does not indicate that behavioral activation is *the* active component of CT, however, and this is a topic for further study. It is also not clear what makes BA or CT effective. Are CT therapists successful because clients are becoming engaged in antidepressant activities? Are BA therapists successful because engaging in new behaviors modifies the client's belief about self and others or increases hopefulness? These questions also are yet to be answered. It is our contention, however, that the behavioral components of cognitive therapy should truly be given their due.

For many therapists who came to cognitive-behavioral therapies from other theoretical orientations, the behavioral "stuff" is often seen as a necessary precursor to "real therapy." Modifying core beliefs and looking at what schemas are activated in different situations is the more attractive form of therapy. It is a belief that some therapy is focused on symptomatic improvement only while other therapy changes "deep" structures that makes behavioral treatment less appealing to some. Hopefully, we have begun to convince a few, or to challenge others to see that deep and lasting change is happening all of the time in the lives of our clients. They are continually shaped by the contexts of their lives, as are we as therapists. By helping clients to modify the context, to reengage in their lives, and to activate themselves rather than passively walk through life avoiding aversive experiences, we can help clients to make lasting change. Rather than going "deeply" into clients' minds, we try to move "broadly" with them through their life situations.

We are not suggesting that therapists do away with cognitive interventions. There are several ways that BA can be used in cognitive therapy, even as it is developed in this manual. The traditional use of behavioral activation in cognitive therapy is to use it first to activate a client, but primarily to change the client's beliefs. Beck and colleagues (1979) recommend assigning behavioral experiments to encourage clients to test their beliefs. Even if one wishes to continue to practice cognitive therapy as one's primary intervention, utilizing the BA ideas about avoidance patterns and the need for approach behaviors may enhance client compliance with behavioral assignments or make behavioral assignments more effective. This would mean that BA is added to CT or to other therapies because it works in a technically eclectic way. A third way that BA could be added to CT is from a philosophical perspective. The contextualist philosophy could be added to CT, and in this fashion changing a client's thinking would be seen as another way to shift the context and to increase the likelihood of the client contacting positive reinforcers in his or her environment.

In many cases, however, BA is sufficient and clients will be treated efficiently and with a therapy that allows them to break patterns of behavior that exacerbate their vulnerability to depressive episodes. Clients seem to appreciate the validation that comes from the therapist agreeing that sometimes the situations of life are troublesome, rather than search for evidence that the client is overreacting. We encourage cognitive therapists to look at the context of their clients' lives. Helping clients to change avoidant behaviors may, in fact, lead to cognitive change. Foa and Kozak (1997) suggest this in the treatment of obsessive-compulsive disorders. BA does not undo a cognitive-behavioral understanding of behavior change and emotion regulation, although there is no emphasis on a necessary cognitive precursor to emotion. Clients do indeed interpret their experiences in idiosyncratic ways. We would expect nothing else given the varied learning histories from which our clients come. However, our analysis suggests that it is, in fact, the life of depressed people, and not only their interpretations, that precede or maintain depression.

BA provides a functional analytic alternative for therapists and clients. However, competent cognitive therapists can practice BA in its complete form if they can begin to think of the function of their clients' thinking and acting and attend to the active change ingredients of BA. The components have always been a part of the therapy. Our hope is that therapists will embrace a focus on working with clients to evaluate the function of their behaviors (including private events like thinking) and through that functional analysis to develop action plans that will help clients to engage, face their lives, and solve problems that may seem insurmountable. We think that some clients may then begin to look at their lives and their abilities differently. It is the experience of new behavior that is important. If an entire treatment focuses on activation, without any access to cognition or modification of beliefs, then that treatment has been good BA, and there may be no need for further treatment. Behavioral activation should not be relegated to use only when clients are "not ready" for cognitive therapy. We await further research to demonstrate the types of clients for which BA alone may be ideally suited as a complete treatment and which clients may benefit from a standard cognitive approach.

SUGGESTIONS FOR FUTURE RESEARCH

There has been much interest in matching treatments to clients, and there have been some promising results that suggest that it is viable, but there is no convincing data available with respect to BA at this time. Empirical data from large group samples often cannot provide specific information about which clients do best with which therapies. BA may be most suitable for clients who are not engaged in important activities, but who recognize this as a problem that can be solved. For clients that want to talk more about their feelings or ideas, cognitive therapy may prove to be a treatment of choice. However, it is difficult to know whether or not the client's ideas about what he or she wants regarding therapy is the best predictor of therapy success. It is possible that a therapy that is initially rejected by a client is the very therapy that the client needs. It would be helpful for future research to evaluate the results of getting people involved in a treatment that might be right for them even if they disagree with the premise of the treatment. Addis and Carpenter (2000) provide a good discussion of this issue.

We have already talked about situations when couple therapy may be the appropriate treatment, and for some individuals a more interpersonal approach, or FAP, might help to improve social relationships that could, in the long run, protect the individual from future relapse. This is all speculative, however, in the absence of data. Overall, BA looks to be as effective as cognitive therapy and Paxil. These data are not yet complete, but the earlier component analysis study of Jacobson, Dobson, and colleagues (1996) provided preliminary results that BA is at least as effective as cognitive therapy.

Treatment outcome studies also measure treatment success with standardized inventories and interviews that focus on the identified diagnosis and may not take other variables into account. This seems particularly true with BA. A client may continue to score in the depressed range on measures of depression, but he or she might have developed a greater level of acceptance and may have made attempts to activate despite the depression. Outcome measures would designate such a client as a treatment failure, but the benefits of the therapy may go unseen. Future research that examines a variety of factors including remission of the identified problem as defined by *DSM-IV*, improvement in social functioning, ability to activate or engage in purposeful activity regardless of change in depression ratings, and improved ability to use techniques learned in therapy to cope and prevent the depression from worsening may also be useful measures of outcome. BA may be an effective treatment and useful for clients to develop an approach to life that allows them to cope in spite of very negative feelings. Should a client truly work from the "outside-in," she may be able to function well in life, even though she feels depressed, and hopefully, over time, as she is reinforced for activating and becomes more engaged in life, her depression will lift. Long-term follow-up of this nature is yet to be done.

CHAPTER 10

Conclusion

W E HAVE PROVIDED AN OVERVIEW of behavioral activation as a complete treatment for depression. Research to date suggests that BA is a useful treatment for depression. It is hoped that researchers from other clinical settings will also evaluate the efficacy of BA and attempt to replicate findings. This chapter reviews the main ideas that have been presented regarding BA.

BEHAVIORAL ACTIVATION WAS DEVELOPED FROM EMPIRICAL FINDINGS

Lewinsohn and colleagues (1984) have used BA as a treatment in its own right in the past, but the treatment also included other elements besides activating clients. The current presentation of BA developed from a component analysis study of cognitive therapy, with behavioral activation being one condition of three. When BA alone was found to be equally efficacious in treating depression as an entire cognitive therapy protocol (Jacobson, Dobson, et al., 1996), further investigations into behavioral activation as a solo treatment for depression were begun.

Although research demonstrated that BA worked in treating depression, the behavior analytic theory that provides an explanation for how BA works was to be found in the writings of Ferster (1973) and Skinner (1957). Lewinsohn (1974) also took a behavioral understanding and developed a treatment based on Ferster's theories regarding depression and low rates of positive reinforcement. Depression is understood to develop as a response to a decrease in or low levels of positive reinforcement or from a chronic history of negative reinforcement and noncontingent punishment. When people experience major life changes, or live with chronic stressors, their bodies respond in a way that has come to be associated with the symptoms of depression. The means by which depressed clients try to cope with dysphoria and other negative symptoms of depression become secondary problems that exacerbate the problem. These secondary problem behaviors prevent the individual from active problem solving and perpetuate escape and avoidance behaviors. When escape and avoidance are the primary functions of the person's behavior, his or her repertoire of responses becomes very narrow. The individual may experience life as very limited, not finding pleasure in activities, and act as if there are no options for finding a way out of the vicious cycle.

BEHAVIORAL ACTIVATION DOES NOT FOLLOW THE MEDICAL MODEL OF DEPRESSION

Popular notions about depression follow a medical model and represent depression as a medical illness. This definition of depression is problematic because it narrowly focuses on biological aspects of depression that are certainly a part of the problem, but cannot adequately explain all of the complex factors that come into play when a person is depressed. We have argued that the relative success of psychotropic medications in treating depression led to assumptions that depression was caused by dysregulation of neurotransmitters. The data have not been consistent in showing that there are significant differences in the brains of so-called normals and in people with behavioral disorders (Valenstein, 1998).

There is also a tendency in western culture to blame individuals whose behavior cannot be attributed to some natural cause. If depression is "caused" by factors other than biological vulnerability, then the individual herself might be held responsible for her problems. The culture of blame encourages people to look for causes of behavior that are outside of their control. This is the pseudoscientific equivalent of "the devil made me do it."

From the perspective on which BA is based, combinations of biological vulnerability, individual learning histories, and life events occasion the onset of depressive symptoms. People behave in characteristic ways to low levels of reinforcement. There may be changes in levels of various neurotransmitters that are part of this process, and medication may help to alleviate some of the symptoms of depression. However, considering depression an illness, rather than a behavioral problem, does little to advance treatments or to understand human behavior.

BEHAVIORAL ACTIVATION IS A
GOAL-FOCUSED, STRUCTURED YET
IDIOGRAPHIC TREATMENT

Although the times suggest an interest in greater and greater structure of therapies, and manuals that tell therapists what to do from session to session, we believe that BA provides a structured therapy that can still be modified for each client. Because we make use of the functional analysis, the treatment may look somewhat different from person to person. Certainly the main elements should be there. Sessions should be structured so that good work is accomplished in 45–50 minutes. The therapist should focus on the client's behavior. Agendas should be set, feedback obtained, and homework assigned and followed up on. Not all clients will be easily focused (as our case examples demonstrate), but with the ingredients of acting rather than feeling, coping rather than avoiding, and being proactive rather than reactive, the therapy can be applied to clients who have differing styles of interpersonal engagement. Because the goal is activation, not cognitive change or disputation, the therapist is, in fact, freer to move with the client as long as there is ultimately a plan for the client to monitor a behavior to observe its function or to change a behavior. Within the structure there is freedom.

The overall goals of BA are to help clients monitor the effects of their behavior in different situations and choose to activate themselves. If major life events have disrupted a routine, the therapist works with the client to reestablish the routine. In cases when clients have never established a good routine and seem to react to life, the therapist helps the client to schedule events in a more ordered fashion. Another important goal of BA is to teach clients to face rather than avoid situations that cause distress. In this way, BA is similar to behavioral treatments of anxiety disorders. In working with clients to act according to a plan rather than a mood or feeling, BA is also similar to other acceptance-based treatments that encourage clients to act in spite of feelings (e.g., Hayes et al., 1999).

Using a functional analysis, the therapist will work with the client to understand the antecedents and consequences to behavior. The client is taught to act toward a goal when trying to change behavior. If the behavior change brings a client closer to a desired goal, then the behavior is likely to be positively reinforced. However, clients are also taught that they can work like a scientist, experimenting with new behaviors and evaluating the outcome. If a client is not making strides toward a goal, no matter how small, then the client is encouraged to try different behaviors and not decide what is the right course of action until observing the results.

BEHAVIORAL ACTIVATION IS A
CONTEXTUAL THERAPY

The theories and techniques that have gone into the development of BA have been around for some time. The work that had been done in the 1970s and 1980s with activity logs and increasing pleasant events by Lewinsohn and his colleagues has been combined with the ideas regarding avoidance behaviors seen in depression presented by Ferster. This is considered a unique contribution of the current BA model in the treatment of depression. The best philosophical model under which this system operates is that of Pepper's 1942 notion of contextualism. Although there are mechanistic elements, certain skills are trained when necessary, the central focus of BA is indeed on context. Context is defined as all that occurs "within" the person, the private events experienced by the person, his or her genetic makeup and vulnerabilities, biological factors, and the external environment. Activating clients in a structured fashion enables them to interact with their external environments in ways that increase the likelihood of positively reinforced behaviors. If their mood improves, or if they get a job done that they needed to get done, we would say that the reinforcement contingencies are working in their favor. From the perspective of contextualism, where the criteria for "truth" is the practical, (i.e., what works) we would say we have met the goal.

Because the therapy is contextual, BA therapists teach clients to look at their depression in the full context of their lives. Rather than believing that the client has an illness, BA therapists look to the life of the client to find antecedents to the depression. In this way BA keeps both therapist and client focused on context rather than only at cognitive or psychological factors in the development and maintenance of depression. This is not a new concept, nor is it unique from cognitive-behavior therapy at large. Perhaps where it differs is in the degree to which clients' life contexts are examined and taken as critical elements in the maintenance of depression. However, the emphasis on activation has been demonstrated to be a sufficient treatment and our insistence that therapists coach clients to be active and therefore increase opportunities for positive reinforcement has produced consistent antidepressant effects.

The history of the individual is an important aspect of the context. People behave in certain ways in one context because they have behaved similarly in similar contexts in times past. The history is always a part of the present context, as well as current life circumstances. Thus there are transactions between the individual and the environment that continue to shift the context that occasion certain behaviors and consequences.

The BA therapist attempts to capitalize on this by working with the client to become more and more engaged in action that will increase the possibility of shifting environmental circumstances. There is an attempt at expanding the client's behavioral repertoire so that she will behave in a fashion whereby her behavior will be positively reinforced and the repertoire will continue to expand, resulting in a greater likelihood of attaining life goals and finding satisfaction.

BEHAVIORAL ACTIVATION PRIMARILY FOCUSES ON AVOIDANCE PATTERNS AS TREATMENT TARGETS

Although it has always been seen as a process involved in the anxiety disorders, escape and avoidance behaviors have not been thoroughly evaluated in the treatment of depression. Holahan, Moos, and Bonin (1999) have demonstrated that clients who use an avoidant coping strategy tend to be more vulnerable to depression than those who use a more active problem-solving approach (see also Holahan & Moos, 1987). BA targets avoidance as a primary problem to combat in therapy.

The BA therapist tries to teach clients a new strategy for approaching problems in living by using the acronym ACTION to teach clients to monitor their avoidant behavior and evaluate outcomes of integrating new behaviors into their repertoire. The use of the idea of a TRAP, in which the client looks for the triggers to a particular depressive response and the resulting avoidance pattern, also focuses clients on their avoidant behavior and encourages them to practice alternative coping strategies to get back on TRAC(k). Targeting avoidance is a method for breaking the control of behavior via a negative reinforcement schedule. Clients may also feel more in control of their lives when they actively respond to the various changes and challenges in their lives.

BEHAVIORAL ACTIVATION THERAPISTS ASSUME VARIABILITY RATHER THAN STABILITY IN CLIENT BEHAVIOR

Unlike therapeutic ideas that search for underlying, stable causes of behavior, the BA therapist assumes variability of behavior. People behave in one way in certain contexts, then behave in dissimilar ways in a different context. The person is seen as an historical act, rather than as having fixed schemata or personality characteristics that exist apart from the overall context of behavior. For the BA therapist, then, when a client says that they are incompetent, for example, the question would be, "When are you competent?" "Under what circumstances have you noticed that you behaved incompetently?" "What has been different during times when you think that you behaved in a somewhat competent manner?" The therapist would ask about contingencies and behavioral variables rather than assuming that the client maintained a stable idea about him or herself.

In BA the client's report of a certain experience is also taken at face value. The example of a client saying "I'm incompetent" would suggest to the BA therapist that the client was reporting a "fact" based on his or her personal history. However, the statement would not be taken as indicative of a personality variable but as an accurate accounting of some experience. The therapist then would assist the client to look for ways to become competent. Using a functional analysis, the therapist would also want to try to ascertain the function of the client's statement. When a client says "I'm incompetent," she may want reassurance from the therapist. The therapist would not want to reinforce such a roundabout request and should be aware that even client statements have a function, and clients need to be directed to use appropriate behaviors to achieve desired goals. If the goal is actually to be reassured, the client can be encouraged to ask a direct question of the therapist, rather than making a statement that serves as a hidden request. Finding such functional relationships is not an easy task, and the therapist and client must collaborate to try to hypothesize about the function of a variety of client behaviors without getting bogged down in looking for "hidden meanings" in all client statements.

BEHAVIORAL ACTIVATION MAY BE USED ALONE OR IN COMBINATION WITH OTHER TREATMENTS

Although the current research being conducted on behavioral activation suggests that it is a sufficient treatment for depression, there is no set requirement that it be used alone. BA has always been a part of cognitive therapy. In cognitive therapy, it has been used in order to both activate very depressed clients and to help clients to change beliefs and assumptions. Using the functional analysis as part of cognitive therapy can aid cognitive therapists in developing better behavioral experiments (Beck et al., 1979) for clients to test beliefs. The theoretical interpretation of what is occurring may be different in cognitive therapy than in BA alone. In BA, thoughts are not recognized as mediators of behavior. Thoughts and emotions may serve as establishing operations (Michael, 1993; Dougher & Hackbert, 2000) that make certain things reinforcing to the client, but they are not considered necessary for behavior change. In cognitive therapy, the goal would be to change thinking.

BA can also be used with clients who are on medication for depression, but the therapist needs to be careful to help the client continue to work from a contextual perspective, looking at commitment to action rather than waiting for an internal change to stimulate action. For some clients, BA can be combined with conjoint therapy with a significant other. If some form of behavioral couple therapy is involved, there would be consistency in philosophy since behavioral approaches to couple therapy are contextual (Addis & Jacobson, 1991).

BEHAVIORAL ACTIVATION IS ONE OF SEVERAL NEW TREATMENTS THAT FOCUS ON CONTEXT

BA is not unique to treatments that take a contextual approach to therapy. It is a new addition to the group of contextual approaches that are slowly gaining empirical support. Contextual treatments such as acceptance and commitment therapy (Hayes et al., 1999) and functional analytic psychotherapy (Kohlenberg & Tsai, 1991) are broad based treatments that can be used to treat a variety of client problems. The understanding of context is somewhat different in each of these approaches, as is the target of treatment. This makes perfect sense from a contextualist perspective. Differing histories of different researchers and clinicians will lead to different ways of looking at a problem and will lead to a variety of attempts at solutions. Whereas BA targets activity as the treatment goal, ACT focuses more on freeing clients from the literality of verbal behavior (Wilson & Hayes, 2000) and FAP uses the relationship between therapist and client as the primary means of modifying clinically relevant behaviors.

Dialetical behavior therapy (Linehan, 1993) can also be considered one of the contextual therapies in the treatment of borderline personality disorder. The DBT approach to treatment is also being expanded for use in the treatment of other disorders. Approaches like cognitive therapy have not ignored context completely, but there has been an emphasis on what goes on in the mind of the individual. Some of the constructivist approaches to cognitive therapy (Neimeyer & Mahoney, 1995) have similarities to contextual approaches, although there are subtle differences, and a continued emphasis on the interpretation of experience rather than on behavior in context.

Jacobson referred to the contextualist approach as a "third wave" in psychology. Third in that it was a movement following the evolution of behavior therapy to cognitive-behavior therapy, and now contextualism and a resurgence of functional approaches to psychotherapy. BA therapists function within this new wave of treatment approaches. The future of BA and other contextual approaches relies on continued empirical support.

In the science of psychology, it is good when history repeats itself. Out of the building blocks gathered by many great thinkers, BA has developed, like a small cottage where many find the tools to cope with depression and begin, once more, to live active lives. BA, like other psychological ideas, will hopefully grow and change. There may be incorporations into other contextual approaches or updates on the BA treatment. The initial success of the treatment has been a hopeful sign to those of us who have conducted this therapy with depressed clients. What once looked like withholding treatment (i.e., cognitive therapy) in order to focus only on behavioral techniques has now become a well-articulated, and complete treatment for people suffering from major depressive disorder. So far, it works, and in the context in which BA has been studied and implemented, that is the criterion that matters.

Appendices

Sample Activity Chart

Below is an example of an activity chart used in behavioral activation. Therapists or clients can make charts of their own of any size and therapists can request that clients monitor a variety of behaviors.

What were you doing? How were you feeling? (Note: Feelings such as mad, sad, glad, scared) Who were you with? Rate the intensity of feeling on a 1–10 scale.							
	Sun.	Mon.	Tues.	Wed.	Thurs.	Fri.	Sat.
12:00 a.m.							
1:00 a.m.							
2:00 a.m.							
3:00 a.m.							
4:00 a.m.							
5:00 a.m.							
6:00 a.m.							
7:00 a.m.							
8:00 a.m.							
9:00 a.m.	Shower, calm, 1						
10:00 a.m.	B'fast, sad, 5						
11:00 a.m.							
12:00 p.m.							

↓   ↓

Beginning Activation Therapy for Depression: A Self-Help Manual*

DEPRESSION IS A PROBLEM that can be a vicious cycle for many people. You may be experiencing depression for the first time or you may have had the experience for many years. Depression can feel like you have an illness. The symptoms of depression are: being slowed down mentally and physically, tiring easily, having feelings of guilt and self-blame, having the blues. As you feel more depressed you may do less and less and blame yourself for doing less. You may feel unmotivated or "lazy." As it becomes more difficult to do things, you become more and more depressed.

Although depression has been called the "common cold" of psychological problems, it is important to realize that your depression is not the result of some personal defect or mental illness process. Depression is often a signal that something needs to be changed in your life. Most people can recognize some incident or series of incidents that have triggered the onset of their depression. Common incidents concern the loss of a loved one, the loss of a dream, lack of achievement, daily struggles that seem insurmountable, or interpersonal difficulties. When people get depressed, rather than change the situations in their lives that may make them feel better, they tend to shut down and withdraw from the world. Gradually the depression worsens, and there are then not only situational problems but the depression itself has become a problem. It is at this point that many people enter therapy.

---

*This self-help manual is adapted from a manual used for the behavioral activation research condition in the Treatment for Depression study at the University of Washington, Center for Clinical Research. It has been changed to accommodate usage with nonresearch participants and follows the rationale as presented in this manuscript.

COPING WITH THE PROBLEM

Several different treatments for depression have been developed. One effective treatment is called behavioral activation. With your therapist you will work toward breaking the cycle of depression by engaging in activities that will lead to improved productivity and mood. You will not just engage in any activity, however. Your therapist will help you to identify the following things that may be related to your depression: actions in your life that you have stopped engaging in since you became depressed but wish to become involved in again; actions that you have taken to withdraw from the world and others around you; and the major situations in your life that you would like to change in order to live more productively. Your therapist will work with you to guide your activity toward specific goals that the two of you determine will help you to cope with your depression and begin to live a more satisfying life. It may not be possible to change situations in your life that led to your depression without first stopping the process of withdrawal and inactivity that you may have fallen into since you have begun to feel depressed. You can break the cycle of depression through guided activity.

Activity is more than "just doing it," as the saying goes. When people feel depressed, doing the kinds of things that will keep life moving and on track feels difficult, if not impossible. This is why it is good to have a coach or a guide in the person of your therapist. The activities that are meaningful to you and to your life are what are important. For example, one person may enjoy living in a clean environment, but feels too depressed to wash dishes. If he washes the dishes, despite how he feels, he may still feel blue or sad, but may have a very slight improvement in mood because his house is cleaner. Likewise, a woman who has a surly boss who makes unreasonable demands may withdraw and not assert her position with the boss. Asserting herself with her boss would be an activity that she would benefit from doing. Activities in behavioral activation are varied, and your therapist will help you to find the right activities that have a chance of helping to alleviate your depression or make you feel more in control of your life.

The advantages of becoming active in spite of feeling depressed are clear.

1. Guided activity can lead to improvement in mood. Activating yourself regardless of the depression can give you a sense of control in your life. You might find that some activities are enjoyable once you try them, even if you initially may think that nothing

brings any enjoyment. Even those activities that aren't pleasurable can give you a sense that you have achieved something worthwhile.

2. Guided activity can break the cycle of fatigue. Often when people are depressed they feel tired and fatigued. This can be a way of withdrawing from the world. Paradoxically, staying in bed and getting extra sleep often results in feeling more tired. Guided activity, even when you feel very fatigued, can make you feel more energized and refreshed. It can have the opposite effect when you are depressed than when you are fatigued for other reasons. For example, when you are depressed and feel fatigued, if you engage in an activity like housework, you may end up feeling good about the accomplishment and have more energy to do other activities. On the other hand, if you are not depressed, but have been working long hours and need to take a break and you do housework the activity may make you even more tired because your body is telling you that you need rest. When you are depressed, even though your body tells you that you need a rest, you need to activate.

3. Guided activity can lead to feeling motivated. Many people who are depressed believe that they "just need to become motivated" but the very symptoms of depression often block such motivation. Therefore, if the person waits to become motivated they wait in vain. Ironically, engaging in activity even when you feel unmotivated to do so can lead to feeling motivated. We call this working from the "outside-in." In other words, you don't wait to feel like doing something prior to doing it, you engage in an activity because you have committed to doing so.

Engaging in activity when you are depressed is not easy. It may be difficult for you to organize your time properly or to get involved in activities that you normally enjoy. Sometimes activity becomes so difficult when you are depressed that even the most basic things feel extremely hard. Your therapist understands this and will work with you to help you to recognize the things that get in the way of activating and help you to overcome those obstacles.

The treatment will help you to overcome problems in your life that inhibit your productive activity. You will learn how to monitor your life, to look at your daily activities like a rich tapestry. You will learn how certain feelings are connected to certain activities. You will learn how to increase activities that make you feel better. Activities oriented toward improving the quality of your life might make you feel less depressed either because they bring more enjoyment or because you simply feel more productive and in control. Your therapist will teach you how to plan activities, how to recognize traps that inhibit productive activity, and how to incorporate new activities into your daily routines so that they become new habits that lead to improvements in the quality of your life. Your therapist will instruct you in the use of daily schedules and activity charts that will help you in this process. You will be asked to continue the work begun in sessions during the week between therapy sessions. You and your therapist will agree on assignments that will aid in the process of becoming more active. Your therapist will be your coach. You may find that becoming activated as a way of coping with depression allows you to operate more effectively in the world and that your life will begin to feel like it is back on track. Taking the first step and coming to therapy has been your first guided activity. Further steps may be easier than you imagine.

References

Addis, M. E. (1997). Evaluating the treatment manual as a means of disseminating empirically validated psychotherapies. *Clinical Psychology: Science and Practice, 4*, 1–11.

Addis, M. E., & Carpenter, K. M. (2000). The treatment rationale in cognitive behavioral therapy: Psychological mechanisms and clinical guidelines. *Cognitive and Behavioral Practice, 7*(2), 147–156.

Addis, M. E., & Jacobson, N. S. (1991). Integration of cognitive therapy and behavioral marital therapy for depression. *Journal of Psychotherapy Integration, 1*(4), 249–264.

Addis, M. E., & Jacobson, N. S. (1996). Reasons for depression and outcome of cognitive-behavioral psychotherapies. *Journal of Consulting and Clinical Psychology, 64*(6), 1417–1424.

Agency for Health Care Policy and Research (1993). Depression is a treatable illness. *USDHS: Publication NO AHCPR 93-0553.*

American Psychiatric Association. (1994). *Diagnostic and statistical manual of mental disorders* (4th ed.). Washington, DC: Author.

Antonuccio, D. O., Danton, W. G., DeNelsky, G. Y., Greenberg, R. P., & Gordon, J. S. (1999). Raising questions about antidepressants. *Psychotherapy and Psychosomatics, 68*, 3–14.

Antonuccio, D. O., Thomas, M., & Danton, W. G. (1997). A cost-effectiveness analysis of cognitive behavior therapy and fluoxetine (prozac) in the treatment of depression. *Behavior Therapy, 28*, 187–210.

Bandura, A. (1969). *Principles of behavior modification.* New York: Holt, Rinehart & Winston.

Bandura, A. (1977). *Social learning theory.* Englewood Cliffs, NJ: Prentice-Hall.

Barlow, D. H. (1988). *Anxiety and its disorders: The nature and treatment of anxiety and panic.* New York: Guilford.

Baum, W. M. (1994). *Understanding behaviorism: Science, behavior, and culture.* New York: HarperCollins.

Beach, S. R. H., Fincham, F. D., & Katz, J. (1998). Marital therapy in the treatment of depression: Toward a third generation of therapy and research. *Clinical Psychology Review, 18*(6), 635–661.

Beck, A. T. (1976). *Cognitive therapy and the emotional disorders.* New York: New American Library.

Beck, A. T. (1983). Cognitive therapy of depression: New perspectives. In P. J. Clayton & J. E. Barrett (Eds.), *Treatment of depression: Old controversies and new approaches* (pp. 265–290). New York: Raven.

Beck, A. T., Emery G., & Greenberg, R. L. (1985). *Anxiety disorders: A cognitive perspective.* New York: Basic.

Beck, A. T., Resnick, H. L. P., & Lettieri, D. J. (1986). *The prediction of suicide.* Philadelphia: The Charles Press. (Originally published 1974)

Beck, A. T., Rush, A. J., Shaw, B. F., & Emory, G. (1979). *Cognitive therapy of depression.* New York: Guilford.

Beck, A. T., Ward, C. H., Mendelson, M., Mock, J. E., & Erbaugh, J. K. (1961). An inventory for measuring depression. *Archives of General Psychiatry, 4,* 561–571.

Beck, J. S. (1995). *Cognitive therapy basics and beyond.* New York: Guilford.

Biglan, A., & Dow, M. G. (1981). Toward a second-generation model: a problem-specific approach. In L. P. Rehm (Ed.), *Behavior therapy for depression: Present status and future directions* (pp. 97–121). New York: Academic.

Biglan, A., & Hayes, S. C. (1996). Should the behavioral sciences become more pragmatic? The case for functional contextualism in research on human behavior. *Applied and Preventive Psychology: Current Scientific Perspectives, 5,* 47–57.

Billings, A. G., & Moos, R. H. (1984). Coping, stress, and social resources among adults with unipolar depression. *Journal of Personality and Social Psychology, 46,* 877–891.

Blacker, D. (1996). Maintenance treatment of major depression: A review of the literature. *Harvard Review of Psychiatry, 4,* 1–9.

Brown, G., & Moran, P. (1994). Clinical and psychosocial origins of chronic depressive episodes: I. A community survey. *British Journal of Psychiatry, 165,* 447–456.

Bonger, B. (Ed.) (1992). *Suicide: Guidelines for assessment, management and treatment.* New York: Oxford University Press.

Cautela, J. R., & Wisocki, P. A. (1977). The thought-stopping procedure: Description, application, and learning theory interpretations. *Psychological Record, 1,* 255–264.

Chambless, D. L., Baker, M. J., Baucom, D. H., Beutler, L. E., Calhoun, K. S., Crits-Christoph, P., Daiuto, A., DeRubeis, R., Detweiler, J., Haaga, D. A. F., Johnson, S. B., McCurry, S., Mueser, K. T., Pope, K. S., Sanderson, W. C., Shoham, V., Stickle, T., Wiliams, D. A., & Woody, S. R. (1998). Update on empirically validated therapies, II. *The Clinical Psychologist, 51*(1), 3–16.

Chiesa, M. (1994). *Radical behaviorism: The philosophy and the science.* Boston: Authors Cooperative.

Christensen, A., & Jacobson, N. S. (1994). Who (or what) can do psychotherapy: The status and challenge of nonprofessional therapies. *Psychological Science, 5*(1), 8–14.

Clark, D. A., Beck, A. T., & Alford, B. A. (1999). *Scientific foundations of cognitive theory of depression.* New York: Wiley.

Cohen, S., & Wills, T. (1985). Stress, social support, and the buffering hypothesis. *Psychological Bulletin, 98,* 310–357.

Coyne, J. C. (1976). Toward an interactional description of depression. *Psychiatry, 39,* 28–40.

Coyne, J. C. (1999). Thinking interactionally about depression: a radical restatement. In T. Joiner & J. C. Coyne (Eds.), *The interactional nature of depression* (pp. 365–392). Washington, DC: American Psychological Association.

Dobson, K. S. (1989). A meta-analysis of the efficacy of cognitive therapy for depression. *Journal of Consulting and Clinical Psychology, 57,* 414–419.

Dobson, K. S., & Joffe, R. (1986). The role of activity level and cognition in depressed mood in a university sample. *Journal of Clinical Psychology, 42*(2), 264–271.

Dougher, M. J., & Hackbert, L. (2000). Establishing operations, cognition, and emotion. *The Behavior Analyst, 23,* 11–24.

D'Zurilla, T. J., & Goldfried, M. R. (1971). Problem solving and behavior modification. *Journal of Abnormal Psychology, 78,* 107–126.

D'Zurilla, T. J., & Nezu, A. (1982). Social problem solving in adults. In P. Kendall (Ed.), *Advances in cognitive-behavioral research and therapy, Volume 1* (pp. 201–274). New York: Academic.

Ehlers, C. L., Frank, E., & Kupfer, D. J. (1988). Social zeitgebers and biological rhythms: A unified approach to understanding the etiology of depression. *Archives of General Psychiatry, 45,* 948–952.

Ellis, T. E., & Newman, C. F. (1996). *Choosing to live: How to defeat suicide through cognitive therapy.* Oakland, CA: New Harbinger Publications, Inc.

Fein, S., Paz, V., Rao, N., & Lagrassa, J. (1988). The combination of lithium carbonate and an MAO in refractory depressions. *American Journal of Psychiatry, 145,* 249–250.

Ferster, C. B. (1973). A functional analysis of depression. *American Psychologist, 28,* 857–870.

Ferster, C. B. (1981). A functional analysis of behavior therapy. In L. P. Rehm (Ed.), *Behavior therapy for depression: Present status and future directions* (pp. 181–196). New York: Academic.

Ferster, C. B., & Skinner, B. F. (1957). *Schedules of reinforcement.* Englewood Cliffs, NJ: Prentice-Hall.

Foa, E. B., & Kozak, M. J. (1997). Beyond the efficacy ceiling? Cognitive behavior therapy in search of a theory. *Behavior Therapy, 28,* 601–611.

Follette, W. C., & Jacobson, N. S. (1988). Behavioral marital therapy in the treatment of depressive disorders. In I. H. R. Falloon (Ed.), *Handbook of behavioral family therapy* (pp. 257–284). New York: Guilford.

Free, M. L., & Oei, T. P. S. (1989). Biological and psychological processes in the treatment and maintenance of depression. *Clinical Psychology Review, 9,* 653–688.

Fuchs, C. Z., & Rehm, L. P. (1977). A self-control behavior therapy program for depression. *Journal of Consulting and Clinical Psychology, 45*(2), 206–215.

Geertz, C. (1973). *The interpretation of cultures.* New York: Basic.

Gibson, P. (1994). Gay male and lesbian youth suicide. In G. Remafedi (Ed.), *Death by denial: Studies of suicide in gay and lesbian teenagers* (pp. 15–68). London: Alyson.

Gollan, J. K., Gortner, E. T., & Jacobson, N. S. (1996). Partner relational problems and affective disorders. In F. W. Kaslow (Ed.), *Handbook of relational diagnoses and dysfunctional family patterns* (pp. 322–334). New York: Wiley.

Gollwitzer, P. M. (1999). Implementation intentions: Strong effects of simple plans. *American Psychologist, 54*(7), 493–503.

Gortner, E. T., Gollan, J. K., Dobson, K. S., & Jacobson, N. S. (1998). Cognitive-behavioral treatment for depression: Relapse prevention. *Journal of Consulting and Clinical Psychology, 66*(2), 377–384.

Gottman, J. M. (1979). *Marital interactions: Experimental investigations.* San Diego: Academic.

Hamilton, M. A. (1960). A rating scale for depression. *Journal of Neurology, Neurosurgery, and Psychiatry, 23,* 56–61.

Hammen, C. (1991). Generation of stress in the course of unipolar depression. *Journal of Abnormal Psychology, 100,* 555–561.

Hammen, C. (1999). The emergence of an interpersonal approach to depression. In T. Joiner & J. C. Coyne (Eds.), *The interactional nature of depression* (pp. 21–36). Washington, DC: American Psychological Association.

Hammen, C. L., & Glass, D. R. (1975). Depression, activity, and evaluation of reinforcement. *Journal of Abnormal Psychology, 54*(6), 718–721.

Hayes, S. C. (1994). Content, context, and the types of psychological acceptance. In S. C. Hayes, N. S. Jacobson, V. M. Follette, & M. J. Dougher (Eds.), *Acceptance and change: Content and context in psychotherapy* (pp.13–32). Reno, NV: Context.

Hayes, S. C., Batten, S., Gifford, E., Wilson, K. G., Afairi, N., & McCurry, S. M. (1999). *Acceptance and commitment therapy: An individual psychotherapy manual for the treatment of experiential avoidance*. Reno, NV: Context.

Hayes, S. C., & Brownstein, A. J. (1986). Mentalism, behavior-behavior relations, and a behavior-analytic view of the purposes of science. *The Behavior Analyst, 9*(2), 175–190.

Hayes, S. C., & Hayes, L. J. (1989). The verbal action of the listener as a basis for rule-governance. In S. C. Hayes (Ed.), *Rule-governed behavior: Cognition, contingencies, and instructional control* (pp. 153–190). New York: Plenum.

Hayes, S. C., Hayes, L. J., & Reese, H. W. (1988). Finding the philosophical core: A review of Stephen C. Pepper's world hypotheses. *Journal of the Experimental Analysis of Behavior, 50*, 97–111.

Hayes, S. C., Hayes, L. J., Reese, H. W., & Sarbin, T. R. (1993). *Varieties of scientific contextualism*. Reno, NV: Context.

Hayes, S. C., Jacobson, N. S., Follette, V. M., & Dougher, M. J. (Eds.). (1994). *Acceptance and change: Content and context in psychotherapy*. Reno, NV: Context.

Hayes, S. C., Strosahl, K. D., & Wilson, K. G. (1999). *Acceptance and commitment therapy: An experiential approach to behavior change*. New York: Guilford.

Hayes, S. C., Zettle, R. D., & Rosenfarb, I. (1989). Rule-following. In S. C. Hayes (Ed.), *Rule-governed behavior: Cognition, contingencies, and instructional control* (pp. 191–220). New York: Plenum.

Hineline, P. N., & Wanchisen, B. A. (1989). Correlated hypothesizing and the distinction between contingency-shaped and rule-governed behavior. In S. C. Hayes (Ed.), *Rule-governed behavior: Cognition, contingencies, and instructional control* (pp. 221–268). New York: Plenum.

Hirschfeld, R. M. A., & Schatzberg, A. F. (1994). Long-term management of depression. *American Journal of Medicine, 97*(Suppl. 6A), 33–38.

Hokanson, J. E., Rubert, M. P., Welker, R. A., Hollander, G. R., & Hedeen, C. (1989). Interpersonal concomitants and antecedents of depression among college students. *Journal of Abnormal Psychology, 98*, 209–217.

Holahan, C. J., & Moos, R. H. (1987). Risk, resistance, and psychological distress: A longitudinal analysis with adults and children. *Journal of Abnormal Psychology, 96*, 3–13.

Holahan, C. J., Moos, R. H., & Bonin, L. A. (1999). Social context and depression: An integrative stress and coping framework. In T. Joiner & J. C. Coyne (Eds.), *The interactional nature of depression* (pp. 39–63). Washington DC: American Psychological Association.

Horvath, A. O., & Greenberg, L. S. (Eds.). (1994). *The working alliance: Theory, research, and practice*. New York: Wiley/Interscience.

Horwath, E., Johnson, J., Klerman, G. L., & Weissman, M. M. (1992). Depressive symptoms as relative and attributable risk factors for first-onset major depression. *Archives of General Psychiatry, 49*, 817–823.

Jacobson, N. S. (1994). Contextualism is dead: Long live contextualism. *Family Process, 33*, 97–100.

Jacobson, N. S. (1997a). Can contextualism help? *Behavior Therapy, 28*(3), 435–443.

Jacobson, N. S. (1997b). Advancing behavior therapy means advancing behaviorism. *Behavior Therapy, 28*(4), 629–632.

Jacobson, N. S., & Christensen, A. (1996). *Integrative couple therapy: Promoting acceptance and change*. New York: Norton.

Jacobson, N. S., & Gortner, E. (2000). Can depression be de-medicalized in the 21st century: Scientific revolutions, counter-revolutions and the magnetic field of normal science. *Behaviour Research and Therapy, 38*, 103–117.

Jacobson, N. S., & Margolin, G. (1979). *Marital therapy: Strategies based on social learning and behavior exchange principles*. New York: Brunner/Mazel.

Jacobson, N. S., Dobson, K., Fruzzetti, A. E., Schmaling, K. B., & Salusky, S. (1991). Marital therapy as a treatment for depression. *Journal of Consulting and Clinical Psychology, 59*(4), 547–557.

Jacobson, N. S., Dobson, K., Truax, P. A., Addis, M. E., Koerner, K., Gollan, J. K., Gortner, E., & Prince, S. E. (1996). A component analysis of cognitive-behavioral treatment for depression. *Journal of Consulting and Clinical Psychology, 64*(2), 295–304.

Jacobson, N. S., Martell, C. R., & Dimidjian, S. (in press). Behavioral activation therapy for depression: Returning to contextual roots. *Clinical Psychology: Science and Practice.*

Joiner, T. E. (2000). Depression's vicious scree: Self-propagating and erosive processes in depression chronicity. *Clinical Psychology: Science and Practice, 7*(2), 203–218.

Joiner, T., & Coyne, J. C. (1999). *The interactional nature of depression.* Washington, DC: American Psychological Association.

Just, N., & Alloy, L. B. (1997). The response styles theory of depression: Tests and an extension of the theory. *Journal of Abnormal Psychology, 106*(2), 221–229.

Kanfer, F. H. (1971). The maintenance of behavior by self-generated stimuli and reinforcement. In A. Jacobs & L. B. Sachs (Eds.), *The psychology of private events: Perspectives on covert response systems* (pp. 39–59). New York: Academic.

Kelly, G. A. (1955). *The psychology of personal constructs.* New York: Norton.

Kendler, K. S., Kessler, R. C., Walters, E. E., MacLean, M. C., Neale, M. C., Heath, A. C., & Eaves, L. J. (1995). Stressful life events, genetic liability, and onset of an episode of major depression in women. *American Journal of Psychiatry, 152,* 833–342.

Kendler, K. S., & Karkowski-Shuman, L. (1997). Stressful life events and genetic lability to major depression: Genetic control of exposure to the environment? *Psychological Medicine, 27,* 539–547.

Klerman, G. L., Weissman, M. M., Rounsaville, B. J., & Chevron, E. S. (1984). *Interpersonal psychotherapy of depression.* New York: Basic.

Koerner, K., Prince, S., & Jacobson, N. S. (1994). Enhancing the treatment and prevention of depression in women: The role of integrative behavioral couple therapy. *Behavior Therapy, 25,* 373–390.

Kohlenberg, R. J., & Tsai, M. (1991). *Functional analytic psychotherapy: creating intense and curative therapeutic relationships.* New York: Plenum.

Kupfer, D. J., & Frank, E. (1992). The minimum length of treatment for recovery. In S. A. Montgomery & F. Roulillon (Eds.), *Long-term treatment of depression* (pp. 197–228). New York: Wiley.

Lewinsohn, P. M. (1974). A behavioral approach to depression. In R. M. Friedman & M. M. Katz (Eds.), *The psychology of depression: Contemporary theory and research* (pp. 157–185). New York: Wiley.

Lewinsohn, P. M., Antonuccio, D. O., Steinmetz-Breckenridge, J., & Teri, L. (1984). *The coping with depression course.* Eugene, OR: Castalia.

Lewinsohn, P. M., Biglan, A., & Zeiss, A. S. (1976). Behavioral treatment of depression. In P. O. Davidson (Ed.), *The behavioral management of anxiety, depression and pain* (pp. 91–146). New York: Brunner/Mazel.

Lewinsohn, P. M., & Clarke, G. N. (1999). Psychosocial treatments for adolescent depression. *Clinical Psychology Review, 19*(3), 329–342.

Lewinsohn, P. M., & Graf, M. (1973). Pleasant activities and depression. *Journal of Consulting and Clinical Psychology, 41,* 261–268.

Lewinsohn, P. M., & Libet, J. (1972). Pleasant events, activity schedules and depression. *Journal of Abnormal Psychology, 79,* 291–295.

Lewinsohn, P. M., Weinstein, M. S., & Shaw, D. A. (1969). Depression: A clinical-research approach. In R. D. Rubin & C. M. Franks (Eds.), *Advances in behavior therapy* (pp. 231–240). New York: Academic.

Lewinsohn, P. M., Youngren, M. A., & Grosscup, S. J. (1979). Reinforcement and depression. In R. A. Depue (Ed.), *The psychobiology of depressive disorders: Implications for the effects of stress* (pp. 291–316). New York: Academic.

Linehan, M. M. (1993). *Cognitive-behavioral treatment of borderline personality disorder.* New York: Guilford.

Linehan, M. M. (1997). *Assessment and treatment of suicidal behaviors: Created by Marsha Linehan for Linehan training group.* Unpublished manuscript.

Loftus, E. F. (1980). *Memory: Surprising new insights into how we remember and why we forget.* Reading, MA: Addison-Wesley.

McGrath, E., Keita, G. P., Strickland, B. R., & Russo, N. F. (Eds.). (1990). *Women and depression: Risk factors and treatment issues.* Final report of American Psychological Association Task Force on Women and Depression. Washington, DC: American Psychological Association.

MacPhillamy, D. J., & Lewinsohn, P. M. (1972). The measurement of reinforcing events. *Proceedings of the 80th Annual Convention of the American Psychological Association, 7,* 399–400.

MacPhillamy, D. J., & Lewinsohn, P. M. (1982). The pleasant events schedule: Studies in reliability, validity, and scale intercorrelation. *Journal of Consulting and Clinical Psychology, 50,* 363–380.

Maes, M., & Meltzer, H. Y. (1995). The serotonin hypothesis of major depression. In F. E. Bloom & D. J. Kupfer (Eds.), *Psychopharmacology: The fourth generation of progress* (pp. 933–944). New York: Raven.

Michael, J. (1993). Establishing operations. *The Behavior Analyst, 16,* 191–206.

Neimeyer, R. A., & Mahoney, M. J. (1995). *Constructivism in psychotherapy.* Washington, DC: American Psychological Association.

Nolen-Hoeksema, S. (2000). Further evidence for the role of psychosocial factors in depression chronicity. *Clinical Psychology: Science and Practice, 7*(2), 224–227.

Nolen-Hoeksema, S., Morrow, J., & Fredrickson, B. L. (1993). Response styles and the duration of episodes of depressed mood. *Journal of Abnormal Psychology, 102*(1), 20–28.

Nolen-Hoeksema, S., Parker, L., & Larson, J. (1994). Ruminative coping with depressed mood following loss. *Journal of Personality and Social Psychology, 67,* 92–104.

Pearlson, G. D., & Schlaepfer, T. E. (1995). Brain imaging in mood disorders. In F. E. Bloom & D. J. Kupfer (Eds.), *Psychopharmacology: The fourth generation of progress* (pp. 1019–1027). New York: Raven.

Pepper, S. C. (1942). *World hypotheses.* Berkeley: University of California Press.

Perez, V., Gilaberte, I., Faries, D., Alvarez, E., & Artigas, F. (1997). Randomized, double-blind, placebo-controlled trial of pindolol in combination with fluoxetine antidepressant treatment. *The Lancet, 349,* 1594–1597.

Persons, J. B. (1989). *Cognitive therapy in practice: A case formulation approach.* New York: Norton.

Persons, J. B., Thase, M. E., & Crits-Chritoph, P. (1996). The role of psychotherapy in the treatment of depression: Review of two practice guidelines. *Archives of General Psychiatry, 53,* 283–290.

Prince, S. E., & Jacobson, N. S. (1995). Couple and family therapy for depression. In E. E. Buham & W. R. Leber (Eds.), *Handbook of depression* (pp. 404–424). New York: Guilford.

Rachlin, H. (1991). *Introduction to modern behaviorism.* New York: W. H. Freeman.

Rehm, L. P. (1977). A self-control model of depression. *Behavior Therapy, 8,* 787–804.

Remafedi, G. (1994). The state of knowledge on gay, lesbian, and bisexual youth suicide. In G. Remafedi (Ed.), *Death by denial: Studies of suicide in gay and lesbian teenagers* (pp. 7–14). Boston: Alyson.

Safran, J. D., & Segal, Z. V. (1991). *Interpersonal process in cognitive therapy.* New York: Basic.

Schatzberg A. F. (1996). Treatment of severe depression with the selective serotonin reuptake inhibitors. *Depression, 4,* 182–189.

Schatzberg, A. F., & Schildkraut, J. J. (1995). Recent studies on norepinephrine systems in mood disorders. In F. E. Bloom & D. J. Kupfer (Eds.), *Psychopharmacology: The fourth generation of progress* (pp. 911–920). New York: Raven.

Schrof, J. M., & Schultz, S. (1999, March 8). Melancholy. *U. S. News & World Report,* 56–63.

Siever, L. J., & Davis, K. L. (1985). Overview: Toward a dysregulation hypothesis of depression. *American Journal of Psychiatry, 142*(9), 1017–1031.

Skinner, B. F. (1953). *Science and human behavior.* New York: Free Press.

Skinner, B. F. (1957). *Verbal behavior.* New York: Appleton-Century-Crofts.

Skinner, B. F. (1974). *About behaviorism.* New York: Alfred Knopf.

Staats, A. W. (1995). Paradigmatic behaviorism and paradigmatic behavior therapy. In W. O'Donohue & L. Krasner (Eds.), *Theories of behavior therapy: Exploring behavior change* (pp. 259–294). Washington, DC: American Psychological Association.

Task Force on Promotion and Dissemination of Psychological Procedures. (1995). Training in and dissemination of empirically validated psychological treatment: Report and recommendations. *The Clinical Psychologist, 48,* 3–23.

Teasedale, J. D., Segal, Z., & Williams, M. G. (1995). How does cognitive therapy prevent depressive relapse and why should attentional control (mindfulness) training help? *Behavior Research and Therapy, 33*(1), 25–39.

Thase, M. E., & Rush, A. J. (1995). Treatment-resistant depression. In F. E. Bloom & D. J. Kupfer (Eds.), *Psychopharmacology: The fourth generation of progress* (pp. 1081–1097). New York: Raven.

Thich Nhat Hanh (1996). *The miracle of mindfulness: A manual on meditation.* New York: Beacon.

Tisdelle, D. A., & St. Lawrence, J. S. (1986). Interpersonal problem-solving competency: Review and critique of the literature. *Clinical Psychology Review, 6,* 337–356.

Turkat, I. D. (1985). *Behavioral case formulation.* New York: Plenum.

University of Washington, Department of Psychology, Center for Clinical Research. (1999). *Cognitive and behavioral treatment of depression: A research treatment manual—behavioral activation (BA) condition.* Unpublished manuscript.

Valenstein, E. S. (1998). *Blaming the brain: The truth about drugs and mental health.* New York: Free Press.

Wegner, D. M., & Wheatley, T. (1999). Apparent mental causation: Sources of will. *American Psychologist, 54*(7), 480–492.

Weissman, M. M., & Klerman, G. L. (1985). Sex differences in the epidemiology of depression. *Archives of General Psychiatry, 34,* 98–111.

Wilson, K. G., & Hayes, S. C. (2000). Why it is crucial to understand thinking and feeling: An analysis and application to drug abuse. *The Behavior Analyst, 23*(1), 25–43.

Wirz-Justice, A. (1995). Biological rhythms in mood disorders. In F. E. Bloom & D. J. Kupfer (Eds.), *Psychopharmachology: The fourth generation of progress* (pp. 999–1017). New York: Raven Press.

Wright, R. (1994). *The moral animal.* New York: Vintage.

Zeiss, A. M., Lewinsohn, P. M., & Muñoz, R. F. (1979). Nonspecific improvement effects in depression using interpersonal skills training, pleasant activity schedules, or cognitive training. *Journal of Consulting and Clinical Psychology, 47*(3), 427–439.

Index